UNDERSTANDING JAPANESE SOCIETY

Japanese society is not well understood in the West, but the need to understand Japanese society is becoming increasingly imperative as contacts between the West and Japan increase.

This book provides a comprehensive introduction to all aspects of Japanese society and culture. It begins with the home and family life and goes through various aspects of everyday and ceremonial life to the larger, more complex units such as government and the legal system. It pays particular attention to the way the world is seen, classified and ordered by Japanese people and to the symbolic aspects of Japanese behaviour, particularly ritual behaviour. The book draws on anthropological studies carried out in houses, villages, factories, businesses, schools, hospitals and so forth to show the reality of Japanese society in specific detail. Men, women and children are given equal weight throughout. The book is written so as to be comprehensible to those with no previous knowledge of Japan. **Joy Hendry** is Professor of Social Anthropology at Oxford Brookes University.

The Nissan Institute/Routledge Japanese Studies Series

Understanding Japanese society

Second edition

Joy Hendry

London and New York

First published 1987
by Croom Helm

Reprinted by Routledge 1989, 1991, 1992
11 New Fetter Lane, London EC4P 4EE

Second edition 1995

Simultaneously published in the USA and Canada
by Routledge
29 West 35th Street, New York, NY 10001

© 1987, 1995 Joy Hendry

Typeset by Florencetype Ltd, Stoodleigh, Devon

Printed in Great Britain by
Biddles Ltd, Guildford and King's Lynn

British Library Cataloguing in Publication Data
A catalogue reference for this book is available from the British Library.

Library of Congress Cataloging in Publication Data has been applied for

ISBN 0–415–10259–6 (pbk)

Contents

Figures

Preface to the second edition

In the years since the first edition of Understanding Japanese Society went to press, there have been several interesting changes in Japan. First, the country has entered a new historical period. With the lingering death of the Shōwa Emperor in 1988/9, an era of 63 quite tumultuous years was brought to an end, and his son, whose reign is to be known as Heisei, was enthroned with much ceremony and international interest. In 1993, the new Crown Prince married, following his father's example by choosing a bride from outside the former nobility. Indeed, his bride stood in some ways for the emancipation of Japanese women, for she was, until her engagement, a young diplomat with a brilliant career before her. Some saw the way she gave all this up to become a member of the imperial family as a backward move – my own hope is that she will help to give the imperial institution a vital contemporary role.

Japanese politics has also been going through some major upheavals, and the Liberal Democratic Party, which had remained in power since 1955, had to cede defeat to a coalition of new parties in 1993. The relatively young Prime Minister who took charge managed to push through some long-awaited reforms to the electoral system, but his promises of cleaning up the political system more generally waxed hollow when he resigned in April 1994 on a corruption charge. There followed a minority administration which collapsed after nine weeks, and it was succeeded by a government composed of the old ruling party, the socialists and a minor party, with a socialist as Prime Minister. The electoral reforms have still to be put into practice as this edition goes to press, so it will be interesting to see how they alter the existing system, but I am confident of the fundamental principles described in Chapter 11 and elsewhere in the book, despite these apparent surprises.

More difficult to interpret and predict are the long-term results of the recent changes in Japan which have been brought about by the worldwide recession. The economic situation is also in a state of flux as this second edition goes to press, and the international value of the yen is still high. For business abroad this is good in terms of investment, a process which the Japanese seem to be engaging in in many parts of the world. It is also good for international tourism and it sometimes seems as though the whole world has become a playground for Japan, with the major international airports providing shopping malls for the 'international' goods that Japanese consumers like to buy. Domestic results of the recession are in many ways more severe, but I will have to leave this for economists to interpret.

Importantly for the new edition of this book, which is still largely based on anthropological approaches to understanding Japan, there has been an abundance of new work published in the last few years. These books have deepened our general understanding of social life as Japan moves towards the twenty-first century, and they have documented the various shifts in attitude which have been evident amongst Japanese people during these years. A major focus has been on the various and increasingly sophisticated ideas of internationalisation to be found in Japan, a concern which has oscillated with manifestations of nostalgia for perceptions of traditional life which may or may not have existed in practice. These two themes recur in much of the work published, sometimes with parallel effects, and they will be brought up in the revised versions of various chapters of the book.

Other themes reflect theoretical interests in the study of society more generally. There has been considerable discussion recently about the role of the individual observer in the study of social life, and several books have been published by young Japanese Americans who make quite explicit the way their personal situation has affected their findings, at first sometimes negatively but usually eventually very positively. A collection of papers edited by two longer-standing anthropologists also seeks to identify the cultural and historical influences on studies of Japanese society by examining approaches from ten different countries (Befu and Kreiner 1992). Other writers have explicitly set out to avoid imposing Western assumptions on Japanese society, and one recent focus in this direction has been with the definition of self, viewed strictly from a Japanese perspective (Rosenberger 1992 – see Chapter 3). References at the end of each chapter of this book have increased quite dramatically in response to the new abundance of material available.

Some of the new materials which have appeared represent the results of conferences and gatherings which have brought together anthropologists formerly working more or less in isolation from each other, or at least only with the help of their immediate supervisors and colleagues. The Japan Anthropology Workshop, for example, has met regularly throughout the period, and it has raised various themes and issues to be discussed. Its publications address a range of areas from the relationship between ideology and practice (Goodman and Refsing 1992), through the ceremonial in daily life (Martinez and van Bremen 1994) and the Japanese at play (Raveri and Yamaguchi, in preparation) to notions of nature and their association with consumerism (Asquith and Kalland forthcoming).

Good new collections have also appeared on *Japanese Social Organization* (Lebra 1992), on *Japanese Biographies* (Formanek and Linhart 1992), generally on *Rethinking Japan* (Boscaro, Raveri and Gatti 1990) and an interesting recent contribution which enlightens the extent of Japan's internationalisation is a delightful medley of illustrations of Japanese consumerism entitled *Remade in Japan*, edited by Joseph Tobin. This collection looks like beginning quite a spate of studies in consumerism. Papers presented to a conference on 'Women, Media and Consumption in Japan' are to appear in 1995 in a book edited by Brian Moeran and Lisa Skov, who have also established a 'Consumption Network' to foster other work in the area of consumption in Asia more generally. Another new book on Japanese popular culture is being put together by Lola Martinez, and a collection examining notions of *uchi* and *soto*, edited by Jane Bachnik and Charles Quinn (1994) is appearing in print just as this one goes to press.

Even more recently, studies are being made of the *shinjinrui*, or 'new species' of young people who have emerged in the last few years, of the 'dropouts' from the pressures of the Japanese education system, and of more mature people who have decided to reject the institution of marriage. Studies are also being made of day labourers and of the foreign migrant workers who have surged into Japan during the same period. Results of this work will have to await a third edition, however, for much of it is still in progress, and the publications which will surely appear are not yet written. Another area which looks likely to attract attention in the next few years arises from the more positive conditions for Ainu and other minorities in a world which, since the Year of Indigenous Peoples, is now better recognising the rights of these formerly rejected and mistreated groups. Some initial work is discussed in Chapter 5.

REFERENCES

Asquith, Pamela and Arne Kalland, *The Culture of Nature in Japan* (Curzon and Hawaii University Press, forthcoming)

Bachnik, Jane and Charles Quinn, *Situated Meaning: Inside and Outside in Japanese Self, Society and Language* (Princeton University Press, Princeton, 1994)

Befu, Harumi and Joseph Kreiner, *Othernesses of Japan: Cultural and Historical Influences on Japanese Studies in Ten Countries* (Phillip-Franz-von-Siebold-Stiftung Deutsches Institut für Japanstudien Monographien, Band 1, München, 1992)

Boscaro, Adriana, Massimo Raveri and Francisco Gatti (eds), *Rethinking Japan* (Japan Library, Sandgate, 1990)

Formanek Susanne and Sepp Linhart, *Japanese Biographies: Life Histories, Life Cycles, Life Stages* (Austrian Academy of Science, Vienna, 1992)

Goodman, Roger and Kirsten Refsing, *Ideology and Practice in Modern Japan* (Routledge, London, 1992)

Lebra, Takie Sugiyama, *Japanese Social Organization* (Hawaii University Press, Honolulu 1992)

Martinez, D.P. and Jan van Bremen (eds), *Ceremony and Ritual in Japan* (Routledge: London and New York, 1994)

Raveri, Massimo and Yamaguchi Masao, *Japan at Play* (in preparation).

Tobin, Joseph J. (ed.), *Remade in Japan: Everyday Life and Consumer Taste in a Changing Society* (Yale University Press, New Haven and London, 1992)

Acknowledgements

I would like to thank a number of people for their encouragement and advice during the writing of this book. First of all, the series editor, Arthur Stockwin, who supported the original idea and commented from time to time on the chapters as they appeared. Several other people read all or part of the manuscript of the first edition and made valuable comments about the content or lack of content in particular areas, pointed out errors which slipped in before they went off to be printed, and generally gave up their time to discuss very basic matters. These are Nick Allen, Brian Bocking, Jenny Davidson, Andrew Duff-Cooper, Roger Goodman, James McMullen, Lola Martinez, Minamikata Satoshi and Hiroko, Carolyn Nicholson, Irena and Brian Powell and Ann Waswo. I thank them all, although, of course, I take responsibility for any errors which remain.

For the second edition of the book I received valuable comments and ideas from two anonymous readers, from reviewers and from students and colleagues at the University of Melbourne where I was invited to teach on a course which makes use of the book as a text. I also received helpful comments from several other anthropologists of Japan who use the text, some of whom also sent their recent publications to Australia so that I could keep up with relevant work as it came out. I would like to thank all these people, in particular Pamela Asquith, Roger Goodman, Michelle Hall, John Knight, Wim Lunsing, Heather Macaw, Lola Martinez, Okpyo Moon, Noguchi Sachiko, Arthur Stockwin and James Valentine. Thanks also to Peter Neustupny who located and summarised some legal changes for me, and special thanks to Bill Coaldrake who, with the aid of the Japan Foundation, not only invited me to the University of Melbourne but also made available the time and facilities which allowed me to carry out the revisions.

Thanks again to my colleagues at Oxford Brookes University for their understanding during the terms in which I wrote most of the original book, to the students who have taken the course for the questions they raised and the contributions they made by pursuing their own interests for the purposes of essay writing, and to three Japanese students, Hashimoto Noriaki, Ishii Rumiko and Ohashi Michiko, who attended the course and added their own personal contributions from first-hand experience.

I remain forever indebted to all those people in Japan who have helped me over my own years of study there. A book like this draws on so many diverse experiences that I cannot possibly list everyone who has had a part to play, but I must single out a few names and places. For my initiation to Japanese society in 1971, I must first of all thank all my fellow residents at English House in Shibuya, and other friends made at that time, in particular those who have remained firm friends over the years since then and thus provided me with an intimate diachronic perspective. To them I dedicate the book. Professor Yoshida Teigo has been my anthropological adviser since I first went to do fieldwork in 1975, and he has been an unfailing source of support and advice. Professor Matsunaga Kazuto of Fukuoka University helped me in particular with my first project, Nagashima Nobuhiro of Hitotsubashi University with my second, and Suzuki Takao of Keio University with my third major project. Financial support for these projects was provided by the Economic and Social Research Council, the Japan Foundation, the Daiwa Foundation, and the Nuffield Foundation. During research I have drawn on the help of innumerable people all over Japan, but a special thank you must be made to the people of Kurotsuchi, Fukuoka prefecture, and Tateyama, Chiba prefecture, who have cheerfully and hospitably put up with my longest periods of investigation.

Finally, I must thank my family, especially my children, for putting up without complaint with the reduced attention which the writing and revising of this book has necessarily involved.

NOTE

Japanese names are written in the usual Japanese style, with the surname first.

Introduction

There is plenty of access to information about Japan these days. It features abundantly in radio and television programmes, in newspaper articles, in splendid and spectacular films and in a variety of exhibitions and live concerts, shows and demonstrations. There are also large numbers of Japanese people in most of the major cities of the world, and they are usually happy to talk about and 'explain' their country. The image we receive is one of prosperity, industry and efficiency. We can read about the strength and ingenuity of Japan's economic policies, the success of its management practices, and the astounding, if sometimes shocking, achievements of the education system. We can experience Japanese art. For many foreigners, however, the Japanese people remain inscrutable. How can this be?

One of the problems is that we generally apply our own standards of judgement when we look at Japan. It is, of course, difficult to do anything else. The press is trained to report on matters which are of interest to its consumers, and foreign correspondents are often summoned home when their reporting becomes too 'native'. They need to be tuned in to the perceived needs of their audience. The Japanese themselves are extremely adept at telling people what they think they would like to hear, and they are often quite keen to present a good image of their country even if they have private doubts. This is perhaps a matter of less importance now that they have regained the self-confidence which they lost after the Second World War, but they do tend to spend considerable time comparing themselves with other people when they go abroad, and they are usually able to present aspects of their own society which will be easily assimilated, even if they are somewhat stereotyped.

Academics spend years studying Japan. They learn the language, they visit the country, they read Japanese books and they become experts in an area of Japanese life which happens to appeal to them.

They write accurate and informative books about their particular specialities, and these books are usually good sources for further study, but they are often written for other Japanese specialists, or for specialists in their own particular field. Social anthropology is one such field, and one of its main aims is to understand people on their own terms. Anthropologists try to see the world as the people themselves see it, and then to translate this understanding back into language which their own colleagues can follow. Their work evaporates the inscrutability of any people, and it is only a small step further to write up their findings in language that the lay reader can understand. The aim of this book is to take that step and to introduce the non-specialist (or student) reader to the anthropology of Japan.

Japanese society is here presented, therefore, according to a social anthropological approach. The aim is to introduce the world as it is classified and ordered by Japanese people. The reader is asked to suspend his or her own judgements and assumptions about how people should or should not order their lives, and try to imagine how a Japanese might see things differently. There is, of course, great variety in Japanese society, as there is in any complex, industrialised society, but just as Japanese people learn Japanese as their first language, they also learn to classify the world in a Japanese way, and they learn to perceive things from a Japanese point of view. In other words, an attempt is being made here to present things as they might be seen by someone growing up and living in Japan.

The chapters move from a discussion of small social units, such as the family and neighbourhood, which are experienced by any member of Japanese society, through various aspects of everyday and ceremonial life, such as education, hierarchy and religion, to the larger, more complex institutions like companies, parliament and courts, which impinge in different ways on people's lives, depending on their position in society. Considerable attention is given throughout to the symbolic aspects of Japanese behaviour, the non-verbal ways in which members of Japanese culture communicate with each other, and particularly to the ritual behaviour in which they participate. Some principles will recur from one chapter to another, and the conclusion tries to bring together features common to all the different arenas discussed.

Women have not been given a special, separate chapter as the approach aims to include men, women and children at all stages in proportion to their participation in whatever the area of society being discussed. It is possible that the author's bias may lean slightly towards giving women priority over men, particularly in the ordering of the chapters, but this has the advantage of coinciding to some extent with the order of experience of most Japanese growing up and acquiring their cultural heritage. The bias is not, I think, strong enough to warrant the inclusion of a special compensatory chapter on the subject of 'Japanese men'.

The sources for this book are as far as possible anthropological studies, including those of the author. These are usually based on fieldwork carried out for long periods in the same place, with a circumscribed group of people, so that Japanese life has been experienced at an intimate 'grass-roots' level. Some of these studies have been conducted in a single home, many have focused on one village or urban neighbourhood, and others have investigated a factory, a bank, a school or a wedding parlour. To some extent the content of the chapters has been designed bearing in mind the work available, with appropriate adjustments for the second edition, for I feel that an understanding of these microcosmic views of Japanese society is ultimately the best means to understanding the macrocosmic view which will emerge gradually towards the end of the book.

There are, however, some areas which, although they have been little investigated by anthropologists, nevertheless add an important dimension to an understanding of contemporary Japanese society. To make the book as comprehensive as possible, therefore, an attempt has been made to fill in the gaps by the use of other sources available. The result is eclectic. Nothing has been barred, but I hope that the reader will benefit from this broad approach. In fact, the book was originally based on a series of lectures which were designed for the modular course at Oxford Polytechnic, now Oxford Brookes University. This course enables students to combine two major fields and a number of minor ones in the pursuit of their degrees, so it is particularly appropriate if they can relate the anthropological approach to the other disciplines in which they happen to be interested.

Some of the further reading recommended at the ends of chapters has also been included with the aim of helping readers to pursue their own individual interests and the second edition adds films. The book, as a whole, is intended to open a door, to fill in some details about life in Japan which all Japanese know because they were brought up there, the kinds of things that Japanese people probably wouldn't bother to tell you because they haven't noticed that everyone doesn't think like that. Or if they have, they just assume only Japanese people would understand these things. As will be discussed in Chapter 1, Japanese people tend to think of themselves as rather special and unique. Once the reader is armed with background information like this, it should be possible to achieve a deeper understanding of specialist books in other areas.

The intended audience is fairly broad. There were no prerequisites for the course at the Polytechnic for which the lectures were designed. Many of the students had some background in anthropology, others had taken a module or two about Japan, but there were also students who knew nothing of either area. In the same way, the book makes no assumptions about the reader's knowledge. It could be of value to anyone interested in Japan. It could form a useful companion to anyone planning to visit Japan, anyone posted there by their company, anyone hoping to set up a subsidiary there. It will not provide any details about how to do business in Japan, but it will give potential businessmen and women an insight into the way their Japanese counterparts may be looking at an issue.

This book will also help someone studying the Japanese language to put the fruits of their learning into a social context. It will provide answers to questions which may arise about why things are said in the way they are, why some things don't appear to have an equivalent in Japanese and why there are several different ways of saying apparently simple words like 'come', 'go' and 'eat'. It will also help to explain Japanese words which seem to have no clear translation into English, and in some cases, the understanding of such words will open a revealing window onto the fundamental categories of thought of the native speakers who use the language in their everyday lives. Not many Japanese words have been supplied in the chapters which follow. This is no language textbook, but without an understanding of the words which have been included, no one could claim a good working knowledge of the Japanese language.

1 Sources of Japanese identity
Historical and mythological foundations of Japan

INTRODUCTION

Japanese people are immensely interested in their own culture. The string of islands which comprises their nation is situated at some distance from the Asian mainland, and the inhabitants like to emphasise their uniqueness and homogeneity. Archaeological findings continually push back the dates of the first evidence of human life on these islands, with stages of development to parallel those of other ancient civilisations, and early Chinese history reports the existence of this separate people over the sea. There have been many waves of influence into Japan from the outside, and the contemporary population shows considerable genetic diversity, but this is a people which also seeks from time to time to consolidate its own special identity. Indeed, in the face of the tremendous Euro-American influences of the past century-and-a-half, and more notably since the Second World War, this concern with self-identity has become almost a national obsession.

Hundreds of publications have appeared, by a variety of academics, journalists and amateur intellectuals, each with a theory to explain the special qualities of Japan in contrast with the rest of the world, which they tend to lump together. Many of these books reached the best seller list, and all bookshops have a section or corner for these examples of *Nihonjinron*, or 'theories of Japaneseness'. Television programmes would pick up on some of the more original ideas, featuring interviews and information about the major contributors.

Anthropological studies sometimes got caught up in the genre, the most famous one being *The Chrysanthemum and the Sword*, by Ruth Benedict (1977) who was engaged by the US War Office to understand the enemy during the Second World War. More recently anthropologists analyse the whole phenomenon as an example of 'cultural nationalism' (Yoshino 1992) or a means of filling a 'symbolic vacuum' left when more usual national symbols such as the flag and national anthem were tainted by association with doubts about Japan's role in the the Second World War (Befu 1992).

It is, of course, not unusual for peoples to emphasise their uniqueness. Indeed, this is one of the ways in which groups define themselves as distinct from others surrounding them. In the years during which Japan has become so successfully and so rapidly a major player in the industrialised world she may well have suffered a crisis of identity, and it is significantly with the West that many of the self-defining comparisons are made. Over the centuries Japan has developed her own culture, drawing where it suited her on the outside influences available, but maintaining her own characteristics in spite of enormous incursions of foreign ideas, and the concern with self-identity no doubt displays this persistence yet again.

This chapter will briefly examine some of the sources of this persistent Japanese identity. It will not linger long on the actual origins of the people who live in these islands, but rather summarise some of the geographical features which define the nation, historical events which have influenced it and the mythological stories which have been drawn upon to give the people a symbolic unity. Such a summary will necessarily be cursory, but it should help to explain this concern with identity, as well as providing a useful background for the book's main focus on modern Japanese society. It should also provide a frame of reference for understanding some of the chapters which follow. An excellent historical study of the self-conscious development of national ideology in modern Japan is to be found in Gluck (1985).

GEOGRAPHICAL IDENTITY AND THE EARLIEST INHABITANTS

Japan consists of a chain of islands. There are four main islands, and some 3,900 smaller ones, stretching from the Soya strait dividing Japan from the disputed Kurile Islands of Russia in the north, almost to Taiwan in the south. From tip to tip, the length of the Japanese archipelago is just under 1,900 miles, and at its nearest point to the Asian mainland it is 120 miles from South Korea. There has been some fluctuation in the position of Japan's boundaries but the central islands have enjoyed a degree of isolation which made possible a long continuity of geographical identity. Since there has been written history, they suffered no real occupation by outsiders until after the

the Second World War, and the extraordinary weather conditions which deterred two Mongol invasions in the thirteenth century encouraged the inhabitants to see themselves as being blessed with divine protection.

This is an area of considerable geological disturbance, however, and it is likely that the earliest human beings settled or developed here long before the islands became separated at their extremities from the Asian mainland between 10,000 and 20,000 years ago. The early hunters and gatherers, whose stone tools have remained to mark their existence, may or may not have survived to develop into the ceramic Jōmon people, who are characterised by their ropemarked pottery and mounds of discarded shells, but popular Japanese interpretations of their archaeological findings tend to emphasise the possibility of a continuous line back to these original ancestors (e.g. *Nippon* 1992:12–13).

In fact there are different types and stages of stone tools, each of which may represent distinctive, unrelated groups, and the ceramic remains, too, show considerable variety. There are also several ethnological theories about the origins of the Japanese people, who seem to combine characteristics of the ruling Tungus people of the north and the Austronesian people of the south. These theories have been proposed as a result of studies of similarities in language and social organisation, as well as by the examination of archaeological artefacts.[1] It is more than likely that the islands of Japan have received many diverse influences since their first settlement, but there is a strong sense of continuity, at least at a popular level, and archaeological findings are often reported prominently in the news media.

The introduction of metal tools and rice cultivation came with an influx of people from the mainland about the third century BC, and this new culture gradually spread northwards during the ensuing period, known as Yayoi after an area of Tokyo where the first distinctive pottery remains were found. Although there have also been various theories about the fate of the previous Jōmon people, including the suggestion that they fled north and became the people now known as the Ainu, modern popular Japanese history tends to prefer an emphasis on the blending of the continental influence with the previous indigenous culture (*Nippon* ibid.; *Statistical Handbook of Japan* 1992:2).

It was in fact during the next 600 years or so that many elements developed of what is now regarded as true Japanese tradition. Remains of Yayoi communities show evidence of considerable cooperative activity, often associated with the rice cultivation introduced at this time, and the selective access to bronze and iron metal objects encouraged social divisions and a system of social stratification. In particular, objects began to be assigned a religious significance. The present style of the Ise shrine, which has become the most sacred of Shintō buildings, dates back to this period, as do the mirrors which adorn the innermost sanctum of most Shintō places of worship. The notorious Samurai sword no doubt developed from the splendid spears, which seem to have been buried for ritual protection during this period.

MYTHOLOGICAL ORIGINS OF JAPAN

The symbolic importance of these objects is made clearer when one turns to the mythological foundations of Japanese identity, recorded in eighth-century chronicles and taught as history in Japanese schools until the the Second World War. According to these tales, the islands of Japan were created by a god and goddess named Izanagi and Izanami, who leaned down from the floating bridge of heaven and stirred the ocean with a jewelled spear. The first island was formed from drops of brine which fell from the spear as it was lifted out. The heavenly couple descended to this island, where they gave birth to what is referred to as an Eight Island Country. The sun goddess, Amaterasu, the ultimate ancestress of the imperial line and tutelary deity of the Ise shrine, was then created out of a bronze mirror held in Izanagi's left hand.

During some considerable turmoil which ensued in the heavens, caused particularly by Susano-o, her younger brother, Amaterasu is said at one point to have hidden herself in a cave, thus plunging heaven and earth into darkness. In their efforts to lure her out, the other deities used a bronze mirror again, and another goddess performed a comical dance with the aid of a spear, so that the ensuing laughter aroused Amaterasu's curiosity and she peeped out. Captivated by her own image in the mirror, she was lured out long enough for the cave to be closed behind her, and the world was granted sunlight again. Amongst the paraphernalia used by the gods in this story to entice Amaterasu out of her cave were also some curved jewels, or beads, and, sometime later, when Amaterasu's grandson was sent down to earth to become the first Emperor, she presented him with three gifts, to this day regarded as the Japanese imperial regalia, namely a bronze mirror, a sword, and a curved jewel.

It is this formation of an imperial line, said to be unbroken to the present day, which provides another important source of Japanese identity. Thus, a Japanese engineer, who wrote 'a modern view of Japanese history' to explain his country to foreign friends and colleagues, chose the title *The Emperor's Islands* for his book. The cover sports a modern artistic interpretation of the mirror, sword and jewel, with a photograph of the Imperial Palace in Tokyo reflected in the mirror (Matsumura 1977). Similarly, a foreigner's attempt to explain his Japanese experiences was actually entitled *Mirror, Sword and Jewel* (Singer 1973). When the Emperor Shōwa, known abroad as Hirohito, died in 1989, his funeral was the occasion for the greatest known gathering of heads of state. Similarly, the wedding of his grandson in 1993 attracted worldwide interest.

According to the mythological accounts, the grandchild of Amaterasu and his companions spent six years of battle and adventure moving from the southern island of Kyushu, where many outsiders also first landed, through the Inland Sea, to the Yamato Plain in the central part of the main island of Japan. Here, the tale runs, he established a palace on the first day of spring in 660 BC and became the first Emperor Jimmu. The seventh-century account lists a continuous line of imperial rule from that time, although some of the rulers are said to have lived for well over 100 years, and the records are now seen as written support for a later established supremacy.

HISTORICAL AND ARCHAEOLOGICAL ACCOUNT OF THE ANCIENT PERIOD

The earliest historical accounts of the Japanese people are to be found in ancient Chinese chronicles. In the second and third centuries AD these tell of a country of 100 kingdoms, some 30 of which had sent emissaries to China on business of one sort or another. They speak of an earlier male ruler, but after much warring amongst these kingdoms, the Chinese report that a kingdom named Yamatai had gained supremacy in the third century under the rule of a queen named Pimiko. She is reported to have been hidden in the depths of a great, guarded castle, where she spent most of her time in communication with the gods, allocating the everyday affairs of state to her younger brother. The location of Yamatai, according to Chinese directions, falls in the middle of the Pacific Ocean, and there are at least two possible adjustments to their calculations which would be plausible. One would put this kingdom in the southern part of Japan, where there is later evidence of this type of sister–brother rule, the other in the Yamato Plain, where the existence of a supreme imperial line is eventually documented.

Impressive archaeological remains, in the shape of large tomb mounds, date back to this period and provide very visible evidence of the existence of powerful leaders. The earliest burial mounds were built into natural hills, but these became gradually larger and more elaborate, taking a characteristic keyhole shape, now often observed most effectively from the air. Some thousands of these tombs have been discovered all over the west of Japan, and a recent discovery in Kyushu seems to go back as far as 100 BC, but the largest was built in the fifth century in the Yamato area, now Osaka prefecture. Said to be the tomb of the Emperor Nintoku, this site occupies an area of eighty acres. It is 574 metres long, 300 metres wide, and surrounded by three moats.

There is some argument amongst scholars about exactly when the Yamato rulers gained supremacy over the regional leaders and how far their power extended. However, the archaeological remains and early written accounts provide us with an interesting record of this people, whose larger identity was becoming established. The buried riches of the rulers include ornaments and decorative objects similar to ones found in mainland Asia, and there is also much in the way of military paraphernalia. Many of the tombs were originally decorated with terracotta figures known as *haniwa*, which represented houses, people, animals and objects of local everyday life, and the Chinese reports provide details of the customs and social organisation of the people themselves.

Society was already clearly stratified, with a ruling class which could call on the services of a large and cooperative working class. The latter was organised into hereditary occupationally specialised groups, known as *be*, which provided goods and services for the ruling families, or *uji*, each of which had control over a particular territory. It was for the leaders of these *uji* that the tombs were built, and their contents reveal that, as time passed, the aristocratic lifestyle became increasingly sophisticated. As for the subordinate *be*, however, apart from the craftsmen most of the population was probably involved in the subsistence activities of farming – in particular rice cultivation – and fishing.

The internal organisation of the *uji* was based on related family lines, with a main line, whose head was the leader or chief, and branch lines which were subordinate to the main one. The whole group observed rituals to remember the ancestors who had preceded them. The imperial line which established itself at Yamato was one of these *uji*, who claimed descent from the sun goddess, Amaterasu, and held as symbols of their authority the 'three sacred treasures' of

Figure 1.1 Haniwa such as this helmeted soldier with sword are useful sources of information about pre-historic Japan.

mirror, sword and jewel. It maintained supremacy by using principles between the different *uji* similar to that which were used within them. These thus came to be ranked hierarchically according to the closeness of their relationship to the imperial line.

These principles of social and political organisation provided Japan not only with a symbolic centrality and focus of identity, but also with a blueprint for social order which has persisted through the centuries. Its modern manifestations will be discussed in detail in subsequent chapters. The imperial line did not forever retain *de facto* political power, as will be seen, but it has continued to enjoy special status, and together with the religious foundation on which it was initially based, it has served again and again as a source of Japanese identity, not least in the ultra-nationalistic period preceding the Second World War.

HISTORY RECORDED: THE ARISTOCRATIC AGE[2]

In the seventh century, there was a great influx of cultural influence from China which brought far-reaching changes to Japan and undoubtedly helped to consolidate the hierarchical system which had been established. Along with the written script, which made possible the codification of the imperial supremacy, came the political doctrines and practices of Confucianism, the art and theory of Buddhism and the whole range of technology, arts and philosophy of a highly civilised people. The ruling families of Japan used the new, advanced culture to divide themselves further from the ordinary people, and they gradually became an aristocratic elite which lived an increasingly rich and sophisticated lifestyle.

The head of the chief Yamato family became an absolute ruler in the Chinese imperial style, and everyday affairs were now administered by a bureaucratic system imported almost intact from China. Local offices were established in all the regions, and magnificent capital cities were built, again on a Chinese model. The first of these was at the site of the present city of Nara, but less than a hundred years later a new capital was founded at Heiankyō, now Kyoto. The names of these two capitals are used to refer to the historical periods of this aristocratic age. In 702, a set of laws, known as the Taihō Code, was instituted and promulgated, and a further Yōrō code followed sixteen years later. For the first time, the entire country was brought under a single system of criminal and civil law (*ritsuryō*). The previous *be* were abolished and farmers became free tenants of the state, each entitled to a standardised parcel of land for their own use.

During the 500 years which followed the great incursion of Chinese influence in the seventh century a splendid court life developed in Japan. Arts and etiquette flourished, and the literature of the period remains as testimony of the achievements of the age. Two major historical/mythological chronicles, the *Kojiki* and the *Nihongi*, provide a wealth of information, as well as the written charter for the supremacy of the imperial line. There are also fine collections of early poetry, such as the Man'yōshū and the Kokinshū, and the famous writings of court ladies, the 'Tale of Genji' and 'Pillowbook of Sei Shōnagon', date back to the latter part of this period. Art and architecture also found an outlet in the Buddhist temples which were built throughout the country, although the religious ideas remained for some time the preserve of the ruling elite.

It was during the later part of this aristocratic age that the imperial family gradually lost its political power to a family by the name of Fujiwara, who maintained a 200-year hegemony by means of skilfully arranged marital alliances. A matrilocal residence system was customary at the time, which ensured that if each emperor could be married into a Fujiwara family, the infant princes would also be brought up in a Fujiwara houschold, a system which aided alliances in the next generation. Political power fell more and more into the hands of the Fujiwara regents and chancellors, who succeeded one another almost as regularly as the emperors did, and for generations the emperors were little more than legitimising symbols of the authority of the ruling elite.

In the country at large, the bureaucratic system also began to lose its effectiveness, and the second half of this period witnessed a move away from Chinese models. Effective government became again the preserve of a few influential families. These shared the powers and duties of central government and consolidated their economic base by gradually establishing control over areas of cultivable land. The direct relationship between cultivators and the state was replaced by local bonds of dependence between farmers' families and those of their local superiors, who increasingly took responsibility for protection and law enforcement in their own provinces. The locus of power moved gradually away from the court nobles and into the hands of military leaders.

FEUDALISM AND *BUSHIDŌ*

In stark contrast to the artistic occupations of court life, these provincial rulers were concerned with the acquisition of military skills, and they developed a code of ethics which has become another major source of Japanese pride and identity. The Samurai warriors, as they became, valued deprivation and rigorous discipline in the interest of building an impenetrable inner strength of spirit. They trained themselves to conquer fear and be ready to die at a moment's notice. Relations between them were based on hierarchical principles similar to those described above for the *uji*, and loyalty to the ultimate leader was a paramount virtue. The principles of *bushidō* (or the way of the Samurai warrior) were not specifically articulated until much later, but the military leaders who developed this set of values gradually came also to wield the greater political power throughout Japan.

Towards the end of the twelfth century, a period of civil strife culminated in the establishment of a powerful military headquarters in Kamakura by the ambitious leader of the Minamoto family, named Yoritomo. His supremacy was recognised, albeit somewhat reluctantly, by the emperor of the time, and eventually he was given the title of *shōgun*, commander of the entire military forces. From that time onwards, the powers of the court gradually diminished, and were only occasionally to regain any strength. In the fourteenth century, for example, an imperial uprising succeeded only in transferring effective power to another family, the Ashikagas. In fact, until 1868, the locus of power was to remain more or less efficiently in the hands of a succession of shogunates.

The system which developed during this period has been described as feudal, because it has been seen to resemble the European feudal system as opposed to the bureaucratic arrangements which had been introduced from China in the seventh century. The country became divided into fairly autonomous provinces under the leadership of local lords. These commanded the allegiance of bodies of hierarchically organised supporters to whom, in turn, they granted rights to parcels of land. The farmers who worked the land were obliged to provide their superiors with rice and other foodstuffs, and in exchange they were supposed to receive protection. In practice farmers often suffered incidentally in battles waged between lords for supremacy over a particular area.

THE TOKUGAWA (OR EDO) PERIOD

During the sixteenth century, the first explorers and missionaries arrived in Japan from Europe. They coincided with a period of some considerable strife between lords of different regions of Japan, as has been graphically, if not strictly accurately, described in James Clavell's novel *Shōgun* and depicted in the subsequent TV series. The chief influences were Portuguese and Dutch at this time, but the success of particularly Jesuit missionaries, who were led by St Francis Xavier, was eventually counterproductive. Towards the end of the century, as the country was again brought under unified central control, Christianity was seen as a threat to the new social order which was being created, and the expulsion of the missionaries was ordered. This was only part of an eventual expulsion of all foreigners. Japanese were also banned from travelling abroad, and the country entered a two-and-a-half-century period of self-imposed isolation.

The new unity was in effect established by Toyotomi Hideyoshi, although the subsequent period is named after his eventual successor, Tokugawa Ieyasu, who consolidated Toyotomi's achievements, and whose house remained in power throughout the isolation period. Between them they created and stabilised strict divisions between the various classes of people and reinstated a degree of bureaucracy in the administration of the provinces. The Samurai became a ruling military class, who lived in the castle towns, and they alone were allowed to carry swords. The rest of the population was divided into farmers (at the top), artisans (second) and merchants. The last two also lived in the towns. Priests did not fit clearly into the scheme, although their rank was fairly high, and there were also a few itinerant entertainers and others who remained outside the system. At the very bottom, there were outcaste people who were literally described as 'non-human'.

The capital was established at the city of Edo (now Tokyo), and to maintain the subjugation and support of the local *daimyō* (lords), a system was set up whereby each had to spend part of the year in the capital city, leaving his immediate family there when he returned to his local province. Each class had strict rules by which to live, and all activities, from cultivation to trade, were registered and controlled. Every family was by law expected to be registered with a local Buddhist temple, which also kept a record of deaths as they occurred. It was during this period that the Samurai ethic became a conscious 'way' of life, and, despite the lack of contact with China, Confucianism was again drawn upon to support the carefully regulated, hierarchical system which they guarded.

This period was for two centuries stable and relatively peaceful. In the middle of the nineteenth century, however, when Western ships began to press for access to Japanese ports, the strict social order had already begun to break down. The shogunate and various *daimyō* alike were suffering financial problems, and people at other levels, too, were expressing dissatisfaction. For some years there was a struggle between the Tokugawa supporters, who sought to revamp the shogunate, and new emerging leaders whose aim was to bring the Emperor back into a more powerful position. The latter were eventually successful. The 'Restoration' of the 15-year-old Emperor Meiji in 1868 was the single event which led most effectively to the establishment of a central government and the introduction of Japan to the modern era.

FROM THE MEIJI PERIOD (1868–1912) TO THE SECOND WORLD WAR

During the next 50 years, Japan was again exposed to considerable outside influence. This time the new leaders sent envoys to various European countries to seek models for their innovations, and trade relations were established, or re-established, with willing countries all over the world. A comprehensive railway network was constructed, a post-office system was established and schools were opened throughout the country. Western technology was introduced, and factories and industrial plants began to form the basis of new urban developments. Western material culture also spread quickly, as buildings, vehicles, clothes and even food were imported to suit the changing tastes of the modern population. The old class divisions were abolished, and all became equal in the eyes of the law.

There was considerable discussion and disagreement about the system of government which should be adopted, particularly about the extent to which there should be popular participation, and various European ideas were tried out on an experimental basis. The first political parties were formed in the 1870s by those who wanted to introduce a national assembly, but for some time the Meiji oligarchs resisted, and power remained entirely in their hands. They were also supported by the conscript army which was introduced in 1873. Work began on the drafting of a Constitution in 1882, however, and the posts of prime and cabinet ministers were created in 1885. Eventually, in 1889, a Constitution was promulgated which made provision for a bicameral parliament, with an elected House of Representatives and an aristocratic House of Peers, and a new legal system, based on French and German models, which was acceptable to the outside world.

Even by this time there was something of a reaction to all the European influence, and Japan entered a period of consolidation. She had established various institutions which now corresponded to the models on which they were based, but just as she had done in the period following the great Chinese influence in the seventh century, she set about placing them on a firm Japanese footing. This nationalistic period, which effectively continued until 1945, witnessed some swaying in the balance of power between the oligarchs, the military and the new political parties, but popular participation had only rather sporadic success, and the country was led into a series of wars. There were two successful forays with China and Russia around the turn of the century, which probably helped to inspire the extraordinary self-confidence which was eventually to lead to Japan's own first experience of foreign occupation.

The build-up of extreme nationalism which preceded Japan's attack on Pearl Harbour in 1941 drew on all the resources for national identity which Japan had at her disposal. The Shintō mythological foundations of the nation in the sixth century BC were taught as history in schools during this period, and the people were encouraged to think of themselves as ultimately related through their ancestors to the imperial family. Samurai values of inner strength and self-denial were held up as personal qualities to emulate in the pursuit of the Confucian principles of loyalty and filial piety. The Shintō notions which made service to the state an extreme form of filial piety, to one's ultimate ancestral line, embodied in the Shōwa Emperor, apparently resolved an oft-discussed conflict between the demands of family, on the one hand, and military leaders on the other.

DEFEAT AND SUCCESS

Japan's defeat in the Second World War has become a landmark in world history, not least because it coincided with the first and so far only use of atomic bombs in warfare. The Allied, though predominantly American, Occupation which followed led to another influx of foreign influence into Japan, this time largely from the United States. The defeated people sought again to learn from their evident superiors, and surprised their victors by apparently cooperating with their programmes of demilitarisation and democratisation. Japan's army and navy were first disbanded, and only much later allowed to reform as 'self-defence forces'. A new Constitution was drawn up, which brought the principles of democracy firmly into the legal system, at least in theory. The education system was revised, particularly with the aim of eliminating propaganda and the harmful nationalistic elements, and the state branch of Shintō was abolished.

Many other changes were introduced into Japan. There was a radical land reform programme, which removed land from absentee landlords and allowed those farmers who were actually working it to buy it at very low prices. Incipient organisations, such as labour unions, which had been suppressed, were allowed to develop. Women were given a vote, and the minimum age for male suffrage was lowered from 25 to 20. A period of intense economic hardship followed, as the return of soldiers and overseas administrators combined with a post-war 'baby-boom' to put tremendous pressure on the country's depleted resources. Gradually, however, the Japanese people drew on their cultural strength again.

The tremendous economic success which Japan has achieved since that time is another important element of world history, and a further source of pride in their national identity for her people. With this success has again come the self-confidence to consolidate the imported values with those underlying Japanese values which seem to persist just below the surface, and Japan has again entered a period of reaction to outside influence. Part of this reaction is the search for a cultural heritage which we described at the beginning of the chapter, and which we can probably witness in the drive over the last few years to export Japanese arts and accomplishments to the theatres and galleries of the world. A more sinister aspect of the reaction, however, is a recent reconstruction of nationalistic sentiments by an extreme right-wing section of the population.

A recent anthropological study which addresses specifically the subject of Japanese identity – or, more accurately, Japanese identities – is a book which examines the way rice is often picked as one of the most important cultural symbols. This is despite clear evidence that consumption of this basic food has diminished to small quantities, which historical material shows were never large for the whole population, a population also well aware that the plant was imported from the Asian mainland. Japan's attachment to her own varieties of rice is quite phenomenal, causing entirely uneconomic behaviour in an economically highly developed nation, and the author, Emiko Ohnuki-Tierney (1993) explains how its use in ritual, in commensality, in cosmology and in aesthetics helps to define the hierarchical social structure and the daily organisation of social relations as well as locating the Japanese in relation to other peoples.

CONCLUSION

This has been a brief and very cursory introduction to some of the geographical, historical and mythological factors which have shaped the modern identity of the Japanese people. The aim has been to build up a picture of the cultural heritage on which Japan can draw, and to provide a context for the more detailed examination of aspects of Japanese society which follow. It should be clear that Japan has again and again imported many elements of foreign cultures, picked them over, taken what she wants, and then (Japanised them as she) incorporated these new ideas into the existing system. Time and again things have changed, but a persistent sense of Japanese identity runs steadily through, rather like the imperial line. And although the Japanese are quite good at adapting themselves superficially to a variety of situations, neither their sense of identity nor the persistence of the imperial line seem likely to disappear in the immediate future.

In the chapters which follow, the aim is to present aspects of this Japanese identity in their historical and anthropological contexts. Features of contemporary society will, where possible, be examined for change and persistence and for the way that they combine both more recent and older influences. An attempt will also be made from time to time to put these features in comparative perspective. Just as a concern with national identity and uniqueness is a common preoccupation of people with problems of self-definition, so many other aspects of Japanese society are comparable with broader principles of social life, and, where possible, these will be indicated.

Japan is, of course, composed of many different sorts of people, in many different walks of life, and it is not intended here to suggest that they all have exactly the same identity. The aim has merely been to summarise some of the sources of identity which they share and on which they can draw in perceiving themselves as Japanese. Young people for example, are much more aware of the place of Japan in the wider world than their parents were, and they probably have only a vague idea of the mythological stories which their grandparents were taught as history. The following chapters should make much clearer the extent to which features of Japanese society are shared, and, conversely, the variety which it encompasses.

NOTES

1. (Nakane 1974:64–5). For a more detailed discussion of the cultural origins of the Japanese people, and the various arguments involved, see Befu (1971) and Aikens and Higuchi (1982). Edward Kidder (1985) also provides illustrated descriptions in English of ancient Japan, as does Colcutt, Jansen and Kamakura (1988). Barnes (1993) places Japan in an East Asian context.
2. For the ordering and some of the labelling of the historical sections of this chapter, I must acknowledge a debt to Hall's Chapter 3 in Hall and Beardsley (1965).

REFERENCES

Aikens, C. Melvin and Takayasu Higuchi, *Prehistory of Japan* (Academic Press, New York, 1982)

Aston, W.G. (trans.), *Nihongi: Chronicles of Japan from the Earliest Times to AD 697* (Allen and Unwin, London, 1956)

Barnes, Gina L., *China, Korea and Japan: The Rise of Civilisation in East Asia* (Thames and Hudson, London, 1993)

Befu, Harumi, *Japan: An Anthropological Introduction* (Chandler, San Francisco, 1971), Chapter 1

———, 'Symbols of Nationalism and *Nihonjinron*', in Roger Goodman and Kirsten Refsing (eds), *Ideology and Practice in Modern Japan* (Routledge, London, 1992) pp. 26–46

Benedict, Ruth, *The Chrysanthemum and the Sword* (Routledge and Kegan Paul, London, 1977)

Colcutt, Martin, Marius Jansen and Isao Kamakura, *Cultural Atlas of Japan* (Andromeda, Oxford, 1988)

Gluck, Carol, *Japan's Modern Myths: Ideology in the Late Meiji Period* (Princeton University Press, Princeton, 1985)

Hall, John Witney, 'The Historical Dimension', in John Witney Hall and Richard K. Beardsley, *Twelve Doors to Japan* (McGraw-Hill, New York, 1965), pp. 122–84

Hall, John Witney and Richard K. Beardsley, *Twelve Doors to Japan* (McGraw-Hill, New York, 1965)

Kidder, J. Edward, *Ancient Japan* (Weidenfeld and Nicolson, London, 1965)

Matsumura, Gentaro, *The Emperor's Islands: The Story of Japan* (Lotus Press, Tokyo, 1977)

Nakane, Chie, 'Cultural Anthropology in Japan', in S.J. Siegel (ed.), *Annual Review of Anthropology*, vol. 3 (1974), pp. 57–72

Nippon: A Charted Survey of Japan 1992/3 (Kokuseisha, 1992)

Ohnuki-Tierney, Emiko, *Rice as Self: Japanese Identities through Time* (Princeton University Press, Princeton, 1993)

Singer, Kurt, *Mirror, Sword and Jewel* (Croom Helm, London, 1973)

Tsunoda, Ryusaku (trans.) and L.C. Goodrich (ed.), *Japan in the Chinese Dynastic Histories* (Perkins Asiatic Monographs, no. 2, South Pasadena, 1951)

Yoshino, Kosaku, *Cultural Nationalism in Contemporary Japan* (Routledge, London, 1992)

FURTHER READING

Bowring, R. and P. Kornicki (eds), *The Cambridge Encyclopaedia of Japan* (Cambridge University Press, Cambridge, 1993)

Coaldrake, William H., *Architecture and Authority in Japan* (Routledge, London, 1995)

Hall, John Witney, *Japan from Prehistory to Modern Times* (Tuttle, Tokyo, 1971)

Hunter, Janet, *The Emergence of Modern Japan* (Longman, London, 1989)

Minoru Kawada, *The Origin of Ethnography in Japan: Yanagita Kunio and his Times,* trans. Toshiko Kishida-Ellis (Kegan Paul International, London and New York, 1993)

Mason, Penelope, *History of Japanese Art* (Abrams, New York, 1993)

Milward, R.S., *Japan: The Past in the Present* (Paul Norbury Publications, Tenterden, Kent, 1979)

Morris, Ivan Ira, *The World of the Shining Prince: Court Life in Ancient Japan* (Oxford University Press, Oxford, 1964)

Sansom, Sir George, *A History of Japan*, 3 vols, (Dawson, Folkestone 1958)

Storry, Richard, *A History of Modern Japan* (Penguin Books, Harmonds-worth, 1984)
Varley, H. Paul, *Japanese Culture* (University of Hawaii Press, Honolulu, 1984)

RELATED NOVELS

Clavell, James, *Shōgun* (Dell Publishing Co., New York, 1976)
Endō, Shūsaku, *The Samurai* (Penguin Books, Harmondsworth, 1986)

FILMS

The Passage to Japan (*Fukuzawa Yukichi*) (dir. Sawai Shinichiro)
The 47 Loyal Samurai (*Chūshingura*) (dir. Mizoguchi Kenji)

2 The house and family system

INTRODUCTION

In Japan, as elsewhere, life begins in a family and it is here that one first builds up a picture of the world. Family members are usually the first people we learn to classify, and in many of the small-scale societies with which anthropologists are familiar, everyone in the society is classified as a relative of one sort or another, so that an understanding of kin relations is essential to understanding any social interaction at all. The way in which such relations are defined, however, varies greatly from one society to another, and the principles of definition may even be quite different from the biological ones which are implied in English usage.

Many families in Japan actually look on first sight rather similar to families in Western countries where the usual pattern is for parents and children to live together as a 'nuclear family', sometimes bringing a grandparent into their home when they become too old to manage by themselves. Households in Tokyo and other major cities very often occupy a two- or three-room apartment, and the nuclear family is indeed the most common type, although there are also families with only one parent, and there are families too who live in houses shared between two or three adult generations of the same family. In the country this last type of family is more common than the nuclear family. These facts tell us little about attitudes and obligations to relatives, however.

It is also often the case that kin relations are inextricably associated with other types of relations, so that economic activities, political relations and religious practices can only be understood properly when considered in the context of the kinship system. This is less and less the case in complex societies, where too much family involvement in public life leads to charges of nepotism, and individuals tend to follow their own careers regardless of family connections, but this is a relatively recent phenomenon. An understanding of most societies is aided by an understanding of some of the assumptions made about kin relations, although there may, of course, be great variety in any particular complex society.

The importance of kin relations in Japan should already be clear from the previous chapter, and the model of the whole nation as one great family descended from the Emperor, was drawn upon heavily during the years leading up to the Second World War. In the Meiji period, when Japanese intellectuals were reassessing the whole structure of Japanese life in preparation for the establishment of the new Civil Code, something they described as the 'family system' was a bone of much contention. Some saw the traditional model as essential for the maintenance of orderly social life, others saw it as a major hindrance to the progress they sought in their modern, internationalised world. The Civil Code of 1898 ended up as a compromise, but the debate continued at an intellectual level.

This Japanese 'family system' was based on a model approximated by Samurai families in the nineteenth century, which was an essentially indigenous Japanese system, supported by an overlay of Confucian ideology. By 1890, there was already a growing feeling in conservative quarters that Western influence was getting out of hand, and an imperial rescript on education, issued at that time, made explicit the traditional values of the system. It was to be learned by heart and recited daily by all schoolchildren. Educationalists of the time tended to be traditionalists, and as enrolment in schools was up to 98 per cent by 1909, the dissemination of these ideas was extremely efficient. There were of course variations in the practice of this 'family system', but its principles became common cultural property, and the model of family relations was used explicitly in many other areas of life.

The same 'family system' was blamed for all sorts of evils during the Allied Occupation, and it was virtually demolished legally in the 1947 Constitution. Modern Japanese life has in many areas become rather incompatible with the system in its traditional form, and Japanese social scientists have predicted its total demise for many years. However, deeply held values die hard, and the principles of that old family system have by no means disappeared, even in the urban sprawl. An understanding of the traditional system will pave the way for appreciating its modern manifestations, and will also lay a foundation for later chapters where its value as a model will become evident.

THE *IE*

The basis of 'the family system' is a unit which does not happily translate as 'family' at all. Indeed, the whole notion of a 'family system' was a concept created in the face of outside influence to explain Japanese behaviour in a comparative context. At any one time, the Japanese household may look rather similar to a domestic unit in any number of other societies, but at an ideological level, this unit is better described using the indigenous term *ie*. 'Family' in one of the senses used by European aristocracy, of a continuing 'line' requiring a definite heir in each generation, would be close in sense, but the word 'family' has several other shades of meaning. 'House' is a better translation, because *ie* may also signify a building, and the English term does again have a connotation of continuity, as in the expression 'House of Windsor'.

Continuity is an essential feature of the *ie*. The individual members of a particular house, who need not necessarily always be resident, occupy the roles of the living members of that particular ie. The total membership includes all those who went before: the ancestors, now forgotten as individuals, the recently dead who are remembered and the descendants as yet unborn. It is the duty of the living members at any one time to remember their predecessors, and to ensure that the house will continue after they die. (See Figure 2.1)

Traditionally, the *ie* as a unit was regarded as owning any property which accrued to it, although in the Meiji Civil Code, this property had to be registered in the name of a particular individual. There was usually an occupation associated with the *ie*, and members were expected to contribute to it as they were able, sharing its benefits without individual remuneration. Members were also expected to maintain the status of their particular *ie* within the wider community, and an individual who threatened to bring shame on the house could be cut off from membership. The continuing entity was more important than any individual member, and individual members were expected to find their *raison d'être* in the maintenance and the continuity of the *ie*.

The affairs of the *ie* were ultimately managed by the head, although certain tasks and responsibilities could be delegated to other members. The head was legally responsible for all the members, who were subordinate to him, but again, if any particular head became despotic or detrimental in some other way to the house as a whole, he could be removed according to the decision of a wider family council. Within the house, the head was supposed to be given

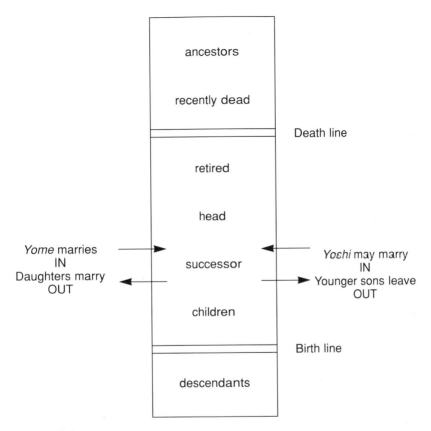

Figure 2.1   Elements of the *ie*.

privileges, like being served first at meals and being allowed to take
the first bath. Relations between members were hierarchically organised along lines of distinction based on age, sex and expectation of
permanency in the house.

In general, the younger members of the house were seen as indebted
to the older members for their upbringing, and in return they were
expected to take care of the older members when they could no longer
manage for themselves. The relations between generations were characterised by Confucian principles of loyalty and benevolence, so that
sons and daughters would personalise their duty to the house as loyalty
to their parents for benevolence received. Women were supposed to
obey men, and a new bride her mother-in-law as well. Relations within
the house were characterised less by love and affection than by duty

and filial piety, and too close a relationship between a husband and wife, for example, could even be seen as detrimental to the house as a whole.

In each generation, one permanent heir would be chosen, and a spouse would be brought in to share the role of continuing the family line. Other members of that generation could stay in the *ie*, or return to it, but if they married they were expected to move out. The system which became codified was that of primogeniture, or inheritance by the eldest son, but there had been a number of regional variations, including first-child inheritance, male or female, in some northern districts, and last-son inheritance in parts of Kyushu.

Again, the ensurance of continuity is more important than the particular means, and all sorts of arrangements could be made to accomplish this aim. If there were no sons, for example, a son-in-law could be married in to take the role of successor, and this position of *yōshi* was a common one for non-inheriting sons from other houses. If there were no children at all, a new spouse could be sought, or a relative's child could be adopted, or the head could take a concubine to produce an heir, who would then be brought up by his wife. It was also permissible, if necessary, to adopt a totally unrelated child, so that the blood connection, while desirable, was not indispensable to the continuity of the *ie*.[1]

The spouse brought in to marry the heir of a particular house was in a somewhat precarious position for a while. Any *ie* was regarded as having its own customs or 'ways', and although marriages were made preferably with houses of a similar standing, an outsider needed to demonstrate fitness to adapt to these ways. An unsuitable wife or *yōshi* could soon be returned to their own house for general lack of fitness, as well as possible barrenness, and this resort could even be taken if an outsider fell ill in middle life and became unable to carry on with his or her expected duties. Again, the *ie* took precedence over its individual members.

RELATIONS BETWEEN *IE*

A preferable possibility for a non-inheriting son was to set up his own house and start a new *ie*. This would be regarded as a branch of the main house, and in some areas there developed a strong wider group of houses which had all at some stage branched off from an original main one. In the north of Japan, these groups still maintain a strict hierarchy based on when they were formed, but in the south such relations tend to be forgotten in a few generations. New possibilities arose for non-inheriting sons as Japan became industrialised and needed workers to move to the developing cities, and the *ie* system was well able to accommodate such changes.

These groups of related houses, known as *dōzoku*, often cooperated in economic activities, and in the north of Japan, the local political community is organised along these lines. In the early period of industrialisation, too, many of Japan's big companies were formed in a similar way. The principle that branch houses owed allegiance to the main ones was exploited in the pre-war image which depicted every house in the nation as ultimately being a branch of the imperial family line. Thus one's allegiance to the *ie* could be translated into a wider allegiance to the Emperor, as head of the original main house, and the nation he represented could be pictured as one great family group. Similar principles operated in the great and small families of earlier periods, too.

THE *IE'S* LEGAL DEMISE

There have, of course, always been regional and occupational variations, particularly in marriage arrangements, and individual families developed their own idiosyncrasies within particular areas. Nevertheless, for centuries, the laws of the time have generally supported such a system, and the Meiji Civil Code introduced centralisation with modifications to the previous regionally varying codes. From about 1881 families were to be registered with the authorities and they were registered as continuing units. Records reveal that families sometimes officially recorded arrangements in line with the new civil code, but in practice continued with something they found preferable in a particular case. For example, first-son inheritance did not suit some families, yet they would register their eldest son as if he were the successor.

In the Civil Code drawn up during the Allied Occupation, the *ie* was abolished as a legal unit, and a nuclear family has now to be registered on its creation at marriage. All children are supposed to have equal rights to inheritance and they share responsibility for the care of their parents. The laws are drawn up according to the Constitution of 1947 which states: 'With regard to choice of spouse, property rights, inheritance, choice of domicile, divorce and other matters pertaining to marriage and the family, laws shall be enacted from the standpoint of individual dignity and the essential equality of the sexes' (Article 24).

It is clear that these values are imported directly from the West, and are at variance with the system described above. It was decided

Main house

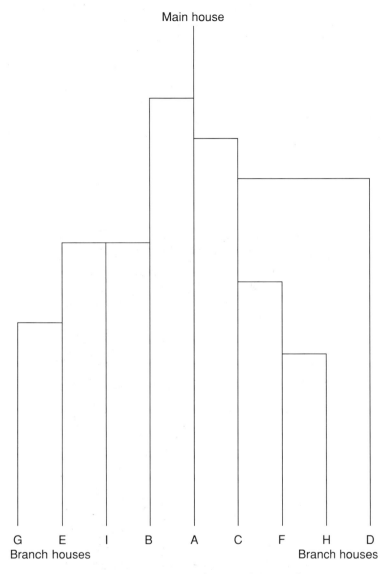

G   E   I   B   A   C   F   H   D
Branch houses   Branch houses

Figure 2.2   Dōzoku hierarchical group (A>B>C>D, etc.).

that the 'family system' was incompatible with the democratic state
which Japan was to become, and it was discarded in legal form, along
with other so-called relics of feudalism. These new values were taught
in schools, and they have often been held up as ideals to be emulated.

In many ways the family has altered in post-war Japan, but just as people coped with the differences between their own ideas and the law in the matter of the inheritance of the eldest son, so they are not necessarily too concerned with the legal code in other matters.

In fact the notion of the *ie* continues to be held quite happily in many parts of Japan, and elsewhere its underlying principles pervade the nuclear families which appear on the surface to be quite independent. One clause in the new Civil Code actually makes provision for a certain amount of continuity, in that one member of a family needs to be chosen to take care of the genealogical records and 'utensils of religious rites' (Article 897). A closer examination of these religious rites will further elucidate the depth of these persistent ideas.

Figure 2.3 Families remember their departed members at the Buddhist altar in the home.

THE RELIGIOUS CHARTER

Within a house, the charter for the continuity of the *ie* takes the form of a Buddhist altar, or *butsudan*, where the memory of the ancestors is preserved. When a member of the house dies, a tablet is made bearing the posthumous name given to him or her by the Buddhist priest who performs the funeral, and this is kept in the altar. Thus altars are found in most houses which have been allocated the responsibility for the care of departed forbears. Offerings are made regularly, and special memorial services are performed for the care of the soul at certain fixed times after death for a period of up to 50 or 60 years.

Once these memorials are complete, the 'recently dead' member of the family joins the general category of ancestor (*senzo*), and is then remembered in company with the other predecessors of the house. Some say that the *senzo* become Shintō deities once the Buddhist memorial rites are complete, and the last memorial should therefore be a celebration rather than an occasion of mourning. In any case, there is an idea that ancestors eventually merge into a kind of single spiritual entity, from which souls emerge for babies who are born, and this notion is distinct from Buddhist ideas found elsewhere.

In practice, the Buddhist altar symbolises the continuity and existence of the *ie*, and visiting members of the house will sometimes walk right past their living relatives to greet ancestors before they acknowledge the human beings present. Gifts received by the house are often presented to the ancestors before they are opened, or placed inside the altar after the wrapping has been removed. Members of the family may consult the ancestors about important decisions, and the doors of the *butsudan* are opened on any special occasion so that the ancestors may participate.

Once a year there is a special festival called *bon* to remember all the souls of departed ancestors, and people travel from all over Japan to visit the homes of their birth and original ancestors. So wives will often leave their marital homes at this time to visit their natal *ie*, and city families travel out to the country to visit the family *butsudan* and renew ties with the relatives of their youth. At New Year, too, similar visits are made, and both occasions are regarded as appropriate for members of branch houses to pay their respects to their ultimate ancestors in the main house.

In many Japanese houses (surveys suggest between 60 per cent and 80 per cent), there is also a Shintō 'god-shelf', which is associated with the imperial ancestress Amaterasu Omikami. Offerings are made here too, and amulets and talismans purchased during visits to Shintō shrines will be kept up on this shelf. The Shintō shelf is cheaper, usually less conspicuous and the offerings are less abundant, but it is hard not to draw a parallel between these two places of reverence. Although no one emphasises these links much today, it seems likely that this 'god-shelf' still serves a symbolic purpose in identifying members of every household with the ultimate ancestors they share as members of the Japanese nation.

DOMESTIC ARRANGEMENTS

In many parts of Japan to this day, members of a family living under one roof will conceptualise their unit as a continuing *ie*. This is particularly the case if the house has been passed down through several generations, and, even if all the generations are not present, a scattered family may see themselves as only temporarily separated. For example, some old people living alone have made a long-term arrangement with one of their children to move back into the family home when they retire from a job which keeps them away. In other cases, couples of two generations may live in close proximity, and this arrangement is not dissimilar from that in the past in which an *inkyō-ya*, or retirement house, was built not far from the main family house in certain regions of Japan. It is said that one needs to be near enough to be able to carry hot soup from one house to the other without having to heat it up again.

'Continuing houses' still flourish where there is an *ie* occupation, or the house owns a portion of its own land. Thus, family businesses may share a building with the family home, and two or more generations may share the burden of the work. Where some considerable investment has been made into the property or business, parents work hard to encourage their children to enter the family business, and there is some evidence that they are often successful. Doctors, for example, must invest a hefty sum if they want to build their own hospitals and clinics, and the benefits are really only reaped in the next generation if their children become doctors. The entrance requirements for medical school are so stringent that medical families often send their pre-kindergarten children to classes to try and give them a head start over their peers.

In rural areas, too, the continuing *ie* is still common, though the success with which continuity is maintained depends on economic circumstances. Farmers, for instance, need a lucrative cash crop, or some additional source of income, if they are to thrive these days. In

Kyushu, where I carried out research myself, the cultivation of tea, and chrysanthemums aided by electric light, were enough of an incentive to keep a son in most houses. According to an anthropological study carried out in a mountainous area which has been converted into a ski resort, a village near enough to the ski slopes to open up a number of family inns has in this way managed to keep many continuing households; another nearby community which still relies on farming and sericulture is rapidly losing its younger generation (Moon 1986).

In these cases, there is usually a physical house which represents the *ie*, and members are at least sometimes resident there together. This is not to say that there has been no change since former times, however, as the arrangements within the house may have altered quite considerably in the last two or three generations. It is more likely, for example, that the younger and older couple will be separated by some solid wall, rather than, as previously, mere flimsy sliding doors, if at all, and it has become common for children to have their own rooms. People say that a couple of generations ago there was much less privacy within the house, although, interestingly, a recent article on home magazines suggests opening up the space in a home as a Western feature designed to promote warm relationships and 'closer ties' (Rosenberger 1992:113–4).

In many Japanese families there is no physical *ie* which has been passed down through the generations. A married couple will live with their children, and their relations with the previous generation will be quite sporadic. Many couples set up home in a rented apartment but with the long-term goal of buying their own free-standing house eventually. Statistics about living arrangements in Japan show a high proportion of these nuclear families but little is known from the figures about how many are entirely independent, and how many still have obligations to their parents. It is not unusual for an elderly parent to come and live with such a family, for example, and it is possibly even more common for an elderly parent to come and live nearby – near enough to carry round hot soup.

In the late 1980s, a new version of intergenerational living became popular in the 'three-storey two-family' house, much advertised in urban areas. These houses may make use of land owned by an older generation and developed into a new house with the salary of their son or daughter and their family. Typically the house is built with a ground floor for the older couple, who will have their own entrance, and an independent kitchen and bathroom, a first floor with the main living rooms of the younger family, and perhaps the parental sleeping area, and a third floor with study-bedrooms for the children. According to William Coaldrake, who has described this type of residence, they have been designed 'within the context of active government policy directed at addressing the perceived needs of Japanese society in the 21st century' (1989:66).

In fact, according to recent statistics, the number of people living alone in Japan has increased quite dramatically. From 1970 to 1990 single-person households increased by 50 per cent and they now represent nearly one-quarter of all households (*Japan Statistical Yearbook* 1992:47). Some of these households are single young people as they have always been, and some are people whose marriages have broken up, but others are an increasing number of people who are choosing not to marry at all. There are also quite a few widows and widowers whose children have left home and who may or may not be near enough to help out.

An alternative for old people is of course an old people's home, and one study draws attention to a recent concern amongst social scientists in Japan about the anticipated 'greying of society' which looms as the expected lifespan grows and the birthrate drops. Demographic predictions suggest a problem outranking those of any Western country, charting some 24 per cent of the population over sixty-five by 2020, and about half of those over seventy-five. Although the decline in family support would appear to have been less sharp and severe than they predicted, there are nevertheless large and growing numbers of old people in Japan who, for whatever reason, are unable or unwilling to rely on relatives to see them through their final years. Alternative forms of care are mostly seen as programmes of welfare, which still carry heavy connotations of failure, but in the last few years several innovative ventures have been fighting to create a new image, summed up somewhat sarcastically as the 'silver business', or the 'silver boom', 'silver' being the designated positive version of 'grey' (Kinoshita and Kiefer 1993).

The book based on this study, *Refuge of the Honored*, makes a clear and readable summary of the contemporary situation, which eventually focuses on one of the earliest 'retirement homes' to be created, and charts its progress through a period of nine formative years. Kinoshita lived in the community with his family, participated in all its activities, daily, seasonal and special, and became a well-known figure to the management and local residents alike. They shared with him as they experienced them the trials and tribulations of creating community life from scratch, and he was able to follow up particular issues over a continuing period to see how they would develop and resolve themselves. The results are laid out in comparison with experiences reported elsewhere, and they are placed in the context of the overall Japanese facilities available for this section of society, as well as of studies carried out in other parts of the world.

Refuge of the Honored documents the retirement lives of relatively affluent members of Japanese society, however, and two papers published by an anthropologist, Diana Bethel (both 1992), report on the state of affairs in an old people's home run by the social welfare system. She makes clear that institutionalisation represents a failure to achieve the Confucion ideal of filial piety for ageing parents to live with their children, and that in their darker moments the residents are only too aware of this, but she also describes well the way that they come to terms with their situation. Some are even pleasantly surprised by the camaraderie that they experience. They try to establish familiar patterns of social life, and engage in traditional practices such as gift-giving amongst themselves.

INTERPERSONAL RELATIONS BETWEEN THE GENERATIONS

Even within a continuing house, there is sometimes conflict about the expectations. The older generations are concerned that their *ie* should continue, partly for the sake of the ancestors, perhaps also for the sake of the household occupation, and for the practical needs that they may have in their old age. Yet they know that the current emphasis on democracy demands that they should give their children the right to choose their own lives.

According to the traditional system a successor would stay in the house. He would spend the early part of his life being trained in the skills required for the household occupation, in the middle years he would work to provide for the other members of the house, and in his old age he could rely on his descendants to support him until he died, and then perform the rites necessary for the welfare of his soul. The lives of women would follow a similar course, once they were married. When young they would also learn the household trade, as well as the arts of domestic management more usually assigned to the female members of the house; then they would marry and spend much time in the service of the menfolk and older women of the house, gradually taking over more and more responsibility as they grew older, until at last they would reach the relatively revered position of grandmother.

In general one gave one's service to the house by taking care of one's senior and junior generations, knowing that one owed one's livelihood to the former, and in the confidence that the latter would reciprocate in later years. It thus comes particularly hard on the older generations, who have given their service, to find that modern ideology no longer supports their case. It is thought to be a poor way to end one's life in an old people's home, and temples where the elderly go to pray for a quick death have become very well attended in recent years (Wöss 1984).

In practice, many old people do still spend their later years with their families, whether it be in the family home, or moving to the home of one of their children. In some cases there will be a successor who regards their care as his duty, or perhaps more accurately, that of his wife. In others the children will share the responsibility by visiting their parents while they can manage by themselves in the family home, and then later by moving the parents into the largest of their houses. Some will be less fortunate, but there is still a strong sense of duty to the older generation in Japan, whether co-residence is practised or not. The three-storey houses with separate entrances would seem to be a good compromise.

As for the younger generation, the duties of the children were various. The successor, usually the eldest son, was expected to make his life within the family, and this applied to an eldest daughter if there were no male offspring to succeed. The other children were freer to make their own lives, although they were expected to make matches with appropriate families when the time came to marry. During the Allied Occupation, when the new Constitution was drawn up and the education system was completely reformed, young people began immediately to receive instruction in the Western ideals of democracy and freedom of the individual.

Children who did not wish to fulfil the family's expectations for them were able to find support for their plans outside the home. In particular, those who did well within the education system were encouraged to go into tertiary education and follow up an individual career. The flexibility of the inheritance system meant that families could cope with this as long as one child was willing to stay. There began to be less insistence that the eldest son should inherit, although the eldest will still usually have first choice if there is a conflict. In some families no final decision will be made about succession until children reach marriageable age. Young people will go off and work or study away from home for a while, and parents will wait in the hope that one of their children will return to bring a bride (or groom) into the family home. If they don't, then the parents may still continue to hope for a return in later life, or at least care in their old age.

Despite the new law that inheritance should be divided equally between all children, family land or property can often not stand division, and non-inheriting children will sign away their rights for the sake of the *ie*, if one of their number agrees to take on the responsibility for the family home. In fact the non-inheriting children are usually given a hand with their own lives. Sons may receive help with house purchase or education, and daughters will customarily receive a large trousseau on marriage. These forms of aid are seen as in lieu of inheritance, and to some extent a relinquishment of the joint responsibility for the older generation, although if something should prevent the successor carrying out his duties, other children may step in to help out.

All these modifications to the relations between generations have in turn modified interpersonal relations within the house. The strictly hierarchical system has inevitably broken down at the ideological level. In practice it was often not quite as strict as it was portrayed, but there is little doubt that the senior generations had more power and authority in the past than they do now, and the younger ones were certainly more burdened with their specific duties. Nevertheless, the reciprocal concern between generations seems to be alive and well in many families, whatever their living arrangements, and the principles of benevolence for loyalty between parent and child have yet to be eradicated at their original level.

Two anthropological studies which have appeared in the last few years document the strong ties of obligation and ideological continuity persisting in certain types of Japanese family regardless of living arrangements. One of these concerns high-powered business families, which stand at the pinnacle of enormous Japanese corporations (Hamabata 1990), the other is about families of the former nobility, officially dissolved in 1947, but evidently still acting, notably through the depth of the family line, as a kind of social elite in Japanese society (Lebra 1993). For different reasons, each of these groups invests considerable effort into perpetuating the family system and both books offer an intimate and highly informative view of the areas of Japanese society they have chosen to highlight.

MALE–FEMALE RELATIONS

According to the Confucian principles which were brought to apply to the indigenous family system, men were superior to women, who were expected to attend to their every need. Marriages were arranged by relatives according to the appropriateness of background and social status, and love between husbands and wives was thought to be inconsistent with the filial piety which demanded that attention be paid to the needs of elders and children before those of a spouse. For men, affairs outside the home were not only accepted, but even expected, whereas until 1908 a woman could be killed with impunity by a husband who discovered her in an adulterous act. A woman was taught that her chief duty in life was obedience, first to her father, then to her husband and his parents, and finally, when widowed, to her son.

Married women were usually also outsiders in the house, and for some time after their marriage they also came under the subjection of their mothers-in-law. In fact the word commonly used for a young wife (*yome*) has the literal meaning of woman of the *ie*, and in the early years of marriage a young wife would be at everyone's beck and call. Women were responsible for cooking, cleaning and washing, but they also took an active part in the household occupation, and small children could well be left to the care of a less able-bodied member of the family, such as a grandmother or grandfather, during much of the day.[2]

In many parts of the country women played a much stronger role than these Confucian ideals would suggest, and in indigenous ideology women have held important ritual roles, such as those described in the previous chapter for the Empress Pimiko. Within a continuing house family decisions are often made in council and the influence of the older women could be considerable, although this obviously varied from house to house. Marriages in the country were based on mutual attraction in pre-Meiji times, rather than the distant unions which were developed by the Samurai class, and although these arranged marriages spread for a while throughout all social classes, love marriages have now become reasonably acceptable. However, in continuing houses, a wife still needs to suit the other members of the family as well.

In nuclear families, especially those of men who work for big companies, it has become common for a woman to stay at home, keep house and attend to the small children, and she is usually entrusted with the family finances as well. Some women take this role so seriously that they are called 'professional housewives', a role very often involving considerable input to the children's education as well as research into household products, the nutritional value of food for the family, and so on. In many parts of Japan housewives have set up cooperatives for buying food directly from producers, partly to cut out the expensive middlemen and partly to have some control over the production process. One of these groups was awarded an international prize for creating an alternative economy based on 'cooperation, human contact and ecological sustainability' in 1989 (Hendry 1993).

However, the role of the grandparents is still strong with regard to child care, and women who do go out to work are often able to draw on this resource, at least for part-time aid. More than 50 per cent of married women do actually go out to work, and many others help in a family business, or take piecework into the home. In continuing houses in the country, the young wife may well be expected to engage in productive work if there are grandparents available to care for children in the home. Otherwise it is common for women to take a period off work while they have small children, and return to some economically productive activity after a few years. Nevertheless, the duty of care within the family falls almost automatically to women, whether it be in times of sickness, injury or senility.

In the past few years women in nuclear families have been seeking more cooperation from their husbands in the running of the home and some men genuinely seem to be making an effort to comply. My own experience includes families where men will take care of the children and prepare the odd meal, but even the most helpful of husbands still take precedence as if by right in case of a clash of interests. A small study I carried out comparing the circumstances of two generations of academic women revealed that, though attitudes had changed significantly, their major domestic support is still being provided by other women (Hendry 1992).

Rosenberger's paper on home magazines (1992) introduces an interesting feature of futuristic living in the 'home automaton' found amongst the high technology of the wealthier homes of Tokyo. This is a control panel which allows remote access to light switches, doors, shutters, bath heaters and rice cookers, which is connected into the telephone system so that a call home can attend to security, comfort and supper before the journey is even undertaken. The development of a machine like this may help working wives to manage their homes from a distance, but it can also make it easier for people to live quite well on their own.

THE FAMILY AS A MODEL

If much of the 'family system' has been modified within the domestic realm, its underlying principles are still used as a model in other areas of society. Perhaps the most basic idea is that of putting the house before individual needs, and this principle has been transferred to many other areas of Japanese life. It will recur in later chapters, but the all-embracing nature of the large Japanese company is a good example, and it has been argued that for company employees the company itself has taken over the traditional role of the *ie*. In the way that parents expected loyalty from their children, a company superior expects total loyalty from his subordinates, and the individual's real family should come second. In exchange, the superior will take care of the individual and his family, if necessary, even to the extent of arranging a marriage for him.

An ethnographic study carried out with employees of the National Railways in Japan, before they were privatised into regional sections, illustrates very clearly the way the family model has been used and manipulated in this way. The image of the family was constantly invoked by the slogan 'One Railroad Family', but the ideology was also open to different interpretations at various different levels among the employees and at different times in their careers. Noguchi (1990) has analysed the system after two longish periods of participant observation, and he has revealed some of the immense complexity found in working relations based on these principles of family cooperation.

The idea of giving loyalty in exchange for benevolence is expected in pairs of relationships in various walks of life, and the expression *oyabun/kobun*, or parent-part/child-part, is used to describe such relations. It applies to teacher/pupil bond, master/apprentice, landlord/tenant, and, in particular, criminal and accomplice. Like the bond between parent and child, these relationships are expected to last, and the beneficiary is expected to consult and visit his benefactor even unto his death if need be. Evidently the family and the ideology associated with it has much in the way of preparation for the world outside. More specific aspects of this preparation will be presented in the chapter which follows.

NOTES

1. For further elaboration of the principles involved, see Bachnik (1983).
2. An article by the historian Kathleen Uno details how much 'reproductive' work men engaged in during the Tokugawa period while women were engaging in 'productive' work (Uno 1991).

REFERENCES

Bachnik, Jane M., 'Recruitment Strategies for Household Succession: Rethinking Japanese Household Organisation', *Man*, vol. 18, no. 1 (1983), pp. 160–82

Bethel, Diana, 'Alienation and Reconnection in a Home for the Elderly', in Joseph Tobin, (ed.), *Remade in Japan* (Yale University Press, New Haven and London, 1992), pp. 126–42
——, 'Life in *Obasuteyama*, or, Inside a Japanese Institution for the Elderly', in T.S. Lebra, *Japanese Social Organisation* (University of Hawaii Press, Honolulu, 1992), pp. 109–34
Coaldrake, William H., 'The Architecture of Reality: Trends in Japanese Housing 1985–1989', in *The Japan Architect*, no. 390 (1989), pp. 61–6
Hamabata, Matthews Masayuki, *Crested Kimono: Power and Love in the Japanese Business Family* (Cornell University Press, Ithaca, 1990)
Hendry, Joy, 'Generational Diversity in a Family Life History: Two Academic Women', in Susanne Formanek and Sepp Linhart (eds), *Japanese Biographies, Life Histories, Life Cycles* (Austrian Academy of Sciences, 1992), pp. 113–25
——, 'The Role of the Professional Housewife', in Janet Hunter (ed.), *Japanese Women Working* (Routledge, London, 1993), pp. 224–41
Kinoshita, Yasuhito and Christie W. Kiefer, *Refuge of the Honored: Social Organization in a Japanese Retirement Community* (University of California Press, Berkeley, 1993)
Lebra, T.S., *Above the Clouds: Status Culture of the Modern Japanese Nobility* (University of California Press, Berkeley, 1993)
Moon, Okpyo, 'Is the *ie* Disappearing in Rural Japan? The Impact of Tourism on a Traditional Japanese Village', in Hendry, Joy and Jonathan Webber (eds), *Interpreting Japanese Society* (Journal of the Anthropological Society of Oxford Occasional Publication, no. 5, Oxford, 1986), pp. 185–97
Noguchi, Paul H. *Delayed Departures, Overdue Arrivals: Industrial Familialism and the Japanese National Railways* (University of Hawaii Press, Honolulu, 1990)
Rosenberger, Nancy, 'Images of the West: Home Style in Japanese Magazines', in Joseph Tobin (ed.) *Remade in Japan: Everyday Life and Consumer Taste in a Changing Society* (Yale University Press, New Haven and London, 1992), pp. 106–25
Uno, Kathleen, 'Women and Changes in the Household Division of Labor' in Bernstein, Gail Lee (ed.), *Recreating Japanese Women* (University of California Press, Berkeley, 1991)
Wöss, Fleur, 'Escape into Death: Old People and their Wish to Die', in Gordon Daniels (ed.), *Europe Interprets Japan* (Paul Norbury, Tenterden, Kent, 1984), pp. 222–9

FURTHER READING

Ariga, Kizaemon, 'The Family in Japan', *Marriage and Family Living*, vol. 16 (1954), pp. 362–73
Beardsley, Richard K., John W. Hall and Robert E. Ward, *Village Japan* (University of Chicago Press, Chicago, 1959), Chapter 9
Bernstein, Gail Lee, *Haruko's World: A Japanese Farm Woman and her Community* (Stanford University Press, Stanford, 1983)
Dore, R.P., *City Life in Japan* (University of California Press, Berkeley, 1971), section III, esp. Chapter 8

Fukutake, Tadashi, *Japanese Rural Society,* trans. R.P. Dore (Cornell University Press, Ithaca, 1972) Chapters III–V

Hendry, Joy, *Marriage in Changing Japan* (Croom Helm, London, 1981), esp. Chapters 1 and 3

Imamura, Anne E., *Urban Japanese Housewives* (Hawaii University Press, Honolulu, 1987)

Jeremy M. and M.E. Robinson, *Ceremony and Symbolism in the Japanese Home* (Manchester University Press, Manchester, 1989)

Nakane, Chie, *Kinship and Economic Organisation in Rural Japan* (London School of Economics Monographs on Social Anthropology, no. 32, University of London: The Athlone Press, London, 1967)

Plath, David, 'My-car-isma: Motorizing the Shōwa Self', *Daedalus* vol. 119, no. 3 (1990), pp. 229–44

RELATED NOVELS

Ariyoshi, Sawako, *The Twilight Years* (Peter Owen, London, 1972)
———*The River Ki* (Kodansha International, Tokyo, 1981)

Enchi, Fumiko, *The Waiting Years* (Kodansha International, Tokyo, 1986)

Futabatei, Shimei, *An Adopted Husband* (Greenwood Press, New York, 1969)

Tanizaki, Junichiro, *The Makioka Sisters* (Picador, London, 1979)

FILMS

The Ballad of the Narayama (*Narayamabushi-Ko*) (dir. Imamura Shōhei)

The Makioka Sisters (*Sasame Yuki*) (dir. Ichikawa Kon, earlier version, Shima Kōji)

3 Socialisation and classification

INTRODUCTION

Having looked at the ideological position of the family in Japanese society in general, we shall now focus in on the very heart of the home to look at the world which is first presented to a Japanese child. Socialisation is the means by which an essentially biological being is converted into a social one, able to communicate with other members of the particular society to which it belongs. A child learns to perceive the world through language, spoken and unspoken, through ritual enacted, and through the total symbolic system which structures and constrains that world. Through socialisation a child learns to classify the world in which it lives, and to impose a system of values upon it.

Much social learning of this sort happens so early that culturally relative categories are often thought to be 'natural' and 'normal' until a person moves out of his or her society of upbringing. Even then, there is a tendency to describe foreigners as 'strange', 'dirty' or even 'stupid', since their assumptions about the world are different. During the Second World War, for example, the Japanese were described as 'pathologically clean' by their enemies in the United States. It is thus interesting to look at the early training of children in a particular society to try and identify important categories being imparted to them. An understanding of these categories can pave the way for a deeper understanding of relations in later life, and headings found in this chapter cover aspects of Japanese interpersonal relations which are also described elsewhere for adult behaviour.

In Japan, the early period is particularly interesting because mothers and other caretakers of small children are quite assiduous in their efforts to train children in the way they regard as fit and proper to do things. 'The soul of the three year old lasts till a hundred', a saying runs, and it is up to the adults around to mould that soul.

There is also a high degree of consistency amongst the adults involved in many of their ideas about how children should be trained There are, of course, regional variations and differences based on social status and occupation, but there are also certain features which seem to be common throughout Japan, no doubt aided by the almost universal influence of television, newspapers and magazines. In this chapter the most important of these common features have been picked out and their role in shaping the child for its membership in society will be discussed.

The socialising role of the kindergarten will also be presented in some detail. Nearly all children are sent to a kindergarten or day nursery for a period of a year or more before they enter school, and this seems to be regarded as an important part of their early education, although it is not compulsory. It is particularly the introduction it provides to interaction with the peer group which is considered important, and it is thought best for this to take place before school entry. Various aspects of relations within this group are quite clearly defined and again appear under headings which could also apply to adult interaction. Many of the principles of the approach used in the family are shared by teachers at this early stage, which provides some continuity in introducing the new experience of life in a large group.

UCHI AND *SOTO*

Some of the earliest acquired ideas which are most difficult to dislodge in any society are those associated with dirt and cleanliness. It is all very well to have an understanding at a theoretical level about different kinds of upbringing, but it is much harder to accept behaviour which one's own early training has presented as revolting or disgusting. It seems likely, therefore, that a system of classification associated with notions of dirt and cleanliness is held rather deeply, as Mary Douglas (1970) has pointed out. In Japanese society the distinction between *uchi* and *soto* is an example of such a deeply held part of the system of classification.

Uchi and *soto* translate roughly as 'inside' and 'outside' respectively, and they are probably first learned by a child in association with the inside and outside of the house in which it lives. They, or parallel words,[1] are also applied to members of one's house as opposed to members of the outside world, and to members of a person's wider groups, such as the community, school or place of work, as opposed to other people outside those groups. The importance of this distinction, and its association with dirt and cleanliness, is illustrated by looking at the ways it is used in training small children.

First of all, *uchi* and *soto* are associated with the clean inside of the house, and the dirty outside world, respectively. Japanese houses almost always have an entrance hall where shoes, polluted with this outside dirt, are removed, and it is one of the few inflexible rules enforced by Japanese adults that small children learn to change their shoes every time they go in and out of the house. The anthropologist, Emiko Ohnuki-Tierney, has discussed this practice (1984: Chapter 2) in terms of the notions of hygiene involved, and she explains that outside is regarded as dirty because that is where germs are thought to be located. This 'outside' is anywhere where there are other people, or other people have been, and the concept is succinctly expressed, she argues, in the term *hitogomi*, which sounds like 'people dirt', although the actual reading of the Chinese characters for the word simply means crowds.

Moreover, this distinction between the physical inside and outside of the house is reinforced by the use of ritualised phrases of greeting or parting which are uttered when one crosses the threshold, or by those remaining behind to greet or see off others who are coming or going. These phrases are fixed and invariable, and adults take special

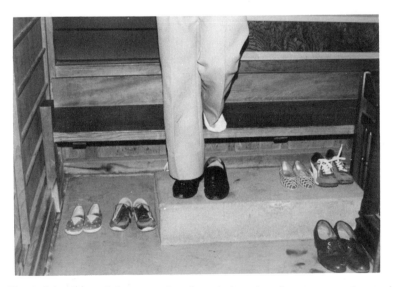

Figure 3.1   A porch for removing shoes is found at the entrance of every Japanese home. It marks clearly the distinction between *uchi* and *soto* worlds.

care to pronounce them carefully with small children, who soon learn to copy them at the appropriate time. Further associations with the supposed pollution of the outside world are expressed in the way children are encouraged when they come in to wash, change, and in some houses, even to gargle, again to eliminate the germs they may have encountered while out.

In the country, children are sometimes held out over the verandah at the side of the house to urinate, and once over the threshold of the front door, anywhere seems to be appropriate for the urine of a small child, even directly in front of the entrance. The toilets of a country house are often physically quite separate from the other rooms, and in most houses a special pair of toilet slippers is provided, which again distinguishes this 'dirty' area from the main part of the house. In the country, too, the gaping hole of the old-fashioned loo is a real danger to children, as is the steep drop often found at the entrance of the house. Thus, an approach too close in either of these directions will elicit negative response from caretakers, encouraging an association of the outside with a danger of falling as well as with possible infection. A similar association will be made in a city house, but for practical reasons it will more likely be concerned with traffic and the anonymity of the city streets.

This association of the outside with danger and fear is actually encouraged in some families, especially by older people, perhaps partly because it seems to work as an effective means of keeping a child close at hand. It is opposed to another association, which is consciously built up, of security with the inside of the home. Parents take trouble to anticipate the needs of babies and small children, to give them in the early years the abundant attention which they see as necessary to create security and trust in a child, and also to elicit cooperation in following the directives of themselves and other adults. Punishments are avoided where possible, but if their use is necessary, they are often associated with the outside world, rather than with members of the inside of the home. Thus threats may be made about demons, policemen and passing strangers, and a severe punishment is to put a child out of the house altogether.

TATEMAE AND *HONNE*

Another way in which the distinction between *uchi* and *soto* is made clear to a child is in the way the behaviour of adults varies depending on whether they are inside or outside the house. Put rather simply, this difference in behaviour corresponds to the difference between *tatemae* or public behaviour, and *honne*, or one's real feelings. In fact, this association is by no means clear cut, because members of the family will have close relationships outside the home, and will behave 'publicly' if outsiders are invited into the house. However, the initial physical distinction is applied gradually to the circle of people with whom the child comes into contact, and it will learn to recognise the *uchi* and *soto* relations of its family by participating in changes of behaviour in appropriate circumstances.

The participation is gradually but firmly encouraged by adults, who will adjust their own levels of politeness according to the situation and instruct the child about how to adjust his or her level, too. Japanese language has quite clear speech levels, which are chosen according to the relationship between the people involved in a conversation, as well as the context in which they find themselves. The use of polite language also makes possible the maintenance of a certain distance between the conversants, therefore protecting the 'inner feelings' from the probings of an outsider. Other distinctions in Japanese which correspond to that between *tatemae* and *honne*, can be translated as 'front' and 'rear', 'face' and 'heart', 'mouth' and 'stomach',[2] and the ability to distinguish between them is regarded as a measure of maturity.

It should be clear, however, that the distinctions are dichotomies only at an ideological level. In practice, there is a range of levels of politeness which varies depending on situations and a variety of relationships, and there are various degrees of closeness as well. A child probably first learns the distinction between the immediate family and the outside world, but will gradually come to recognise wider *uchi* groups, such as relatives, close neighbours, age-mates and so on, as his or her experience broadens. Even for each of these 'inside' groups, a slightly different type of behaviour will be appropriate.

The importance of these distinctions cannot be overemphasised in explaining features of Japanese society, as will be shown in later chapters, for it is in choosing the appropriate 'face' for a particular occasion that one is able successfully to fulfil one's social role in the world. The 'inner self' is recognised, and children are taught to understand their own selves so that they can project this understanding and devise behaviour which will consider the inner feelings of others. The conscious awareness of different sorts of *tatemae* behaviour is only learned gradually, and it is associated with the emphasis placed on another important aspect of Japanese social relations, namely harmony.

HARMONY: RECIPROCITY AND HIERARCHY

The concern of adults to create a secure and attentive environment for a small child is part of this wider emphasis in Japanese society on harmony in social relations. It is, of course, an ideal which may or may not be achieved in practice, but much of an adult's training of children is based on the assumption that one should work towards this ideal. Thus, from the very beginning, one should try to maintain a congenial atmosphere with a small child, teaching it the proper way to behave for the sake of behaving properly, rather than for praise or to avoid punishment. An ideal child is a 'bright', cheerful child (*akarui, meirō*) and, once past the baby stage, a crying child is described as 'strange' or 'peculiar' (*okashii*).

This emphasis on harmony also applies to relations between the child and others with whom it may come into contact, and adults take pains to help children playing together to avoid situations of dispute. If a fight does break out, some time will be spent establishing what happened, and who should apologise, with full consultation of the children involved themselves. An apology must then be made clearly, and accepted by the injured party, so that play can resume happily. Two important principles are drawn upon in establishing guilt in such a case, and the same principles are used in pursuit of the aim of establishing and maintaining harmonious relations. They are the principles of hierarchy and reciprocity.

Reciprocity

Reciprocity is called upon constantly in the way adults teach children to think of others before they act. Essentially it is the principle of 'do as you would be done by' which is being invoked here. Thus a child is exhorted to think of how it would feel if another child were to do to it what it is doing to another child, how it would like it if another child refused to lend a toy when it wanted to borrow one, how it would feel if another child snatched its toy . . . and so on. A child must be trained out of its natural selfishness – the word used for selfish, *wagamama* is made up of *waga* (self) and *mama* (as it is) – rather implying an untrained state. This is part of a wider general encouragement of children to try and put themselves in the shoes of others before acting.

Hierarchy

It is of course asking a lot to expect very small children to project themselves in such a way, and the other important principle, that of hierarchy, helps to resolve this problem. Children are made aware of their relative ages from a very early stage, and in case of dispute, an older child is encouraged to give in to a younger child 'who is not yet old enough to understand'. Such encouragement seems to emphasise the long-term advantages of being older, despite temporary deprival, and it seems to be rather a successful method of solving sibling rivalry, as well as quarrels within the neighbourhood. It has the incidental effect of emphasising the superior role, and the responsibility and benevolence associated with it, before the inferior role. This order of learning must be somewhat more palatable than the reverse.

In the family, older children are addressed by younger ones with a term meaning 'older sister' or 'older brother', sometimes as a suffix to their names, and adults make use of this form of address when eliciting 'good' behaviour, perhaps as a demonstration to a younger child. Similar distinctions are made in the wider circle of children in the neighbourhood, for example, and new children entering the group will always be asked for their ages before play can proceed. When adults ask children to play with babies or their younger siblings, they may use a form of request which can be translated as 'do the favour of . . .', projecting onto the older child a verb which is used for action from a superior to an inferior, and smaller children will learn to ask an older child to play using the converse of this form – from an inferior to a superior.

These verbs, and terms of address, form part of the system of speech levels mentioned above, and it can be seen that the beginnings of such distinctions are being learned very young. The hierarchical distinctions within a house are sometimes thought appropriate ones to emphasise in teaching a child to use polite language, especially where there are three or more generations living together, but the distinction between *uchi* and *soto* may override these differences, so that children will be taught to address the grandparents outside the home more politely than those inside. Speech levels themselves vary greatly with social background, but the general principle of using hierarchy as a means of trying to achieve harmony is widespread.

KINDERGARTEN: EQUALITY

For a period varying between one and several years before children enter school they will attend a kindergarten or day nursery, which is said among other things, to introduce them to 'group life' in preparation for school. The class will form a new 'inside' group for a child, a new *uchi*, to be opposed to the outside world, and various ritual procedures emphasise the nature of the group. Again children must remove their outside shoes when they come into the classroom, usually changing into special indoor shoes, and they may also have to change their clothes. As the day begins there will usually be some routine activity which the children learn and go through together involving elements such as songs, chants, movements in time to music, and the reading of the register. There will be a similar routine at the end of the day as the group breaks up.

In contrast to the basically hierarchical relations found in the home and neighbourhood, when children enter kindergarten the emphasis within the class is on the essential equality of members of the group. The children wear uniform, or at least smocks or aprons to make them alike, and they have identical sets of equipment for their activities. The other children in the class are all referred to as 'friends'. These are not special buddies chosen by each child, but up to 39 other children with whom any one child is now to pass a substantial proportion of each day. Of course, any child will form special attachments, and children will also know their relative ages, strengths and so on, but members of the class are regarded as symbolically equal, and this equality is expressed in several ways.

Duties and privileges, for example, are shared out equally by means of a rota system. Thus children take it in turns to be on duty for break and lunch service which probably involves handing out food and drinks, and also perhaps seeing that the other children are sitting properly before they give the signal to start eating. The children on duty may also be responsible for lining their classmates up for a trip to the hall, and they will probably also take any roles of privilege for the day, like presenting flowers to the altar in an institution with a religious foundation. In this way roles which could, if taken out of context, be interpreted as hierarchical, like service, authority and privilege, are equally distributed among all the members of the class. As will be seen elsewhere in Japanese society, apparent hierarchy is often contextual rather than based on any inherent differences in status.

Again, there is much emphasis on creating and maintaining a congenial environment for small children, and before a child even enters kindergarten much is made of the 'fun' it will have there. This is another part of the emphasis on harmony as an ideal in social relations. Any quarrels are investigated and apologies made. Children are expected to be happy, and anyone who is not, like the crying child, is classed as 'strange' or 'peculiar'. A child who shows reluctance to participate is encouraged to join in, but, if it refuses, it will simply be ignored, as the teacher goes about the business of making life 'fun' for all the other children.

This form of classification sets apart a child who appears to be unhappy, by moving it out of the main group and emphasising its difference from the other children. Taken together with the association already established of security with *uchi*, and fear with *soto*, and the emphasis on equality of members of the group, this form of ostracism is usually rather effective in encouraging participation.[3] The threat of removal from the group is also used as an effective sanction when an individual child fails to comply with the teacher's directives. A small child at this stage is keen to be just like its mates, and teachers take advantage of and encourage this propensity, making it unattractive to be 'different'.

PEER GROUP PRESSURE

Teachers also take advantage of the propensity of children to impose rules upon themselves (cf. Piaget 1932), allowing much of the discipline of the group to be generated by the pressure of the peer group. Thus, for example, at the beginning of the day, the routine in which the children participate is initiated by a tune on the piano or organ, played continuously by the teacher until all the children are sitting, or standing in their positions ready to begin. Those who are slow hold up the whole group, and they are urged by their classmates to hurry up. The same principle is put into practice before break and lunchtime, when the added incentive of hunger ensures rapid cooperation.

In a similar way quarrels are resolved by asking children who witness a dispute to pass judgement on the situation, and decide who was at fault and should therefore apologise. Teachers also appeal to the whole class when pointing out the recalcitrant behaviour of one of their number, asking whether such behaviour is acceptable, and if not, what kind of behaviour is. The personalised collective term *mina-san* is used to address and refer to the whole group and its needs, and an individual whose behaviour is to the detriment of *mina-san* is made to feel most uncomfortable. The children are also encouraged to take care of the kindergarten property in the name of its corporate owners, *mina-san*.

COOPERATION

In general cooperation is also encouraged in a number of other positive ways. Classroom walls are invariably decorated with cooperative creations to which each child has contributed, like nets full of individually fashioned fishes, or woods full of trees. Marching in formation is another cooperative activity practised in some kindergartens, as are orchestras or choirs. The kindergarten where I worked in Chiba prefecture had an eighty-piece orchestra, largely composed of six year olds, which played tolerable renderings of popular Mozart and Vivaldi pieces. The annual sports day usually emphasises cooperation over individual competition, and children are encouraged to exert themselves for the sake of the class, or the area where they live, rather than for their own glory. Popular events include the tug-of-war and the three-, five- or seven-legged races, where cooperation is essential for success.

Stories and plays presented to or put on by the children also tend to emphasise the advantages of cooperation over individual endeavour, and a Japanese version of the 'Three Little Pigs', for example, usually has the first two little pigs escape the attacks of the big bad wolf so that they can join the third pig and cooperate in their efforts to entice him down the chimney into the cooking pot. The more usual version found in England, the home of the story, has the first two little pigs being eaten up for their lack of foresight, whereas the third pig uses his individual cunning and cleverness to defeat the wolf. Television programmes for children often reiterate this theme, as a single hero tries and is unsuccessful in his attempt to defeat the monster, or other alien force until he gains the cooperation of other victims of the danger.

SELF-DEVELOPMENT

It should be emphasised that the development of the individual child is not neglected in all this collective activity. In the home, the child is, of course, given much individual attention, and one of the first things it is taught as a baby is to respond politely, with the term *hai*, to hearing its own name being called. Parents fill in detailed forms about their children's personal attributes, faults, friends, likes and dislikes on entering them into kindergarten, and the teachers come to know their charges very well. They pick out individual children for praise or reprimand, and they seek to find ways of dealing with any individual problems they may have. They also maintain close communication with the parents of each child, and in public kindergartens they visit each child's home at least once a year.

Each child has its own property to take care of in the kindergarten or day nursery, albeit identical to the property of other children, but it must be responsible for its own personal set. It also has personal property at home, and early training includes the specific encouragement to attend to the maintenance and care of these items. Some of the aims of early training, shared by parents and teachers alike, are to develop personal qualities such as perseverance, concentration, effort, independence and self-reliance. Indeed, one of the aims stated by parents in sending their children to pre-school educational establishments is to help them to develop these qualities.

Another often stated aim is that children should learn to think for themselves and understand themselves in order to understand others. By understanding their own needs they are thought to be able to understand the needs of others, and so to work out appropriate behaviour in any situation. They need, parents say, to understand the limits imposed on their self-interest by the needs of others, and the collective needs of the wider group which they join in educational establishments. Thus, a child will gradually learn to exercise self-control in the interest of harmonious social relations.

SELF IN THE WORLD

In fact, an individual child usually learns to enjoy the advantages of its new identity as a member of a collective group, and sees that it is in fact in its own interest in certain circumstances to put self-interest second. This principle is important throughout school life, and indeed, for many Japanese, on into adult life in relations at work or in the local community. The success of the company, for example, is seen to depend on the cooperation of its individual members, and the success of the members is seen as directly dependent on the success of the company to which they belong. Individuals may also express satisfaction in being part of a greater entity such as this.

Several writers have discussed the Japanese concept of self. Some have suggested that the self as an isolable entity is non-existent, since Japanese people are always defining themselves in reference to other people, or to some group. Others discuss the importance of dependence as a quality of human relations in Japan and oppose this with the independence for which we are supposed to strive in Western societies.[4] Some of the arguments are summarised in Smith (1983: Chapter 3), who continues with an excellent alternative discussion of the issue in terms of social interaction and use of language. Lebra (1976: Chapter 8) discusses various ways in which the concept of 'self' is used in Japanese, and argues that individuality is achieved through introspection.

One of the problems is that 'individualism' and 'individuality' have been associated with 'democracy' and other apparently positively valued aspects of Westernisation which were used in the drafting of the 1947 Constitution and new educational tenets. The Japanese words which translate the concepts have quite different connotations, however. The word for individualism (*kojinshugi*) is seen as little different from that for 'selfishness', which, as we have seen, implies an undesirable, untrained state. The word for 'individuality' (*kosei*), on the other hand, has become an ideal, and is sought in the pursuit of personal interests and achievements, perfectly acceptable as long as they don't interfere with one's obligations to others. Brian Moeran (1984) has discussed the 'problem' of individualism in Japanese society in terms of an 'internal cultural debate'.

A book of papers entitled *Japanese Sense of Self*, edited by Nancy Rosenberger (1992), aims to use studies of Japanese lives to contribute to anthropological efforts to understand the issue of self 'outside of Western assumptions'. The editor explains that in this volume the self and the social are studied as interactive rather than as opposing processes, in other words the papers seek to ask: 'how do the self and the social constitute one another?' The papers consider notions such as 'the multiplicity of self, or the multiple and changing positions that constitute self'.

One of the contributions is a chapter from another important book in this area, namely *Crafting Selves* by Dorinne Kondo. Subtitled *Power, Gender, and Discourses of Identity in a Japanese Workplace*, this is an excellent ethnography about life in a Tokyo sweet-making factory. The author spent a year working in this small family business where she came to know well her workmates and their lives in and outside the factory. She constructs a fascinating account of the sources and discourses of self and identity of these people, and throws in a fairly detailed analysis of her own self-identity as a Japanese American working as an anthropologist and therefore investigator in her country of origin.

Two other papers in the Rosenberger book address the importance of learning and practising the moving between these different multiple selves expressed in behaviour appropriate for different situations. The first, by Joseph Tobin, is based again on the study of a kindergarten and focuses on the way children learn to distinguish and move smoothly between the controlled behaviour expected in relatively formal *omote* or *tatemae* situations and the free and easy behaviour of the *ura* or *honne* ones. This paper draws on the work of Doi Takeo in his book *Anatomy of Self* (1986) which examines in great detail the concepts of *omote* and *ura*, and how they relate to one another, but Tobin emphasises that it is the *kejime* or distinction between the two which is important at the kindergarten stage. Jane Bachnik's paper in the Rosenberger volume develops this notion of *kejime* and its importance for 'defining a shifting self in multiple organizational modes' in adult life.

To return to the child in kindergarten, there is probably little choice. Except for extraordinary cases, like that described in note 3 below, individualism is not really an option. One can either be cooperative or be left out, either be happy or laughed at as 'strange' and 'peculiar'. But this cooperative individual is not losing its *individuality* or individual identity by participating in group activities. It is merely demonstrating one of the 'faces' it learns to have for different situations. This 'face' is part of the *tatemae* or 'public' behaviour appropriate in this particular context, and an individual will have several such 'faces' for different situations.

These different 'faces' are reflected in different speech forms used on different occasions, and none of them negates the existence of a complete self using them all. Just as *tatemae* is distinguished from *honne*, one's real feelings or intention, behaviour in the group context may be distinguished from the individual who is acting out a role as member of the group. A child who falls down in front of his or her playmates will make every effort to avoid crying and being called 'strange', despite considerable pain. In another context – perhaps with a kind-hearted grandmother – the tears may be adjudged appropriate to gain sympathy and special treatment. The same fall, if a child was entirely alone, would perhaps be more quickly overcome. These different 'faces' are recognisable in other societies, but they form an integral part of the system of classification in Japan.

CONCLUSION

By looking at the early training of a small child we have in fact only touched upon subjects which other studies have discussed in much greater detail as important 'keys' to understanding Japanese people and their ways of thinking. We have, however, isolated some very important indigenous concepts which will recur in the chapters which follow. By seeing how they are first introduced in childhood, we can, I hope, get a feel for how they are acquired by a native speaker. Armed with this 'feel', we can proceed to venture out into the wider world outside the family.

NOTES

1. In reference to groups of people the terms *miuchi* and *tanin* or *yoso no hito* are often used for 'inside' groups and 'outside' people respectively.
2. *Omote* and *ura, kao* and *kokoro, kuchi* and *hara.*
3. One exception to this rule is the protagonist of the well-known autobiographical story of Totto-chan (Kuroyanagi, 1981/2), now a popular TV personality in Japan. The book, which is sub-titled in English: *The Little Girl at the Window*, tells the story of a child who never managed to fit in to her class at school, and she was eventually moved to another rather special school.
4. The best-known work on this subject is by the psychiatrist Doi Takeo (1973). The essence of the argument is that the concept *amae*, which he translates as 'passive love' or 'dependence', is uniquely Japanese and therefore provides a key to understanding Japanese behaviour. The concept is certainly found elsewhere (e.g. Spanish *mimar* is close), even if there is no easy translation in English, and I have not found the argument particularly helpful from a social point of view. However, a reader with a psychological training might find it useful to follow up.

REFERENCES

Doi, Takeo, *The Anatomy of Dependence,* trans. John Bester (Kodansha International, Tokyo, 1973)
——, *The Anatomy of Self: The Individual Versus Society,* trans. Mark Harbison (Tokyo: Kodansha International, 1986)
Douglas, Mary, *Purity and Danger* (Harmondsworth, Penguin Books, 1970)
Kondo, Dorinne, *Crafting Selves: Power, Gender, and Discourses of Identity in a Japanese Workplace* (University of Chicago Press, Chicago and London, 1990)
Kuroyanagi, Tetsuko, *Madogiwa no Totto-chan* (Kodansha, Tokyo, 1981); trans. D. Britten as *Totto-chan: The Little Girl at the Window* (Kodansha, Tokyo, 1982)
Lebra, Takie Sugiyama, *Japanese Patterns of Behaviour* (University Press of Hawaii, Honolulu, 1976), Chapter 8
Moeran, Brian, 'Individual, Group and *Seishin*: Japan's Internal Cultural Debate', *Man*, vol. 19, no. 2 (1984), pp. 252–66
Ohnuki-Tierney, Emiko, *Illness and Culture in Contemporary Japan* (Cambridge University Press, Cambridge, 1984)
Piaget, J., *The Moral Judgement of the Child* (Routledge and Kegan Paul, London, 1932)
Rosenberger, Nancy (ed.), *Japanese Sense of Self* (Cambridge University Press, Cambridge, 1992)
Smith, Robert J., *Japanese Society: Tradition, Self and the Social Order* (Cambridge University Press, Cambridge, 1983)

FURTHER READING

Bachnik, Jane, 'Time, Space and Person in Japanese Relationships' in Joy Hendry and Jonathan Webber (eds) *Interpreting Japanese Society* (Journal of the Anthropological Society of Oxford Occasional Publication, no. 5, Oxford, 1986), pp. 49–75

Benedict, Ruth, *The Chrysanthemum and the Sword* (Routledge and Kegan Paul, London, 1977), Chapter 12

Hendry, Joy, 'Shoes: The Early Learning of an Important Distinction in Japanese Society' in Gordon Daniels (ed.), *Europe Interprets Japan* (Paul Norbury Publications, Tenterden, Kent, 1984), pp. 215–22

——, *Becoming Japanese: The World of the Pre-school Child* (Manchester University Press, Manchester, 1986)

——, 'Individualism and Individuality: Entry into a Social World' in Roger Goodman and Kirsten Refsing (eds), *Ideology and Practice in Modern Japan* (Routledge, London, 1992).

Koschmann, J. Victor, 'The Idioms of Contemporary Japan VIII: *tatemae to honne*', *The Japan Interpreter* 9 (1974): pp. 98–104

Maretzki, Thomas W. and Hatsumi Maretzki, 'Taira, an Okinawan Village', in Beatrice Whiting (ed.) *Six Cultures* (John Wiley and Sons, New York, 1963), pp. 353–539

Peak, Lois, *Learning to Go to School in Japan: The Transition from Home to Preschool Life* (University of California Press, Berkeley and Los Angeles, 1991)

Wagatsuma, Hiroshi and George A. De Vos, *Heritage of Endurance: Family Patterns and Delinquency Formation in Urban Japan* (University of California Press, Berkeley, 1984)

RELATED NOVEL

Ishiguro, Kazuo, *Pale View of Hills* (Penguin, Harmondsworth, 1983)

4   Community and neighbourhood

INTRODUCTION

Outside the family, the next unit of social organisation which Japanese people experience, whatever their walk of life, is the neighbourhood. The nature of this unit will, of course, vary considerably according to its location, but there are again certain expectations among neighbours which seem to be characteristically Japanese, and they may be used as a yardstick even where there is little consistency with actual behaviour. Indeed the English word 'community' has recently been adopted into Japanese to refer to some of these expectations, often in an effort to establish them where they are perceived to be lacking.

One example of common neighbourly behaviour follows on well from the previous chapter, for it is generally in the neighbourhood that children make their first friends. Where physically possible, children are allowed out to play in the immediate vicinity of their house from the age of about three. This early freedom is made possible by the cooperation of adults living in the area who keep an informal eye on any clusters of tiny playmates who should happen to be roaming nearby. It is, of course, not possible for families who live on major roads to participate in such activities, but even in the largest cities, there are plenty of residential areas with quiet unsurfaced roads, and blocks of flats often have an enclosed play area attached to them.

When children begin to go to school, or even kindergarten, they will often line up together at a certain time each morning to walk to school as a group. The older children will then be responsible for taking care of the smaller ones as they walk through the streets. In rural areas, too, children will cross the fields in crocodile formation, or, in more remote regions, they will take a bus together. Even within the school, children from each neighbourhood will meet from time to time to discuss activities within their own community, and rules may be drawn up for the holidays based on the children's own ideas about how best they should behave. This group forms another experience of *uchi* affiliation.

Such neighbourly cooperation is not limited to children. Adults participate in neighbourly activities in a wide variety of ways, more or less compulsorily, depending on where they live and how long they or their forbears have been in the community. Until the modern period, 90 per cent of the population of Japan lived in rural villages, and these paid taxes as a unit to their feudal lords. Villagers were not very free to move out of their own area, but there was considerable autonomy within the communities, and they developed very effective ways of living together on a long-term basis. Towns, too, were composed of neighbourhoods which developed their own identities within the wider area to which they belonged, and even today, the residential areas of cities are divided into distinct units, which draw on the fund of historical tradition to support their current organisation.

A Japanese expression defines the immediate neighbours on whom one might need to depend in times of emergency. This literally translates as 'the three houses opposite and one on either side' (*mukōsangen ryōdonari*). It is generally thought to be important to maintain good relations with at least this minimal group, even if people have very little to do with the wider community, and people sometimes lament the breakdown of the system in urban apartment complexes. However, families moving into a new house or apartment will often take small token gifts round to their close neighbours in order to establish relations with them, and housewives in most areas tend to establish quite close links with their neighbours.

This chapter will be devoted to presenting the principles, the variety and some of the consequences of this neighbourly interaction, which will be seen to set the scene for further communication. A community is a good focus for anthropological study, for it is possible for an individual observer to participate quite effectively in the inter-actions of neighbours, and an anthropological training prepares such an observer to understand communication in a face-to-face group of this sort.[1] There are a number of books and articles by anthropologists which are based on the life of specific communities in Japan. Some of these are listed at the end of the chapter. They will be referred to from time to time, but a good way to understand how neighbourly life works in Japan is to read about one or more cases in detail. Only then will the reader get a real feel for the combination of security and constraint this implies.

JAPAN'S ADMINISTRATIVE DIVISIONS

Japan is divided, for administrative purposes, into 47 prefectures, with prefectural offices, and municipal bodies encompassing 652 cities, 1,997 towns and 607 'villages', each with its own autonomous government and elected assembly (*Japan Statistical Handbook* March 1984). The English terms used here are somewhat misleading, however, as the towns and cities often include quite rural areas within their boundaries, and the 'villages' are usually collections of sparsely scattered small communities. Thus a small 'city' may well include within its boundaries a central area which resembles an English town, and a number of outlying settlements which would probably be classed in English as villages. The term 'village' will subsequently be used here for the type of settlement which the word would normally evoke in English.

In fact, these settlements usually form the smallest sub-divisions of the wider administrative zones in a rural area, and the corresponding unit of urban areas, which may have the same name in Japanese (*chōnai*), will here be called a neighbourhood. These smaller units are used, for example, for the purposes of postal addresses, policing and school allocation, but also to maintain a register of every resident and his or her original home if that is different from the present one. Often these administrative units coincide with more natural divisions, but they are revised from time to time, and older allegiances tend to survive in certain situations. A degree of local autonomy, even at the neighbourhood level, makes it difficult to generalise for the whole of Japan, and it is proposed here to describe first a stable rural unit, which will demonstrate maximum neighbourhood interaction, and then consider some of the variety found in other areas.

A RURAL COMMUNITY

It seems appropriate to start with a rural community, for the production of Japan's long-held staple, rice, requires considerable cooperation, and the mechanisms developed for this purpose underlie neighbourly relations in no small way. The crucial process of transplanting the seedlings from boxes to fields requires artificial flooding, and this needs to be carried out in conjunction with all the other farmers who share the same sources for their irrigation channels. The water supply needs to be monitored carefully during the early period, and if one family takes more than their share it could spell disaster for their neighbours. The practice during the feudal period of assessing a whole community for its quota of tax, to be paid in rice, meant that those who had more often had to subsidise those who had less, so it was in everybody's interest for each family to have a successful harvest.

In modern rural communities the economic base is usually very different. With the use of machines, chemical fertilizers and insecticides, rice production has become increasingly efficient and therefore less time-consuming, so that fewer people are required to provide the country's needs which are anyway diminishing rapidly as rice consumption drops. There is also less need for cooperation to accomplish the basic tasks of production. Cash crops, such as tea, fruit, flowers and vegetables, have become more prevalent, but in many areas, populations have been greatly depleted by young people especially moving off to work in cities. Elsewhere, a substantial proportion of villagers commute to a nearby town to work, and in the northern snowy areas some spend the entire winter away seeking seasonal work in an urban area.

The community which will be described in some detail below has managed to adapt very well to modern circumstances, so it will provide a good base line for comparison. It is largely agricultural, with several families specialising in the production of tea and/or chrysanthemums. Many families do have at least one member who goes out of the village to work, and several practise no agriculture at all. Nevertheless, every house participates in agricultural festivals, and most of them are continuing *ie* with ancestors who lived in the same village before the present occupants. The current residents have thus inherited much of their neighbourly interaction from their forebears, and the following description is a modern example of a stable unit of the type which was common in pre-industrial Japan.

The basic unit of population in such a community is the *ie*, and questions about the size of the community are usually answered in numbers of houses. At village meetings only one member of each house is required to attend, and the same principle operates for all village obligations and communal activities. Much neighbourly interaction is also carried out between houses, rather than between individuals, and people tend to refer to one another as 'the grandmother of House X', or 'the father of House Y', and so on.

Our village coincides with a local administrative unit of the 'city' to which it belongs, and all communication with the city hall is carried out through the head of the village. This person is elected by an assembly of the village (or neighbourhood) association (*chōnaikai*) which is made up of the heads of the houses within the community. He is responsible for the collection and payment of taxes for the whole community, for road and path repair within the village, and where possible, for the settlement of disputes which arise between the villagers.

In practice, the first of these tasks is carried out by the houses in strict rotation. The village is divided up into three smaller groups, in each of which one house is responsible for tax collection each month. A member of the house concerned goes round to all the other houses and collects up the money, which he or she then hands over to the village head, who passes it on to the appropriate authority. The way in which this responsibility for tax collection moves round to everybody in turn resembles the way tasks are shared out in the kindergarten, and it probably has a similarly equalising effect, despite other hierarchical differences. It certainly seems to ensure payment, for the village's taxes are usually paid in full. In the past, if one house could not afford for some reason to pay their taxes, their neighbours would chip in to help out, a measure designed to avoid bringing shame on the whole community. Even now, the poorer residents of a community may be allocated a lower sum to contribute to community funds, or even be excused payment altogether.

The order in which houses take on the responsibility for tax collection is also the order followed by a 'circulating notice board', which brings news from the city hall, from the head of the village, or from a house in the group wishing to circulate news about something to all its neighbours. This board is brought to the door by the previous person on the route, and it must be stamped as seen, and carried round to its next destination. This regular circulation of news ensures that every house keeps in touch with at least two other houses, and it also ensures that the authorities can maintain contact efficiently and cheaply with every house in their administrative zone.

The repair of roads and paths within the village is another task shared out equally among the houses. The village assembly will decide on a particular day to carry it out, and every house is expected to send a member along to participate. The materials will have been ordered in advance, and the work is usually completed within a few hours. Most houses comply with the directive, but there is a standard fine charged if one should fail to do so. Streams and smaller paths are taken care of in a similar way by the houses that use them.

Security is a concern of the community as a whole, and young men of the village serve for a few years in a voluntary body which stands ready to help out in case of need. Usually their active role is in fire-fighting, and they meet once a month to check the village fire engine and practise the drill for using it. This is an important supplement to

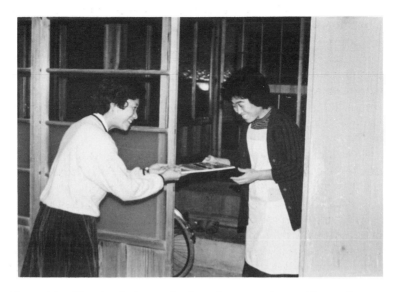

Figure 4.1 The circulating notice board ensures that residents of a community are kept informed about events taking place there. It also keeps neighbours in touch.

the professional fire service operated at city level, for members of the group are usually working in the neighbourhood and can be very quickly on the scene if they are required. The prevalence of wood and paper in Japanese houses means that swift action is essential in case of fire to prevent it spreading throughout a neighbourhood. The same group would be ready to act in case of other disasters such as floods or earthquakes.

Another task of the whole community is the care of the places of worship in the village. These include the shrine of the tutelary deity, who is thought to protect the residents of the community, and a couple of other sacred places, which are situated within the village boundaries. Groups of houses take responsibility in turn for each of these places, cleaning the buildings, maintaining the grounds and celebrating the periodic festivals associated with them. The largest festivals involve the whole community, but they are organised by the groups of houses to whose charge they fall in any particular year. This charge is passed on ceremonially after the major festival.

That this is a neighbourly duty as much as a religious one is illustrated in the way that even houses which have turned to a new religion are expected to take part. If they refuse, they are ostracised to some extent for their failure to cooperate. Formal ostracism is used occasionally in Japanese communities to express disapproval of some action regarded as antisocial. This *mura hachibu*, or 'village eighth-part' was very effective in pre-modern closed communities, because neighbours would cut off all communication except that absolutely necessary for survival (the 'eighth-part'), and few families could survive such an ordeal without conforming. It can be seen that the tactics of the kindergarten have a tried and tested basis in traditional village life.

At a more microscopic level, strong links are developed between immediate neighbours within this wider community. These houses are usually close enough for frequent chance interaction, and they are also the ones to whom one turns in times of need. A death in one house will bring representatives round immediately from the closest neighbours to take over the practical arrangements for the funeral, and a birth will likewise elicit visits and practical help, if necessary. Similar participation is virtually automatic on the occasions of marriage, house-building, sickness or disaster such as fire.

Participation on these occasions may well be much wider than the immediate neighbours, but these often have a special role in helping with practical arrangements. There is considerable exchange of gifts between these immediate houses too, as any special occasion will be marked by the presentation of gifts, and food is often distributed in return. Such exchanges also mark relations between villagers on a wider scale for major events, and a fire, house-building or a funeral usually brings the whole community into the system. Ultimately, however, the closest neighbours are those on whom one can rely in an emergency, and people offer their help freely because they know that they may need help in the future.

On an individual level, villagers have further allegiances in the neighbourhood to their age-mates, those people with whom they have moved through school, and in the case of women who have married into the community, those who arrived at around the same time. In the part of Kyushu where this village is located, these groups are very strong, often starting during childhood, meeting regularly, but adjusting to suit changing circumstances and composition of the group. They form another strong support group in times of need or celebration, and they are often an individual's closest companions.

These groups have also had wider functions, such as regular saving on a group basis for particular purposes like sending their members at least once during their lifetimes to the shrine of the imperial ancestress at Ise. Nowadays villagers are usually able to afford to make that particular trip without group saving, but the principle of saving for group activities, such as travel or visits together to holy places, continues. A traditionally exciting event in the lives of young people is going away for a few days with their age-mates on the proceeds of regular savings begun at an early age by their mothers.

Another series of groups based on age are for members of the community as they pass through particular stages in their lives. These groups resemble those found in other parts of the world which anthropologists have called age-grades. In this community there is a children's group, nowadays largely for members of primary school, a youth group, for young people between the ages of school-leaving and marriage, and two groups for old people of retirement age. Elsewhere, there are groups for men 'in the prime of life'. Except for the older people, these groups have usually had an important role to play in the organising and carrying out of local festivals, and nowadays they often have sporting and social events together as well. The old people's groups have recently been revived all over the country as part of a national concern with the welfare of the burgeoning numbers of retired people in Japan. In many areas, these groups have taken responsibility for various tasks of benefit to the whole community, and they also have sporting and social events, notably a game called 'gateball', which resembles croquet.

Similar groups with particular tasks in the community are formed on other principles. There is a strong 'housewives' group', which usually has one member from each house, so that the older wife will be the regular member, but she can be replaced by her daughter-in-law if she is unable to attend for some reason. Elsewhere, there are groups for the young wives too. There are also PTA groups associated with the primary and middle schools attended by the children. Nowadays these groups, like the old people's one, form local branches of nationwide organisations, and the same applies to the youth groups and the fire-fighting corps. All of them have social and educational activities. Those members of the community engaged in agricultural and horticultural work also belong to local branches of their unions, which provide a variety of services associated with their economic interests. There is also a women's branch of the agricultural union which meets to order domestic supplies in bulk, and may act as a consumer interest group somewhat like the cooperative groups mentioned in the previous chapter.

Finally, at a more informal level, there are various places where neighbours meet regularly to exchange news and gossip about each other. In this particular community there are two shops and a communal bath house, as well as a children's play area in the shrine compound. In the country it is customary for families whose children are proposing to marry to visit the village of the other party and ask around in shops and other public places about the family concerned. Since marriage is very important for the continuity of the *ie*, this is another strong incentive for neighbours to keep on good terms with each other and fulfil the obligations expected of them. Shops may also provide something of an outlet for pent up frustrations, and two fish shops in the area seem to attract senior and junior generations of housewives separately, so that problems of intergenerational conflict may be aired.

It can be seen in this one case that community life appears to involve an almost endless series of demands and obligations, and in fact there are further groups which have not been mentioned. Any one house will be constantly called upon to send members to participate in tasks, activities and exchanges, and in many cases there is little choice but to join in. On the other hand, membership in such a community brings security in the face of danger, comfort in times of need, and entertainment and social life to the very doorstep. Like the kindergarten child, villagers have little choice about participating, but they also realise the advantages of belonging to such a community. Recently, many villagers have tended to move away to a city for a period when they are young, but a substantial number return later and settle down in the village.

VARIETY IN RURAL JAPAN

The description given above refers largely to one particular community in provincial Kyushu. I have chosen to do this because it is easier to understand the various overlapping obligations and interactions involved in community life by considering one case in particular. Many of the activities will vary slightly in different parts of Japan, as will be seen if any of the other ethnographies listed below are consulted. A useful reference source of such variation was compiled by the Japanese anthropologists, Nagashima Nobuhiro and Tomoeda Hiroyasu (1984) in *Regional Differences in Japanese Rural Culture*.

According to reports of nationwide surveys of rural Japan, however, the type of community activity described above is disappearing in many areas, largely due to the decline in the numbers of people involved in agriculture. In many areas, young people leave their villages, or commute to work in towns and cities, and they are not, therefore, available to participate in the many activities of community life. With regard to the upkeep of village roads, for example, a survey by the Ministry of Agriculture, Forestry and Fisheries reports that while in 1955, 94 per cent of village communities carried out road repair as a communal task, this proportion had dropped to 74 per cent by 1970, and 68 per cent by 1980.[2] In some cases, this is due to the fact that roads have been paved by the local authorities, but the unavailability of residents also plays a part.

A similar decline has been noted in the proportion of houses participating in production-related activities. In the 1950s and 1960s, farming families organised themselves into local groups to study and develop new techniques, as well as to purchase agricultural materials and sell their produce efficiently. The number of villages with branches of such organisations increased from 53 per cent in 1955 to 83 per cent in 1960, but since then a decline has set in so that the number decreased to 80 per cent in 1970, and only 66 per cent in 1980. Branches of women's groups and youth groups have also declined (Hasumi 1985:7).

To some extent this decline may be related to the diversification of economic interests in rural areas. Particularly where there are attractive natural resources, or slopes conducive to the establishment of ski resorts, some communities have been able to concentrate on tourism. An anthropological study carried out in two communities in Gunma prefecture illustrates the changes which have occurred as a result of such developments. This study compares a community that is declining because of its continuing agricultural interests with one that is thriving through the development of country inns to accommodate skiers coming to use the nearby slopes. The nature of community life has changed in both cases, but the reasons are different, and the operators of country inns are still greatly involved in neighbourly interaction (see Moon 1984).

Another thriving community described recently by an anthropologist is the village of Kuzaki in Mie prefecture, where fishing and diving used to form the basis of the economy which was stimulated by its status as provider of sacred offerings for the Ise shrine. Here too tourism has become an important source of income, which encourages the diving activities, since the female divers are one of the major attractions to tourists, and allows the villagers not only to remain and make an adequate living in their own village, but also to keep their religious activities separate from the tourist gaze (Martinez 1990).

Elsewhere too the economic base has been strengthened by outside factors, but with greater internal effect. In a village in Kyushu, studied by another anthropologist, the life of rural potters was profoundly altered by the popularity of their products in the wider world (Moeran 1984). In this case, and that of the country inns, a conflict arose between the previous emphasis on cooperative activity, and the new inducements to compete with neighbouring houses. In both cases, the country people are encouraged to retain their 'traditional' ways by visitors from urban areas who enjoy finding their ethnic identity relatively unscathed in such communities. Nevertheless, the element of competition which is introduced as outsiders pick and choose amongst inns, pots or whatever, would seem to be eroding the very 'traditions' they seek to maintain.

A detailed anthropological account of changes which took place in an ordinary rural community in Shikoku, the smallest of Japan's four main islands, is to be found in *Kurusu*, by Robert Smith (1978). This book is based on two studies carried out in 1951/2, in the first place, and 1975 for a return visit. It was thus able to document changes in agricultural and other activities, and the related modifications which were made in material goods, family relations and community solidarity in a first-hand report. However, since this study was completed, things may well have changed again. A striking account of change is also to be found in Norbeck's 'timelapse' study of an island which has been incorporated into urban expansion into the ocean (Norbeck 1978).

In the 1980s there was a nationwide movement to try and revitalise Japan's countryside and grants were made to rural municipalities to give them an incentive. Some tried to attract visitors, either as tourists if there were enough local attractions or as adoptive fictitious 'relatives', offering cityfolk who had no country ties a way to keep in touch with their rural roots. Both schemes drew on the wave of nostalgia which was washing over the country (see also Bestor 1989, Moeran 1984, Martinez 1990 and Robertson 1991). The scheme to attract 'relatives' offered people the opportunity not only to visit the area and be taken care of in rural surroundings, but also to receive regular parcels of country produce when they returned to the city.

John Knight, an anthropologist who worked in an extremely rural area in Wakayama prefecture, made this village revival movement the focus of his research (Knight 1992). He has published an interesting article pointing out how the parallel Japanese interest in internationalisation is now reflected in some of the strategies adopted by rural municipalities. Some have set up direct exchange arrangements with localities in other parts of the world, others have adopted features of foreign culture to give themselves a special attraction to visitors. In one case, a local community with a noted interest in Denmark purchased the whole Danish pavilion from the 1992 Seville Exposition so that it could be reconstructed within their boundaries. Elsewhere, a holiday in a Swiss pension is the attraction (Knight 1993).

In 1985 a Japanese countryman reported on the changes which had taken place in his rural community in central Japan during a period of twenty years while he was living in Tokyo. The population had actually increased from the count of houses, but many of the residents now commute to work outside the village, so there is less opportunity for communication and cooperation between them. This factor is compounded by modern methods of house construction, which have done away with open verandahs where passers-by could stop for a chat without going through the formalities of removing shoes and entering the house. In the early 1970s, the author found fewer than half the households represented at local hamlet meetings, but since then, community values have been revitalised. Attendance at such events has increased again, and shrine festivals and temple ceremonies are positively flourishing in recent years (Horikoshi 1985).

Festivals bring members of a community out together to celebrate local events, and since they often involve carrying or pulling a portable shrine around the whole neighbourhood, they also serve to strengthen the residents' perceptions of their boundaries within a wider area. There seems to be an expansion of these activities recently in many parts of Japan. In Kyushu, where I have myself attended the same festivals in different years, I have noticed a marked increase in size, both in numbers of people and vehicles involved, and in evidence of local spending on the occasion. In many areas people have been reported using some of their recent affluence to build splendid new floats and portable shrines, and these activities seem to have been encouraged by competition between adjacent communities.

URBAN NEIGHBOURHOODS

This kind of competition is found particularly in urban areas, where there are few natural geographical features to distinguish neighbourhoods. Here there are no problems of depopulation, and often the modern communities are relatively new. An interesting anthropological study carried out in a Tokyo neighbourhood describes very forcibly how traditional features of neighbourhood organisation are invoked to justify modern social organisation, although there is ample evidence to show that this so-called tradition is not based on historical continuity (Bestor 1985).

Figure 4.2   Community festivals invariably include the sound of drums.
Local participants vie for places in the musicians' seats.

Bestor's study of a Tokyo neighbourhood illustrates a situation
where there is considerable conflict between the local government's
ideas for and demands on the local people and their own activities
organised through the effective *chōnaikai*. It also illustrates that the
neighbourhood is not merely a small administrative unit of local
government but retains a degree of autonomy, too. For example, when
the official boundaries of the community were altered in a way that did
not suit local arrangements, they were just ignored for all practical
purposes except house-numbering. The need for cooperation at a local
level has made it possible for the community to maintain its own
cohesion here.

Further differences even extend to conflicts about the official
ward-office policy on 'community building', which ironically seems to
be based on pre-existing models. This is part of a nationwide effort
to encourage a 'return' to more local autonomy for the 'Komyuniti'.
The use of the English word in Japanese gives the whole project an
intentionally global air, but it has often been interpreted as a rather
devious way of cutting back on public spending and avoiding the
adequate development of social welfare provision.

In fact, in urban areas many organisations are found with the same
names and apparent functions as those already described for a rural

community. The *chōnaikai* has already been mentioned, and Bestor's study also lists a women's group, a senior citizens' group, a festival committee, a merchants' association, PTAs, school alumni clubs, politicians' support groups, a volunteer fire brigade, and various groups based on hobbies. A new community which I visited in Chiba city, although less than ten years had passed since the first houses were built, had already organised very effective groups for house-wives' and children's activities, and had a very strong consumer protection organisation.

In the urban neighbourhood of another city in Chiba prefecture where I lived in the late 1980s, camaraderie was so low that the portable shrine by-passed this zone during the local festival. Never-theless, the circulating notice board was delivered, most people paid their neighbourhood dues, and there was a reasonable turn-out on the appropriate Sunday to clean the communal ditches which ran along the roadside. People also took a gift of money to houses where a funeral was being held, but it was interesting here that the criteria for contribution were based strictly on membership in an administra-tive district, rather than on neighbourly proximity, so that a nextdoor neighbour might not appear with a gift if they happened to live over the administrative boundary.

Another interesting community facility I noticed in this area, although they are widespread elsewhere too, are the loud speakers situated throughout the inhabited area. These are used to make announcements about emergencies, for example, to advise of approaching inclement weather conditions, and during our stay we were reassured about a volcanic eruption on a nearby island which had set our shutters shuddering in a strange and, at first, inexplicable way. These were also used to play the opening bars of Beethoven's *Fifth Symphony* at dusk, apparently to advise children playing outside that it was time to be returning home.

The interests of city dwellers may be quite different from those of rural communities, however, and the activities of the groups are tailored accordingly. The *chōnaikai* still operates to disseminate information from local government offices to the residents through a circulating notice board, but taxes are taken care of individually. It may also be more necessary to lobby the local government on behalf of its members when their community is part of a wider urban complex. In an anthropological study carried out in western Japan in an area which was an amalgamation of an old village and a newly developed housing complex, Ben-Ari (1991) describes the way neighbours organised themselves into a citizens' action group to secure acceptable services for their community, both from the developer and from the local government. In this area, the local group has called itself *jichikai*, a word which emphasises its self-governing aspect, and perhaps helps to distinguish it conceptually from some of the older functions of neighbourhood groups, when they were used as agents of political control, as, for example, during the Second World War.

Figure 4.3 Cooperative efforts produce 10,000 school lunches a day at this municipal centre. Each of these large cauldrons holds 1,000 helpings.

Ben-Ari's study also makes clear an important difference between new communities, where outsiders are continuously moving in, and those with houses going back through generations. It is the degree to which neighbours feel obliged to participate in local activities. In the country people may complain about the obligations they feel to participate in communal activities but, when asked, most of them do join in. In newer communities people are more at liberty to avoid participation. Evidently the ultimate sanction of *mura hachibu* would have considerably less force in an urban area, although informal ostracism may well continue.

Nevertheless, in Bestor's Tokyo community, the *chōnaikai* has roles to play which could affect any resident. When someone dies, there is specific aid with the funeral arrangements. If there is a fire, again the *chōnaikai* will help out, as it would for any disaster, and there are regular drills in preparation for such eventualities. They participate in traffic safety campaigns, maintain street lights in back alleys and spray the whole area with pesticide in the hot summers. Other local groups organise children's outings, trips for adults, and a series of annual events including a New Year's party, a springtime cherry-blossom viewing party, a summer folk-dance festival, and an autumn festival for the local Shintō deity. Even if the constraints are, to some extent, relaxed in the cities, the security and possibility of involvement in the neighbourhood may still remain very strong.

In another recent study carried out in a commuter 'bed-town', which encompasses a number of older communities within the wider metropolitan area of Tokyo, Jennifer Robertson (1991) found participation in local events and activities different for natives and newcomers. Sometimes this involved exclusion from the long-standing associations of all but families established for several generations, and a tier of relative natives, or relative newcomers, running a parallel but different set of organisations in the middle. A picture emerges of deep and divisive rifts despite a local community-building movement which draws on the harmony which was supposed to exist amongst the pioneering occupants of the original seventeenth and eighteenth-century communities.

There is, of course, much variation in different urban areas, and where residents are mostly commuters, local activities will be more important to housewives and children than to men (see, for example, Vogel 1963). The Chiba community already mentioned illustrates this type of community, and the groups which have formed there reflect these interests. PTA groups provide opportunities for women with small children to meet one another, especially when they are new to the area, and the schools themselves bring local children into regular contact. In a community with shopkeepers and small businesses (like the one described by Bestor) these same children may well continue into adulthood in the same area, and their long-standing relationships will assist them in pursuing neighbourhood activities throughout their lives.

CONCLUSION

Whether the community is new or old, Japan has a rich fund of models for neighbourly interaction, and it is not difficult for the demands of local circumstances to be tackled by drawing on these models, whether at an ideological level, or in practice. The principles of knowing and caring about one's neighbours have been strongly upheld in Japanese community life, and evidence seems to suggest that these are still held to be important. In new neighbourhoods, as in apartment complexes, women in particular complain of loneliness and a lack of neighbourhood interaction. Elsewhere, it is no doubt women like these who are drawing on the traditions of neighbourhood interaction to solve their own problems of isolation.

Various aspects of the system of classification outlined in previous chapters have re-emerged here. For long-term communities, the *uchi/soto* distinction is clearly applied again at this level, as it is in most areas for housewives and children. The importance of reciprocity is made very clear, and the strict sharing of duties between houses reiterates the principles of equality and cooperation. There are, of course, sometimes hierarchical differences between houses based on the *dōzoku* relations, discussed in Chapter 1, or other factors, such as economic resources, but this chapter has concentrated attention on the neighbourhood as a conceptual unit, and at this level, at least, houses are for most purposes treated equally.

NOTES

1. Some of the advantages of such a study are outlined in my introduction to *Interpreting Japanese Society*, a collection of papers written by anthropologists of Japan (Hendry and Webber 1986).
2. Hasumi Otohiko 'Rural Society in Post-war Japan, Part II', *The Japan Foundation Newsletter*, vol. 12, no. 6 (April 1985), pp. 1–7. This and Part I in the previous issue of *The Japan Foundation Newsletter* provide an excellent summary of the changes which have taken place in rural Japan since 1945.

REFERENCES

Ben-Ari, Eyal, *Changing Japanese Suburbia: A Study of Two Present Day Localities* (Kegan Paul International, Tokyo, 1991)
Bestor, Theodore C., 'Tradition and Japanese Social Organisation: Institutional Development in a Tokyo Neighbourhood', *Ethnology* vol. 24, no. 2 (1985), pp. 121–35
———, *Neighbourhood Tokyo* (Stanford University Press, Stanford, 1989)
Hasumi, Ohtohiko, 'Rural Society in Post-war Japan, Part II', *The Japan Foundation Newsletter* vol. 12, no. 6 (April 1985), pp. 1–7
Hendry, Joy and Jonathan Webber (eds), *Interpreting Japanese Society* (Journal of the Anthropoligical Society of Oxford Occasional Publication, no. 5, Oxford, 1986)
Horikoshi, Hisamoto, 'The Changing Rural Landscape: A Township over Two Decades' *Japan Foundation Newsletter* vol. 13, no. 1 (June 1985), pp. 1–11

Knight, John, 'Rural Depopulation, Tourism and "Village Revival" in Wakayama, Japan' (PhD. thesis, University of London, 1992)

———, 'Rural *Kokusaika*? Foreign Motifs and Village Revival in Japan' in *Japan Forum*, vol. 5, no. 2 (1993), pp. 203–16

Martinez, D.P., 'Tourism and the *Ama*: the Search for a Real Japan', in Eyal Ben-Ari, Brian Moeran and James Valentine (eds), *Unwrapping Japan* (Manchester University Press, Manchester, 1990), pp. 97–116

Moon, Okpyo, *From Paddy Field to Ski Slope* (Manchester University Press, Manchester, 1989)

———, 'Is the *ie* Disappearing in Rural Japan?' in Joy Hendry and Jonathan Webber (eds), *Interpreting Japanese Society* (Journal of the Anthropological Society of Oxford Occasional Publication, no. 5, Oxford, 1986), pp. 185–97

Moeran, Brian, *Lost Innocence* (University of California Press, Berkeley, 1984)

Nagashima, Nobuhiro and Hiroyasu Tomoeda (eds), *Regional Differences in Japanese Rural Culture* (Senri Ethnological Studies, no. 14, National Museum of Ethnology, 1984)

Norbeck, Edward, *From Country to City: The Urbanisation of a Japanese Hamlet* (The University of Utah Press, Salt Lake City, 1978)

Robertson, Jennifer, *Native and Newcomer: Making and Remaking a Japanese City* (University of California Press, Berkeley, Los Angeles and Oxford, 1991)

Smith, Robert, *Kurusu: The Price of Progress in a Japanese Village 1951–1975* (Stanford University Press, Stanford, 1978)

Vogel, Ezra F. *Japan's New Middle Class* (University of California Press, Berkeley, 1963), Chapter 6

FURTHER READING

Beardsley, Richard K., John W. Hall and Robert E. Ward, *Village Japan* (The University of Chicago Press, Chicago, 1959), Chapter 10

Cornell, John B. and Robert J. Smith, *Two Japanese Villages* (Greenwood Press, New York, 1969)

Dore, R.P., *City Life in Japan: A Study of a Tokyo Ward* (University of California Press, Berkeley, 1958)

Dore, Ronald, *Shinohata: A Portrait of a Japanese Village* (Allen Lane, London, 1978)

Embree, John, *Suye Mura: A Japanese Village* (The University of Chicago Press, Chicago, 1939)

Fukutake, Tadashi, *Japanese Rural Society* (Cornell University Press, Ithaca 1972), Part III

Kalland, Arne, *Shingu, a Japanese Fishing Community* (London and Malmo: Curzon Press Ltd, 1980)

Kalland, Arne and B. Moeran, *Endangered Culture: Japanese Whaling in a Cultural Perspective* (London and Malmo: Curzon Press, 1992)

Moeran, Brian, *Okubo Diary* (Stanford University Press, Stanford, 1985)

Moore, R.M., *Japanese Agriculture: Patterns of Rural Development* (Westview Press, Boulder, San Francisco and London, 1990)

Nakane, Chie, *Kinship and Economic Organisation in Rural Japan* (Athlone Press, London, 1967), Chapter 2

Norbeck, Edward, *Takashima: A Japanese Fishing Community* (University of Utah Press, Salt Lake City, 1954)

Smith, Robert J. and Ella Lury Wiswell, *The Women of Suye Mura* (The University of Chicago Press, Chicago, 1982)

Yoshida, Teigo, 'Cultural Integration and Change in Japanese Villages' *American Anthropologist*, vol. 65 (1963), pp. 102–16

FILM

Ballad of Narayama (dir. Imamura Shōhei, 1982)

5 Status and stratification in the wider world

INTRODUCTION

Hierarchy is one of the most important principles of classification in any society, as anthropologists have shown, but it is important to recognise that the assumptions one brings to the subject from one's own background may need radical revision in a different cultural context. Louis Dumont has illustrated this clearly in his introduction to *Homo Hierarchicus* (1980), a detailed study of the Indian caste system, where he points out that the emphasis on equality in modern Western society may blind its members and prejudice them against a proper understanding of his subject matter. He draws on the classic studies of Tocqueville and Talcott Parsons to show that hierarchy is an inevitable part of social life, but he goes on to emphasise that this hierarchy may be 'quite independent of natural inequalities or the distribution of power' (1980:20). This point is important to bear in mind in the case of the Japanese.

In the previous chapter very little mention was made of hierarchical differences; the emphasis was on cooperation and reciprocity in interaction between houses. In one symbolic sense, membership in a community involves relations of equality, as each house takes a turn to carry out certain duties, and each sends one member to community gatherings. Hierarchical relations also exist within communities, and these are based on a variety of factors, some of which will emerge in the following pages, but the simultaneous expressions of equality should not be forgotten as we turn our attention towards Japanese notions of hierarchy.

Hierarchical ranking runs through Japanese life, ordering individuals, groups, institutions, material objects, even foods, but at any particular level there will be a certain equality as well. Thus, in contrast with their attitude to the outside world, Japanese people tend to regard themselves as homogeneous, as all equally Japanese. Yet within their own cultural milieu very great differences may be expressed and their boundaries are by no means clear cut. Similarly, members of a particular company, when dealing with outsiders, will express an equality among themselves as members of that company. Ultimately, the *uchi/soto* distinction may override hierarchical differences in some contexts.

Nevertheless, notions of hierarchy are extremely important in Japan. The first experiences of the concept have already been described as they affect children. Here hierarchy is based largely on age difference, benevolence being expected of the superior role, an idea probably learned earlier than the deference later demanded of the inferior one. Relations within the house have also been discussed, and here further principles of sex and expectation of permanency as a member of the inside group may also play a part, although these factors are subject to regional variation and recent change. The further group allegiance, as a child enters a kindergarten, introduces the symbolic equality mentioned above, and with these early models we are well equipped to examine the notion of hierarchy more widely. This chapter will open with a description of some of the manifestations of hierarchy in modern Japan, move on to consider some of the historical foundations for them and finally return to discussing the principles behind them.

EXPRESSIONS OF HIERARCHY IN MODERN JAPAN

There is no doubt that hierarchical differences affect interaction between Japanese people in their everyday lives. Indeed, in many situations it is difficult to know how to behave unless one can place the other people present in a hierarchical order in relation to oneself. This begins from the moment of greeting, for bowing is a good example of the expression of status differences. One bows more deeply to a superior than to an inferior, and one should stay down longer than one's superior. An amusing situation arises where the relation is unclear, for each side will try to stay down longer, assuming that it is better to err on the inferior side than on the superior. The custom of exchanging name cards on meeting a new person helps to resolve such problems.

Speech in Japanese also varies depending on the relationship between the partners engaged in a conversation. The complicated system of speech levels, already mentioned in the discussion about *tatemae* and *honne*, makes it possible to show different degrees of respect or self-deprecation, and the choice of inappropriate levels can sound very offensive. Verb endings vary and some common words, such as 'go', 'come' and 'speak', have completely different forms according to the degree of politeness being used. It is virtually impossible to have a conversation without making a decision about the appropriate level to use.

Terms of address will also vary. The example of the family has already been given, where brothers and sisters are always distinguished according to whether they are older or younger, and this same model is transferred into wider relations between children. As a general principle in the house, inferior members address superior ones with a term of relationship, while superior ones may use personal names, and this same form of distinction is carried into the world at large. Within specific institutions, where members occupy named positions in the hierarchical scale, they will be addressed by these titles by more junior members, whom they in turn will address by name. Interesting modifications to the language have occurred in Hawaiian Japanese, where, presumably in response to the American cultural milieu, English words like 'brother' and 'sister' have been adopted to replace some of the Japanese words which imply differences of status.

Again in Japan, on any formal occasion, and a good number of less formal ones, seating in a room is decided according to an appropriate hierarchical order. In a traditional Japanese house, there is a principal post in the main room and on one side of this is a special raised alcove called a *tokonoma*. In this space are placed various beautiful objects, usually a hanging scroll, and a flower arrangement as well as other objects of significance to the family. The Buddhist altar may well be on the other side of the principal post. A similar arrangement is found in many of the rooms of Japanese restaurants and inns. This area marks the top of the room, and it is therefore necessary for decisions to be made about how people will sit in relation to it. There are various rules which govern this procedure, and there may be differences of opinion about which should prevail. A show of modesty is usually in order, too, so that some shuffling may precede the final arrangement.

Another expression of hierarchical difference is to be found in the non-reciprocal exchange of gifts. Within a community, as described in the previous chapter, houses keep a record of the gifts they receive in order to maintain overall reciprocity with each other. Some houses receive a large number of gifts which they do not need to return, however, and these are associated with expressions of debt or goodwill in a hierarchical relationship. It is common in many societies for gifts to be used in symbolic ways such as this, and there is usually something intangible going in the other direction. Thus students take gifts to their teachers as an expression of gratitude for learning imparted. Shop-keepers and tradesmen present small gifts to their customers at certain times of the year as thanks for their continued support. And as many gifts move between people and houses as there are different relation-ships of this sort. The wrapping of this type of gift usually makes clear its purpose and value so that some people even keep a store of received gifts to present again when the appropriate moment arises.

HIERARCHY IN JAPANESE HISTORY

There have been clear differences of status in Japan since at least as far back as the Tomb period. Some of the environmental factors involved have already been discussed, and archaeological evidence remains to testify to the material ways in which these differences were marked. Since the emergence of a dominant imperial family, with an apparently unbroken line of descent to the present day, there has always been some kind of nobility set apart from the common people, even if its practical role has gone through several changes. The impe-rial family illustrates a special case of the general principle that lines of demarcation are based on membership in a family or *ie*, a common means of distinction which may well go back further. It certainly seems likely that such acquired status has been important throughout the historical period, although it is important to remember that this is not always based on kin connections.

In varying degrees throughout Japanese history it has also been possible to achieve status by individual or cooperative effort. The early warring periods illustrate such competition for dominance between groups, competition which has been repeated again and again at various times throughout the subsequent years. In the intervals, relatively stable periods have been marked by a greater emphasis on inherited status. The courtly Heian period is one such example, as is the 200-odd years of Tokugawa rule, during which Japan was closed to the outside world. Within larger groups relations have been based on a combination of earned and inherited character-istics, each being recognised in different ways according to the group and to the time. Chance for mobility within the system has also been a variable factor.

In the period immediately preceding the Meiji Restoration, Japanese society was divided into four clear classes. The Samurai warriors were at the top, followed by peasants, artisans and merchants, in that order. Everyone was supposed to remain within their own class, continue the work of their forebears and marry within their own social category. Samurai warriors were empowered to take immediate retaliation in the case of overt expressions of rebellion against the system by using the swords they always carried to decapitate the offender. Above the Samurai, and perhaps closer to the gods than to other people and their affairs, were members of the nobility, which included the imperial family. The anthropologist, T.S. Lebra (1993) has recently published an ethnography of the descendants of these families entitled *Above the Clouds*.

At the other end of the scale were the outcastes, human beings who were regarded, literally, as non-people, almost animals. Another interesting study, *The Monkey as Mirror*, discusses the development of this class of people in a long historical context (Ohnuki-Tierney 1987) and reveals changing attitudes to the top and bottom of the hierarchical system in Japan over the centuries. It should be borne in mind also, however, that Japanese attitudes to animals, and the distinction between humans and animals, are rather different to those held in Western societies. Pamela Asquith has written about this issue, and in one interesting article discusses the way human beings pray for the souls of the monkeys with whom they have worked (Asquith 1990).

In fact, despite the rules, it was not impossible for individuals or families to cross these apparently rigid barriers. Sometimes this would be for economic necessity. The warriors, at the top of the scale, placed very little value on material wealth, indeed they prided themselves on their frugality. Consequently they were often bad at managing the property which they did own. Merchants, on the other hand, although they were officially at the bottom of the scale, were able to use their wealth to become effective landowners by helping families who fell into debt. It was not unheard of for a judicial marriage, which would benefit both sides, to be arranged between two such families. Priests and scholars could also float within the system to some extent, and there were itinerant travellers whose status was also unclearly defined,[1] but on the whole self-betterment was not encouraged, and people were expected to know their place, even within the four major divisions, and stay within it.

Although the divisions were abolished at the beginning of the Meiji period, the legacy of this system is expressed by Ruth Benedict in her classic anthropological study of Japan *The Chrysanthemum and the Sword* (1977). In a chapter entitled 'Taking One's Proper Station', she discusses some of the hierarchical attitudes and assumptions with which the Japanese entered the Second World War, tracing them back to the rigidity of the 'caste system' of the Tokugawa period. She, like Dumont, points out an important distinction between the fixed position one occupies according to the rules of hierarchy, and the quite different degree of dominance or power that one may wield behind the scenes (1977:39). The two are quite separate, and the latter gives no right to violate the former. This is an important aspect of Japanese hierarchy which has by no means disappeared.

There have now been many changes, of course, and during the modern period much new ideology has been imported to rival the older ideas. In the early days European influence was particularly strong among intellectuals, and ideas of equality and individual freedom were behind many of the new institutions which were introduced. During the Meiji period, when class divisions were abolished, universal education was introduced throughout the country and opportunities were opened up at all levels in the new industries which were beginning to develop. After the Second World War there was a further influx of ideology which came with the Allied Occupation. The new Constitution brought so-called democracy to Japan, and American ideas of equality and freedom flowed intoxicatingly through the defeated nation.

As elsewhere in the industrialising world, a higher status could now be achieved legitimately through individual effort. Nowadays a person's occupation no longer depends solely on the family position into which he or she is born or adopted, although this may still play an influential part. Gradually the importance of personal connections in gaining employment has been supplemented by the opportunities provided through the education system. It is now possible for a Japanese child from any background to rise to a position of great eminence in society, given ability and perseverance, and the effects and effectiveness of this meritocratic educational system will be discussed in the next chapter. Nevertheless, despite greater opportunities for mobility, it is evident that some aspects of a rigid hierarchical order remain.

A particularly striking example is to be found in the way certain groups in society are still persistently discriminated against despite legislation and various efforts to eradicate the phenomenon. Almost in the same way that the imperial family has remained removed at the top end of the social scale throughout various historical changes among the ordinary people, there are still groups at the bottom that could well be described as 'outcaste'. These are the 'non-human' people of the Tokugawa period, the Eta, or *burakumin*, who were associated with defiling occupations, such as burying the dead and tanning the hides of animals. The former is polluting in a Shintō view, the latter in a Buddhist order of things. Nowadays, the same people are still a class apart, whatever their occupations, and 'regular Japanese' are most careful not to marry them and 'pollute' their own blood lines. One of the factors working against integration for these people is the system of family registration, described in the previous chapter, by which 'outcaste' people can often be recognised from their areas of origin.

There is a similar attitude to certain other minority groups in Japan, and they are discriminated against in other ways, too. Families of Korean extraction are a good example, for if they retain their Korean nationality they are denied full rights of Japanese citizens, even when they have been born and entirely educated in Japan. Like children of mixed blood, they are treated as social inferiors by many ordinary Japanese. People of Ainu origin may suffer a similar fate, although there has been evidence in the last few years that they are benefiting from a worldwide interest in the rights of indigenous people to regain some of their culture. Although a few years ago it was thought that most of the Ainu had been incorporated into the wider society, a study made in 1993 by Jane Wilkinson[2] would suggest that quite a lot of them were lying low until their status as 'original Japanese' improved.

A poignant representation of the experience of one *ainoko*, or 'half' Japanese, i.e., children born during the Occupation, usually of Japanese mothers and American fathers, has recently been published in a book by Norma Field (1991) called *In the Realm of the Dying Emperor*. Field is a scholar of Japanese literature, usually resident in the United States, but she happened to be spending a year in Japan with her relatives when the Shōwa Emperor fell terminally ill and eventually died. The book she has written is highly critical of Japanese society, and she focuses her attention on three individuals who took a stand against the establishment, which in 1988/9 was strongly polarised around the imperial system. One of these people was an ordinary Okinawan who burned a Japanese flag, another was a Christian woman who objected to the Shintō enshrinement (and deification) of her deceased husband, and the third was the Mayor of Nagasaki who made a public criticism of the dying Emperor.

The hue and cry which surrounded each of these cases, and the ostracism the protagonists experienced, well illustrates the discrimination meted out to people who adopt a posture which falls outside the boundaries of acceptable behaviour in Japan. The book also recounts the gestures of support these people received, quoting in full some of the letters written to the mayor of Nagasaki, for example, so that the logic of each protest is well attested, but it also clearly identifies several lines of discriminatory demarcation in Japanese society. Personal information about Norma Field's own life is very revealing of the case of the *ainoko*, but there is also a wealth of detail about the ambiguous situation in which the Okinawans find themselves, officially Japanese, but with a different language and cultural background, and with a much longer experience of occupation, and about the plight of Christians in a society whose dominant values are at odds with the ethical basis of their religion. The Nagasaki Mayor comes from a family which practised Christianity in secret throughout the Tokugawa period, and his grandfather was tortured for revealing his beliefs in the Meiji period.

Field's book is in many ways pure ethnography. It illustrates with eloquence the theoretical principles outlined by James Valentine (1990) in his paper on the significance of marginality in Japanese society. A neat summary of the categories of people who are regularly set apart, notably by the Japanese media, Valentine's paper also places the Japanese case in the context of anthropological and sociological work on the subject. In a society which emphasises form and clear lines of demarcation between *uchi* and *soto*, people who don't fit in are clearly threatening. One way of resolving the situation is to try and adopt an appropriate *tatemae* for most situations, and the characters discussed by Field had succeeded through most of their lives in doing just that. It was at the moment when they stood out and expressed *honne* views that they incurred disapproval. Another strategy is to try and 'pass' as a member of mainstream society, but the risk of discovery must take a toll, a point well illustrated in a novel (and film) about a *burakumin* who lives for some time as a regular school teacher (Shimazaki 1974).

Apart from discrimination, however, people in marginal positions sometimes benefit from their special status, and many *ainoko* have more recently been chosen to appear on television programmes, apparently for their appealing looks. There is also sometimes power attached to the ambiguous or liminal, as will be discussed further at the end of the next chapter in a consideration of a new marginal group of Japanese, namely those who have lived abroad, and many minority groups around the world have received long-awaited benefits in the last few years. Ohnuki-Tierney's historical study of the *burakumin*, or 'special status people' as she calls them, suggests that though today they may be seen as scapegoats, in the past they played an important mediating role (1987).

PRINCIPLES OF HIERARCHICAL ORDER

Relativity

Apart from these rigid divisions, then, what are the principles under-lying modern expressions of hierarchical difference? This is no simple matter to explain, since various factors are involved and in different situations different principles may take precedence. Indeed, one of the first things to note about Japanese hierarchy is that it is to some extent relative to the situation. As was explained for *tatemae* behaviour, a single individual may have different faces for different occasions, and it is theoretically possible for the relationship between two individuals to be reversed in different arenas. This relativity also makes possible the apparently contradictory idea outlined above that notions of equality may be expressed under certain circumstances among groups or people ranked in other ways hierarchically.

It was mentioned above that members of an inside group may express such equality in relation to outsiders, and a straightforward example of the relativity of expressions of hierarchy may be given with regard to seating arrangements when entertaining guests. Guests (outsiders) will be placed above members of the group responsible for organising the occasion (insiders), and the latter may de-emphasise their own hierarchical distinctions in expressing deference to the guests. For example, at a formal family celebration guests may sit in hierarchical order round the outside of an arrangement of tables, while members of the inside group will circulate, regardless of their own distinctions, round the inside of the tables where they can greet each of the guests in turn. In another house, the same people will be ordered quite differently.

To give another example in quite a different context it may be useful to introduce the notion of the company or other institution as an inside group. This is no exaggeration of the concept, as will be developed later, and the word *uchi* is used to describe one's own company, school or other place of attachment and the other people who belong to it. In conversation with outsiders, one is expected to use self-deprecatory speech forms not only for oneself, but also for all the other members of one's own inside group, however high-ranking their position. Within the group, clear-cut hierarchical distinctions may well still be rigidly maintained. The *uchi/soto* distinction, taught so carefully at the level of the house, also underlies the principles of relative ranking, and it would seem useful to continue by distinguishing between ranking within and ranking outside of such social groups.

Ranking within social groups

The principles of ranking within the most intimate *uchi* of the family were discussed earlier, and this model may be used again at an ideological level throughout society. Benevolence from a person in a superior role is to be reciprocated with deference and loyalty from a partner in an inferior role. Typically, a young person will become attached in whatever walk of life to a senior, who will help him[3] in the early stages of his career. Gradually he builds up a debt to the senior, which may be likened to that which a child has towards a parent, a debt which must be repaid with long-term loyalty and support. The senior should therefore be able for ever to rely on such a junior to do his bidding at all times. This type of relationship is not infrequently described by the expression *oyabun/kobun* (parent-part/child-part), a phrase which has been translated as a relationship of patronage (Dore 1971:70).

R.P. Dore discussed this type of relationship in several arenas in his book *City Life in Japan* (1971), and the following quotation nicely illustrates the above principles in a practical arrangement within a company:

A, who gets his job in the United Glass and Steel Corporation through the influence of B who was, perhaps, at the same High School with A's uncle, is thereafter marked as B's man. This not only means that B is the obvious man to ask to be his marriage go-between, the obvious man to go to for advice when he is in trouble over a girl, or the obvious man to ask for a loan, nor only that he takes it as a matter of course that he is expected to run personal errands for B, or even for B's wife. It means also that he will join the rank and file of the B group in its cold war against the X group and the Y group within the firm, and that his own chances of success will depend on the B group's maintaining its power.

(Dore 1971:207)

It may be less likely now than it was in the 1950s, when Dore was writing, that a man would join a large company through the influence of his uncle, but Clark's more recent book (1979) would suggest that such links still played an important part then, and he was writing about a company where personnel often move around the country. In smaller, local companies this type of recruitment is probably still the most prevalent. Even when no such links initially exist, Clark points out that similar long-term relations may be established when a senior man acts as a go-between at a junior's wedding (1979:199).

The rival groups within a firm, which are mentioned at the end of Dore's quote, are also ranked informally within the larger group, but whereas the relationships between individuals within them are fixed hierarchically, the relationships between groups may fluctuate. They are also subject to fission, particularly if a person at the top of the group dies or retires. Such factions (or *habatsu* as they are called in Japanese) are also to be found in many other spheres such as political parties, self-defence forces, theatrical groups and underworld gangs.

This kind of organisational structure has been strikingly described by Nakane Chie, a retired Japanese professor of social anthropology at Tokyo University. In her book entitled *Japanese Society* (1973), she isolates the *oyabun/kobun* type of relationship as the basic structural principle on which Japanese social organisation rests. She represents this 'vertical principle' diagrammatically as shown in Figure 5.1 (Nakane 1973:43). In this case, *B* and *C* are both in an inferior relationship with respect to *A*, and she emphasises that their relationships with *A* are more important than their relationships with each other. The *A/B* relationship here corresponds to Dore's *B/A* relationship above.

Figure 5.1   Nakane's basic model

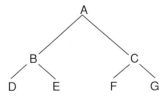

Figure 5.2   Nakane's elaborated model

This 'inverted V', as she terms the shape, may be regarded as a building block for larger groups, where a leader A may have several *kobun* in the structural position of B and C, who in turn may have *kobun* of their own as shown in Figure 5.2 (1973:44).

While the leader, A, remains in the original position of being the ultimate *oyabun* of a group, relations within that group are very effectively maintained, since A can rely on B and C, who can rely on D, E, F, and G, who can in turn rely on their *kobun* to carry out any tasks required. Similarly, in the reverse direction, the *kobun* have close relationships with superiors to whom they turn for help and advice. New members can be recruited to the lower levels, and the same principle can work effectively throughout a large organisation. Examples can be found in many areas of Japanese life, and apart from those mentioned above as having factions, Nakane claims that a structure such as this also characterises new religious groups such as Sōka Gakkai, as well as many educational establishments including those for traditional Japanese arts.

Once A is removed, however, for whatever reason, Nakane points out that there is no clear way to decide who shall be the successor. The relationship between B and C is unspecified, since each is related individually to A, so that it is at this point that fission may occur and two (or more) factions emerge. Subsequent relations between these factions may well be delicate, and a number of outcomes are possible. Within a large company, Nakane argues that the formal administrative organisation will usually preserve the overall group, even if efficiency is temporarily impaired when this informal hierarchy collapses. In some organisations, however, this type of hierarchy is the chief organisational principle. The headship may then be a hereditary position, such as in *nō* theatrical groups and schools for flower arrangement and tea ceremony. In political parties, on the other hand, future leadership depends very heavily on relations between factions, and an understanding of these principles of organisation is essential to making sense of Japanese politics.

Nakane also discusses the qualities required for leadership in such arrangements, and she points out that the ability to inspire loyalty is more important than personal merit. Indeed, such a system works rather well if the leader has some weakness so that he is obliged to rely on his subordinates in some respects. A good leader is also expected to know and respect the feelings of his subordinates. These characteristics are important for leadership in other societies, and some of the specific requirements of leadership in particular Japanese arenas will be discussed in later chapters, but it is useful to distinguish here between superiority of this kind and superiority based directly on merit.

In varying degrees, people are accorded status or superiority according to their personal abilities, but in a structure like the one described above it is not possible to move ahead of one's senior however distinguished one may become in any particular field. A group organised in this way takes a kind of collective responsibility for tasks assigned to it, and each member contributes to the best of his or her ability, allowing the group as a whole to receive any praise or criticism which may accrue. Thus talented members of such a group may be appreciated and respected for their abilities, but this respect is quite different from that based on length of service, and it is the latter which maintains the smooth working cohesion of the group. Nakane gives a striking example of how Japanese scientific research teams carry out projects more efficiently if they are connected in this way, even if they come new to a field, rather than if they are composed of experts who were previously unknown to one another.

Relations between groups

Nakane goes on to apply her model to relations between groups. Just as *ie* are ranked within a community, she argues, other associations become ranked throughout the social structure. Thus companies, for example, are also assigned positions in a hierarchy, and their members, whatever their rank, all share to a degree the status accorded their company in the outside world. This ranking is found particularly amongst companies in the same fields, and members of the company are, therefore, encouraged to work hard to improve the company's position, and so improve their own status outside. This rivalry takes place particularly between companies involved in similar enterprises. Interdependent companies, on the other hand, may develop long-term links not unlike those between human beings, sometimes even referred to as *oya/ko* relations. Some small companies may prefer to maintain several non-exclusive allegiances, however.

Schools and universities, too, are ranked amongst themselves, and high-ranking schools are able to supply high-ranking universities, who will in turn supply high-ranking companies. The system is self-perpetuating, since the best schools are able to choose from the best applicants. A particularly prestigious career is in the civil service, where ministries are also ranked, and most graduates entering the top ministries are from the top university, which is Tokyo. At this level it seems that even the faculties are ranked. The education system will be discussed in more detail in the next chapter, but it can be seen already that this is where the big opportunity comes for social mobility.

Ranking outside groups

An individual's overall status in the world outside his or her *uchi* groups depends to a large extent on membership in and therefore association with those certain groups. In the more stable areas, where families have been living in close contact for generations, there is still considerable weight attached to the depth of family background, and the position of one's *ie* in some long-standing hierarchical scale, whether it be part of a *dōzoku* system or association with the owner-ship of land. Various schemes of land reform have removed much in the way of material support for this last form of ranking, but it takes more than a generation or two to forget such differences of status, and members of old landowning families have often been able to use their status to make their mark in some other way. One such avenue to success has been through local, or even national, politics.

In the more complex and changing society of urban areas an indi-vidual's status will be more affected by associations beyond the immediate neighbourhood, unless of course the housing complex belongs to a particular company, in which case the two will coincide. In mixed areas individual householders will derive most of their status from their institutional attachments, and Nakane has argued that companies and other occupational groups have merely taken over the function of the *ie* in this respect. As a result a family takes its position in society from the attachment of its head to an outside institution, which may well demand the same total commitment of the individual as used to be accorded to the *ie*. Nakane sees this as consistent, since the *ie* used to be the chief occupational group, and she emphasises further that since the principles described above are based on the family model, new occupational groups may be likened to large ie. The company may also take over some of the functions of the neighbourhood, for example by helping out in times of need.

Nakane's model has been criticised for trying to be too all-embracing, among other things (see, for example, Sugimoto and Mouer 1981, 1986), and *Japanese Society* has no references or bibli-ography. Examples are cited in a rather anecdotal way, sometimes distorted slightly to emphasise a point, and occasionally the general-isations are very sweeping. Nevertheless, the principle outlined is very pervasive, and Nakane is able to draw on her experiences in India, Europe and the United States to compare its operation in practice with different hierarchical principles found elsewhere. She constantly reiterates, for example, the way the Japanese vertical principle differs from that underlying a caste or class system, and she examines some of the consequences of these differences. It is a book to be recommended, but it is a good idea to bear in mind that it is a structural analysis, rather than a direct description of behaviour, and its manifestations in practice may be quite various. Nor is it supposed (or intended) to account for all Japanese behaviour everywhere. The above analysis, for example, is much more appropriately applied to the behaviour of men than of women, although women may of course become involved in such vertical relations as well.

In the circles of a Japanese housewife, however, it is less likely that people will be ranked quite so rigidly. For one thing, there are various criteria by which ranking is assessed, and several conflicting influences may operate between the same people. On the one hand, a wife inherits her status from her husband's occupational position, especially in company housing, but on the other, she usually has various attributes of her own which play a part. For instance, a woman's educational and occupational background will influence her ranking among other women, as will her current activities. In groups which centre around a traditional hobby such as flower arranging or tea ceremony, for example, there may be a ranking system not unlike that described above, and common interest groups such as the PTA or the Women's Group have office-holders among their ranks.

Since many of the groups housewives join are based on local allegiances, it is quite likely that the same women will meet in different arenas. Thus a woman who is a low-ranking pupil in one context may well hold a position of office in another. Sometimes women who have achieved teaching qualifications in different arts will exchange lessons. These examples illustrate the contextual nature of hierarchy discussed earlier, and in particular situations the vertical principle may well underlie formal interaction. However, since housewives in a neighbourhood are likely to meet in all sorts of situations, they need a more general way to communicate. Age is important again here, and women of within about ten years of each other are often reciprocal in their use of deferential language, or they drop the respect forms altogether, in either case implying a relationship of some equality.

This brings us back to the underlying equality of houses in a neighbourhood, and in purely casual exchanges within a local context men

of a similar age also often tend towards egalitarianism in their treatment of each other, whatever their outside connections. Indeed, in
some village gatherings, when there is no special seating order
demanded by the occasion, everyone will sit in age order, although
the men will probably place themselves above the women. Except for
the male/female divide, this is an egalitarian form of hierarchy since
everyone grows old eventually, and it accords with the principles
outlined in the previous chapter. The studies cited there by Moeran
(1984) and by Moon (1984) discuss the problems which arose in their
communities when some families seemed to be more concerned with
making themselves rich than with cooperating with their neighbours.

Ultimately, the *oyabun/kobun* type of hierarchical ordering also
brings advancement in a rather egalitarian way, especially in large
organisations. The principles are similar to those used among small
children. Those who have been there the longest are given superior
status along with the privileges and responsibilities that entails,
because of that fact alone. With children hierarchy is simply based on
age, and every child who is old enough to be aware of the system has
inferiors as well as superiors. As time passes, he or she moves up
through the ranks. Similarly, in any of the groups mentioned above a
person automatically moves up. This type of ranking is independent
of natural inequalities and may also bear little relation to the distribution of power.

Like children again, the individuals involved in such relationships
come to know one another very well, and their actual relations in day-
to-day life depend also on factors such as personality, skills and mutual
understanding. Relations between men and women have not been
mentioned much in this chapter, largely because the principles above
are basically independent of gender. Within the specific contexts of the
family and the bar or nightclub, relations are necessarily intersexual.
The former case has been discussed in Chapter 1, but it is worth emphasising that husband/wife relations are a good example of the need to
separate status and power, since the husband will almost always be
accorded slightly more status than his wife, although the wife may have
considerable power, particularly in family matters.

The case of bars and nightclubs is more complex, since female
attendants play a somewhat ambiguous role. The customers are
usually men, but are anyway treated as guests, and are therefore
accorded status on that ground alone. Women who own such establishments are referred to as *mama-san*, and part of their role is a motherly one, but they often have or have had male patrons who have
helped them to establish themselves. In geisha circles, there is also

usually a strict hierarchy, as elsewhere, among the women, and customers, too, may be ranked for preferential service (Dalby 1983). This is a subject which will be discussed in more detail in Chapter 10. On the whole, gender as an index of hierarchy is swamped in Japanese society by the many other measures in use.

STATUS MANIPULATION – WRAPPING

We have talked about the manifestation of ranking in Japanese society and we have outlined its historical basis. We have also analysed its principles of operation, inside and outside social groups. Throughout, however, we have mentioned the dual nature of Japanese hierarchy, the balance of achieved and acquired status in any system of ranking and the need to distinguish between formal status or authority and the exercise of power. In this last section I would like to consider some of the strategies used in Japanese society to gain advantage in the more fluid matters of status distinction which ultimately allow a measure of power in interpersonal relations.

My own research has been directed to this end over the last few years and much of it was carried out with housewives, although the principles I unearth are quite applicable to interaction between men, too. Because of the relative freedom of status allocation amongst housewives, there may be more opportunity for manipulation than amongst employees who take their chief role in life from their firm, but each situation offers its own framework for the exercise of power. I started out by looking at polite and respectful language in Japanese, but the subject opened out into other forms of presentation, and eventually I decided that the process was epitomised in the non-verbal signals transmitted by the beautiful wrapping which is used when presenting gifts in Japan (Hendry 1993).

I first of all found that language is very important in determining relative status. People make judgements about one another depending on their ability to use the polite forms appropriately, and it is said by some that this skill can only be acquired as a child, so that family background may have an indirect benefit. The skilful use of speech levels can go much further than this, however, and it is clear that those who use them most effectively are able to manipulate others around them to comply with their expectations. A person who is most successful in this respect is one who is able to adjust their mode of speaking with clarity, but also with subtlety. In other words, the way something is said – the way it is wrapped in appropriate language – is as important, sometimes more important, than what is said.

My findings did not stop with language. In working with house-wives, I noticed that the same principles apply to mode of dress, or 'wrapping' of the body, the way a room is prepared, or 'wrapping' of space, even the way time is organised, and, of course, the way gifts are presented. The wrapping represents the degree of formality and it expresses the system of etiquette, but it also offers opportunities for manipulation, not *of* the system, but through it. These principles are of course found in any society, but the Japanese advantage in dealing with members of many other societies is their relative awareness of the power of wrapping. Elsewhere there is often a propensity to disregard 'wrapping' as mere adornment and to seek to rip it off in an effort to reveal what lies beneath. In Japan this may well be a mistake.

In attempting to explain the way 'wrapping' may be used to manip-ulate status and exercise power, I have made comparisons with other societies studied by anthropologists, mainly in the Pacific region. Their common feature is a reluctance to bring difference of opinion too far out into the open in continuing relationships, and various means are used to communicate at a more subtle, often ritualised level. The emphasis on harmony in Japanese relationships is indica-tive of this type of system. It doesn't mean that there are no disputes, or indeed, that everyone is living in an orderly, contented fashion. Not at all! It simply means that polite, harmonious interaction is an appro-priate way to wrap one's communication, whether it be pleasant or severely barbed.

CONCLUSION

Clearly hierarchical differences are important in Japanese society, if somewhat complicated to describe. To summarise, it is necessary to remember the way in which any individual may be involved in a number of different hierarchical dyads in different situations and contexts. It is also important to distinguish between differences of status based on a position in some scale of seniority, and possibly quite independent distinctions of merit or power. The importance of merit in order to achieve status has become particularly marked in recent years, and some of the consequences of this change will emerge in the next chapter.

Finally, it is perhaps worth restating the complementary impor-tance of equality as a Japanese value. Even in measures of hierarchy, it has been shown that the possibilities are fairly distributed, and status comes eventually to those who serve long and well. There is a great emphasis placed in Japan on being like others and fitting in well. An often quoted proverb is that 'the nail which sticks out will be knocked in'. Once one has gained a clear place in the world, one has little chance of altering it. This puts all the more pressure on the years when one's chances are still open. These years will form the subject matter of the next chapter.

NOTES

1. The anthropologist Jacob Raz has carried out interesting fieldwork with descendants of these groups. A good source is Raz 1992.
2. A report of this study should appear in the forthcoming volume of essays edited by Pamela Asquith and Arne Kalland.
3. The gendered pronouns are used advisedly here because this kind of ranking within groups applies much more to a male life strategy than to a female one. However, it is not impossible for a woman to adopt such a role too.

REFERENCES

Asquith, P.J., 'The Japanese Idea of Soul in Animals and Objects as Evidenced by *Kuyō* Services', in Donald J. Daly and Tom T. Sekine (eds) *Discovering Japan* (Captus University Publications, North York, Ontario, Canada, 1990), pp. 181–8

Asquith, Pamela and Arne Kalland, *The Culture of Nature in Japan* (Curzon and Hawaii University Press, forthcoming)

Benedict, Ruth, *The Chrysanthemum and the Sword* (Routledge and Kegan Paul, London, 1977)

Clark, Rodney, *The Japanese Company* (Yale University Press, New Haven, 1979)

Dalby, Liza Crihfield, *Geisha* (California University Press, Berkeley, 1983)

De Vos, George, and Hiroshi Wagatsuma, *Japan's Invisible Race* (University of California Press, Berkeley, 1966)

Dore, R.P., *City Life in Japan* (University of California Press, Berkeley, 1971)

Dumont, Louis, *Homo Hierarchicus: The Caste System and its Implications* (University of Chicago Press, Chicago, 1980)

Field, Norma, *In the Realm of the Dying Emperor* (Pantheon Books, New York, 1991).

Hendry, Joy, *Wrapping Culture: Politeness, Presentation and Power in Japan and Other Societies* (Clarendon Press, Oxford, 1993)

Ishino, Iwao, 'The *oyabun–kobun*: A Japanese Ritual Kinship Institution', *American Anthropologist*, vol. 55 (1953), pp. 695–707

Lebra, Takie Sugiyama, *Japanese Patterns of Behaviour* (University Press of Hawaii, Honolulu, 1976)

———, *Above the Clouds: Status Culture of the Modern Japanese Nobility* (University of California Press, Berkeley, 1993)

Nakane, Chie, *Japanese Society* (Pelican, Harmondsworth, 1973)

Ohnuki-Tierney, Emiko, *Monkey as Mirror: Symbolic Transformations in Ritual and History* (Princeton University Press, Princeton, 1987)

Sugimoto, Yoshio and Ross E. Mouer, 'Japanese Society: Stereotypes and Realities' (*Papers of the Japanese Studies Centre*, no. 1, Monash University, Melbourne, 1981)

———, *Images of Japanese Society* (Kegan Paul International, Tokyo, 1986)

Valentine, James, 'On the Borderlines: The Significance of Marginality in Japanese Society', in Eyal Ben-Ari, Brian Moeran and James Valentine (eds), *Unwrapping Japan* (Manchester University Press, Manchester, 1990), pp. 36–57

FURTHER READING

Dalby, Liza Crihfield, *Kimono Fashioning Culture* (Yale University Press, New Haven, 1993)

Donoghue, John D., *Pariah Persistence in Changing Japan* (University Press of America, Washington DC., 1977)

Hane Mikiso, *Peasants, Rebels and Outcastes: The Underside of Modern Japan* (Pantheon Books, New York, 1982)

Lee, Chang-soo and Devos G., *Koreans in Japan: Ethnic Conflict and Accommodation* (University of California Press, Berkeley, 1984)

Neary, Ian, *Political Protest and Social Control in Pre-War Japan: The Origins of Buraku Liberation* (Manchester University Press, Manchester, 1989)

Ouwehand, Cornelius, *Hateruma: Socio-religious Aspects of a South Ryukyuan Island Culture* (Brill, Leiden, 1985).

Raz, Jacob, *Aspects of Otherness in Japanese Culture*, (Institute for the Study of Languages and Cultures of Asia and Africa, Tokyo, 1992)

White, Merry, *The Japanese Overseas: Can They Go Home Again?* (The Free Press, New York, 1988)

Yoshino, Roger, and Murakoshi Sueo, *The Invisible Visible Minority: Japan's Burakumin* (Buraku Kaiho Kenkyusho, Osaka, 1977)

RELATED NOVEL AND FILM

Shimazaki Tōson, *The Broken Commandment* (Tokyo University Press, Tokyo, 1974); filmed as *The Outcast* (*Hakai*) (dir. Ichikawa Kon)

6   The education system

INTRODUCTION

We shall return now to the world of a child growing up, but this time we are able to look at the provisions made for the child in the context of a broader knowledge about the society for which it is being prepared. In some of the 'continuing houses' described in Chapter 1, an eldest son may be assured of a future occupation so long as he is willing to follow in the footsteps of his forbears, and if the business of the *ie* prospers his younger brothers may be provided for as well. A daughter without brothers may be in the same position. In the modern world, however, this customary practice is no longer possible for many families, and parents look instead to the education system to provide their children with the qualifications necessary for finding themselves a niche in the world.

As has been shown in the previous chapter, the quality of this 'niche' is often settled rather early in life, since the nature of the hierarchical system makes it difficult to achieve spectacular advances in mid-career. This statement is not true of all occupations and professions, as later chapters will reveal, but many parents see the success of their children at school as of paramount importance for their future prospects. This is a clear opportunity for children to work towards goals beyond the confines of their present situation; and for parents well established in careers which they cannot pass on, this is also the only avenue for continuity.

For the children themselves school life becomes almost their whole life. Chapter 2 described how kindergarten or day nursery prepares a child for a new identity as a member of a class and as a cooperating member of a peer group of equals. This peer group now takes its place at the bottom of a clearly defined hierarchy, and children will, from the time they enter school, identify themselves with their class. It is much more common in Japan for children to be asked which school year they are in, rather than how old they are, and an answer to the question places the child at a stage of development recognisable to anyone. They are then identified by other children as seniors or juniors in the system and appropriate behaviour ensues.

School uniforms or badges are worn for many public occasions unconnected with school, and the wider world is thus able to classify these younger members according to the occupation proper to their age. Much of the responsibility for children passes to the hands of their teachers, and an accident or incident involving a child is as likely to be reported to the school as to the child's parents. Unseemly behaviour, even if out of school hours, reflects badly on the school, and teachers would certainly want to be involved in any disciplinary action which arose. During the school holidays, children are expected to attend school at regular intervals, and various activities are arranged to occupy the period when they are not there. Too much free time for children is seen as dangerous. School trips are also a regular feature of a child's life.

It is evident, then, that school has an important shaping influence for a person growing up in Japan, and the system of classification imparted already by parents and kindergarten teachers provides a basis for further development and elaboration. The emphasis on the importance of the right environment for a child's development continues, and one of the underlying assumptions of the system is that every child should have an equal chance to share the benefits of the system. The following sections will examine the overall official education system and its characteristics, supplementary institutions which are associated with it, some of the consequences of the system for children and their families, and recent moves for change in the light of criticism, particularly from outside.

COMPREHENSIVE EDUCATION FOR ALL

Since the turn of the century, Japan has had a school attendance record of above 98 per cent, and there is consequently a rate of literacy as high as any in the world. Since centralised universal education was introduced in the Meiji period, the possibilities for attendance have gradually increased, both at the earlier compulsory levels, and for those who wish to pursue their studies further. The present system was crystallised after the Second World War. It aims to be egalitarian and co-educational for the period of compulsory schooling, which comprises six years of primary school and three years of middle school, and meritocratic for three further years of high school and the range of universities and colleges which follow.

For the first nine years most children attend their local public schools, and there are clearly defined catchment areas which should not be crossed. As was mentioned in Chapter 4, primary school children from any particular neighbourhood may gather at a fixed meeting point each day to walk to school together, and from time to time various activities within the school are organised along neighbourhood lines. All children enter school the April after their sixth birthday, and they move up together each year, regardless of their academic performance. Thus the *uchi* group which probably formed rather casually in the neighbourhood, and may well have been reinforced at kindergarten or day nursery, is quite likely to stay together until graduation from middle school. However, by middle school, cohorts from more than one primary school will have come together, and the primary *uchi* group will by then be expanded to include other factors such as belonging to the same class or club.

Throughout the nation, tuition at this compulsory level is provided for all in subjects outlined by the Ministry of Education without much streaming according to ability. Teachers have detailed plans which they must follow, so that children in the same grade may on any particular day be covering the same ground in Hokkaido as they are in Kyushu. Even the textbooks must be approved by the Ministry, and their writers are occasionally instructed to rewrite whole passages to reflect the image that the Ministry deems appropriate. Courses in morals and social studies form part of the curriculum, and at the primary level children all over Japan are being socialised through this education in a rather uniform way. In secondary schools teachers have more autonomy in how they deal with the morals' course, which is often the subject of political controversy.

The content of all these courses is not unchanging, and the textbooks in use before the Second World War were banned by the Occupation Government because they helped to propagate the nationalistic fervour which led Japan into defeat. They taught Japanese mythology as history, encouraging all Japanese people everywhere to think of themselves as belonging to branches of the imperial line and thus descended ultimately from the imperial ancestress Amaterasu. Shintō ideology was also banned from schools in the immediate postwar period, and the values which were subsequently taught were for a while distinctly Western, mostly American, with the lives of heroes such as Benjamin Franklin being held up as models for the children. Gradually the courses have become more 'Japanese' in content, and

Figure 6.1 Classes of up to 45 children are managed by dividing them into smaller groups which work together and take collective responsibility for their activities.

suitable Japanese heroes have been brought in to localise the value system being advocated. However, the content of school textbooks remains a topic of considerable controversy, and another issue has been the objections of China and Korea to the way Japan represents her actions during the time of imperial expansion.

Order is maintained in elementary schools in much the same way as it is in kindergarten, with teachers allowing the force of peer pressure to play a strong contributory part. A 'homeroom' class is perceived as a group of equals throughout the system, with duties and privileges being shared out as fairly as possible. On the whole, discipline is good, and children effectively keep themselves in order in the way outlined already in Chapter 2. Throughout the school system classes are divided up into small groups, which are responsible collectively for various tasks. The behaviour of each member therefore contributes to the overall ability of the group, and the children learn to help one another. The principle of considering the needs of the collectivity as well as one's own personal desires thus continues to be emphasised throughout the education system.

William Cummings's book *Education and Equality in Japan* (1980) provides considerable information about how the principles of equality are being inculcated in Japanese schools. To give just a couple of examples, he cites the way the children themselves take it in turns to bring food over to the classroom and serve it out for lunch, and the way they are also responsible, with their teachers, for the cleaning of the premises. He regards such activities as part of the children's moral education, because they learn that 'no work, not even the dirty work of cleaning is too low for a student; that all should share equally in common tasks; the maintenance of the school is everyone's responsibility' (1980:117). He points out that Japanese teachers aim to 'develop "whole people", rather than some narrow aspect of individual potential' (1980:104), and much time is spent in non-academic activities such as music and sports.

Cummings is mostly concerned with education at primary level, and his major thesis, that Japan's schools have had a transforming egalitarian effect on society, would seem to reflect this emphasis. Children are aware of their seniors and juniors, according to school year, but since all move through the system together it is only a matter of time before any child reaches the top class. They are also aware of differences of ability, but these are played down or channelled into group benefit, and competition between individual children is not encouraged at this stage, even during the school sports day. Amongst the children themselves, there are inevitable comparisons, however, and when they move through to middle school, in the April after their twelfth birthday, they become more important.

A clear understanding of middle school education depends on an understanding of the differences in the high school system, which are discussed in the following section, and there we encounter the opposing hierarchical principle again. The middle schools prepare pupils for the more serious academic instruction they will receive when they go on to high school, but they also continue to attend to the development of the child as a whole person. Two articles have recently appeared which discuss in some detail the role middle schools have of 'guiding' their charges through puberty, especially in their extracurricular activities, and emphasising the importance of the hierarchical dyadic relationships they make. They now refer to their schoolmates in other classes as seniors or juniors, especially where club activities are concerned, and the consequent expectations and responsibilities are part of the education process (Fukuzawa 1994, LeTendre 1994).

SELECTION FOR HIGH SCHOOL AND BEYOND

Although some 95.4 per cent (in 1991) of middle school graduates move on into high schools, there is at this stage a considerable range of schools available. The best qualified students are able to continue in the academically oriented schools, which are ranked in any area for their success in placing graduating students in good universities. There are also a number of vocational high schools which include training in commercial and technical skills, domestic science and fields of local importance such as agriculture or forestry, and there is sometimes also a night high school, so that students can work during the day. In most areas there is also a variety of private high schools, which are sometimes of lower status than the public ones, but which provide an academic track for children who fail to gain access to the best public schools. Although it was not intended when the system was designed, some of these private schools have become more prestigious than the local public schools.

In stark contrast to the previous emphasis on equality of education, entry into high school is based on merit and is fiercely competitive. At this stage students are free to apply to any of the high schools within commuting distance of their homes, and acceptance is based on the results of an entrance exam set by the school, sometimes together with a report from their middle school. Typically, there are far more applications for the academic high schools than there are places, although teachers try to advise pupils to apply where they are most likely to succeed. The graduates of these schools are likely to gain admission to correspondingly prestigious universities and, as was discussed in the previous chapter, the quality of one's university is reflected in the quality of employment which one can then go on to obtain. Since the system also favours those who remain in the same employment for life, this sorting at the high school stage is evidently immensely important.

An excellent anthropological analysis of the high school system and its social context is provided in Thomas Rohlen's book *Japan's High Schools* (1983), which is based on research carried out in the city of Kobe. Rohlen spent six to eight weeks in each of five high schools, which range across the spectrum of possibilities. He found, however, that the vast majority of children, in whatever high school, were still hoping to gain entrance to university or, at least, to a two-year junior college, and their studies were largely orientated towards this goal. Although the specialist and night schools were built to prepare less academic children for practical employment, the emphasis on gaining a university qualification is so strong in Japan, that few high school students seemed realistically to be pursuing alternative careers.

This is not the case everywhere. Indeed, in the rural area of Kyushu where I carried out my own fieldwork, children are less concerned with university entrance and their parents are happy for them to remain in the family business. The agricultural and commercial high schools are considered to be quite acceptable choices, and when parents can afford it, girls often choose a private school which specialises in home economics. Those children who do well enough to enter an academic high school are not discouraged, and if they then go on to a good university, they and their parents are praised by the neighbours. If an only son takes up employment in a distant prestigious company, however, the success may be double-edged for the parents, for their house and sometimes quite substantial property is left without a successor.

Rohlen's description is supported by research carried out in Tokyo and other large cities, however, and by the seemingly endless stream of articles which appear in the press, both in Japan and abroad, about the competitive nature of Japanese university entrance. At this stage, admission is based almost entirely on success in an exam set by the university concerned, and the difficulty of the exams reflects the prestige of the university. Results obtained during the period a student is attending university may play only a small part in the subsequent employment secured (especially in humanities), so that the major pressure is on the pupils applying for entrance. Since some high schools have a much better reputation than others for gaining places for their pupils, this means that some of this pressure is transferred back to the sorting for high schools.

In theory the system is a meritocracy, providing equal opportunities to all children to enter the school which reflects their ability and willingness to work hard. But in practice there are other factors involved. Rohlen found a striking correspondence between socioeconomic circumstances and the high school attended. He administered questionnaires to second-year pupils in each of the five schools, and found unmistakable correlations between the prestige of the school and the education of the parents, the facilities at home for study and the general stability of their families. It is evident that the emphasis on equality so thoroughly instilled in the early years is heavily tempered by the time a child enters high school. Indeed, Rohlen comments that he can think of no other inclusive social institution in Japan that comes closer to a simple class structure than the structure of urban high schools in cities like Kobe (1983:129).

SUPPLEMENTARY EDUCATIONAL AIDS

This evidence of inequality in high school populations is also related to the use made by many families of the supplementary educational facilities which abound in Japan. The most common form of supplement to the public system is found in classes held after school for tutoring students in particular subjects. For some families these classes start before their children even go to school. At this stage they follow quite a variety of pursuits, which may represent the development of individual interests, including music, art and martial arts such as *kendo*, but a minority of children will already be studying academically orientated subjects such as English or maths. Primary school pupils often go to classes to learn the abacus, or the piano, but by the middle school level, when pupils are preparing for high school entrance, the emphasis focuses on preparation for exams in the compulsory subjects.

From this stage onwards, until a university place has been secured, some children will spend several evenings a week rehearsing the basics of maths and English until nine or ten at night, and then return home to study alone until the early morning. These classes cost money, of course, and some families are able to afford better ones than others. Nor is it every family which has the space to allow each child his or her own work room. Those who do have the resources may even opt for a private middle school since, particularly in urban areas, there are certain schools which have a better reputation than others for gaining places in the better high schools. The same applies to some of the public middle schools, and since children are supposed to be allocated to these on the basis of residence, it is not unheard of for children to be lodged, in theory or in practice, with friends or relatives in the appropriate part of the city. Some country families even move mother and children to Tokyo solely for the sake of the children's education.

Although most children in Japan attend public primary schools, in areas where some middle schools have a particularly good reputation, competition for entry has encouraged affluent parents to seek private primary schools to prepare their children for middle school entrance, and since these, too, are under pressure for entry, there are even kindergartens which aim to prepare children to enter prestigious primary schools. The system most aspired to in Tokyo is sometimes called an escalator system, for some of the prestigious universities have schools of all levels attached to them, and a child who gains entry at the bottom has a very good chance of moving smoothly through to the top. The problem now becomes one of gaining entry to the kindergarten. In Tokyo there are even tutorial institutions which accept children of one, two and three years of age for preparation for kindergarten entry. One such school provides one teacher for every two children, and according to an article published in early 1986, charges 15,000 yen as a pre-entry examination fee, 80,000 yen for admission, and a monthly tuition fee ranging from 26,000 yen to 70,000 yen depending on the days attended (£1.00 = approx 240 yen at the time). Classes are from 9.30 a.m. to 1 p.m., for one to four days a week (Ohki 1986:10). There is no question here that a wealthy elite is being separated off at a very early age.

In some kindergartens it is felt that the problems which can arise in trying to assess children of three years of age are too great, however, and they choose instead to test the mothers. This is not entirely inappropriate, for mothers in Japan often become very involved in the education of their children. The wives of company employees in particular seem to make a career of the supervision of their children's education. When children are very small many mothers spend time studying manuals of advice on the best ways to bring up their children, but the most dedicated will continue to purchase publications supplementary to the school courses in order to keep one step ahead and therefore help their offspring for as long as they are able. They will spend time discussing their child's progress with the homeroom teacher and generally contributing to the school's welfare through the Parent–Teacher Association. They will avidly consume all the statistics and opinions which regularly appear in the media, and devise strategies to win for their child the best possible advantages to be gained from the supplementary educational facilities available.

Vogel's chapter entitled 'The Gateway to Salary: Infernal Entrance Examinations' in *Japan's New Middle Class* (1971) is a valuable discussion of the ways and means that families may use to help their children through the education system. It includes a very vivid description of the involvement of the mothers in the district of Tokyo where he carried out research. He describes, for example, how some mothers queue all night just to put in applications for university entrance exams on behalf of their sons, although the time of an application makes no difference to its success. Others mock such dedication, but get up to catch a 4 a.m. train to the university campus (1971:48). Vogel argues that the mother's own status within the community is very much bound up with the educational success of her children (1971:55).

Such mothers form something of an elite within the system at large, however, and there are also many mothers who go back to work once their children enter school, as well as those who work as far as possible throughout their childbearing period. In three-generation houses, as has already been mentioned, it is often the grandparents who are left to care for the children. On the whole, a strong contributory factor here would seem to be the occupation of the father. There is an obvious economic connection, in that the 'education mama', as such mothers have become known, must be supported financially in order to be fully active in this respect, but it seems likely that more than this is involved. This is the ability or otherwise of the family to pass on its lifestyle to its children. The children of employees of large, prestigious companies must do well in the exam system if they are to follow in their fathers' footsteps. The fathers can help economically, but the role of manipulating the system is taken on by their (maintained) wives.

As a kind of safety net for families whose children fail to gain a place in the university of their choice directly from high school, there is another last-ditch series of private cram schools which provide intensive training for one or more years for second and subsequent sittings of the entrance exams. Rohlen quotes figures (1983:84) which suggest that a quarter to a third of the applicants for higher education in any one year are from these 'cram schools', and this proportion is roughly equal to the number of students who fail to gain a place. The potential success of such endeavour is indicated, however, in his figures for the 1980 entrance exams to Tokyo University, which occupies the pinnacle in the university hierarchy. Of the successful applicants, 35 per cent were taking the test for the second time, and 10 per cent for the third time or more (1983:86–7).

Another 'aid' to teachers helping parents and children to make decisions about which high school or university to choose when making applications is supplied by companies which offer tests on a commercial basis. These tests are modelled on the school and university entrance tests, and classify the children who take them in comparison with their peers. A ranking for each examinee may then be compared with figures published by the same companies about what ranking is necessary for entry to particular universities or high schools. Some pupils will take these tests as regularly as once a month as they work hard to improve their scores. The results have apparently become so influential in recent years that middle school teachers rely very heavily on them in advising parents where to place their children's applications for high school entry. To the children themselves such competitiveness must seem to erode the previous ideology of equality, which they were taught was so important.

SOME CONSEQUENCES OF THE EDUCATION SYSTEM FOR SOCIALISATION

How, then, does all this emphasis on entrance examinations affect the lives of children in Japan? What are some of the important socialising factors involved? Articles in foreign newspapers have tended to emphasise the strain of keeping up, the lack of time to play, and they are quick to report the high rate of suicide among school children in Japan. There has been a good deal of fuss in the Japanese and foreign press alike about violence in school and at home, particularly involving middle school pupils, and the problems some school children suffer at the hands of their classmates. Bullying seems to have replaced examination pressure as a major cause of child suicide and school refusal in recent reports, and special centres have been set up to provide phone-in help for victims.

An interesting article by the medical anthropologist Margaret Lock (1988) examines in some detail the phenomenon of school refusal, a subject which has been a particular focus of attention recently in the Japanese mass media. Lock cites cases which have been diagnosed as a specific 'syndrome' and she reports on the treatment administered, but her article also places Japanese attention to this phenomenon in the context of contemporary ideas about the breakdown of traditional social values. Blame is laid at the door of the 'fragile nuclear family' or the 'new middle class', including a 'selfish' mother and/or an absent father, despite the lack of hard evidence to show any such correlations.

The press coverage accorded these unpleasant aspects of school life would seem to be directly related to the shock they deliver to the more usual expectations of the audiences concerned The British press finds Japanese schools unbearably uniform and seizes on examples of rebellion as signs of pathology in a social system which seems to deny the very individuality which is regarded as so important in the West. In Japan these incidents are news because they undermine the order which has been such an all-pervading part of the education system. In other advanced industrialised nations violence and bullying in schools are often so commonplace that they cause little or no stir in the outside world. In Japan the incidence of violence in schools has recently put particular pressure on long-standing committees set up to discuss reform in the education system (which will be considered in the next section).

On the whole, Japan's schools, at all levels, are still extremely ordered. They occupy children directly or indirectly for a substantial proportion of their lives. They teach them self-discipline and control as well as the subjects on the curriculum, and they allocate to them in an efficient and systematic way the roles which await them in the adult world. The system is so clear cut that special schools and classes have been created for the re-adjustment of Japanese children who spend even short periods abroad. These 'returnees' are perceived as posing a serious threat to the tight order of Japanese educational institutions, as is shown in the work of another anthropologist, Roger Goodman (1990)

Goodman set out to examine the 'problems' children returning to Japan after a period overseas were perceived to encounter. He actually found that the facilities available to them are quite substantial and impressive, not least the places reserved for them in the best universities, and some people apparently even send their children to school abroad so that they may qualify. The parents of these returnee schoolchildren are also seen to suffer from the disadvantage of having been sent away from Japan (see White 1988) and, as many of them occupy high-ranking positions, they have been in a position to use this apparent problem to lobby to turn the perceived disadvantage for their children into an advantage.

Goodmans's analysis reveals as much about Japan's power structures, and the way they operate, as about the fate of these children, and his book addresses the important contemporary issue of Japan's attempts at internationalisation. Much is revealed here about the division which persists in attitudes of powerful Japanese to the outside world, between those who value the force for change these children represent and those who are concerned about their loss of 'Japaneseness'. This division is shown to be part of a long-standing ambiguity noted elsewhere in Japan's representations of the outside world (see also Hendry 1991).

As Rohlen has pointed out, Japanese schools 'in a very real sense pace society'. They teach rhythms and segmentation of time which 'complement very neatly indeed the working order of industry and modern organisation' (1983:168); 'they are best understood as shaping generations of disciplined workers for a technomeritocratic system that requires highly socialized individuals capable of performing reliably in a rigorous, hierarchical, and finely tuned organizational environment' (1983:209). His overwhelming image of high school classes is one of boredom – of children sitting still and listening to their teacher, of accumulating facts but having little opportunity to discuss them, of having views, but not needing to express them, of possibly resenting the authority of teachers, but of learning not to challenge it (1983:246). They have been well trained to have a *tatemae* face for the classroom, whatever their inner thoughts on a subject.

In such an environment diligence is a highly prized quality. Longstanding Japanese virtues of self-control, dedication and singularity of purpose are admired and rewarded, and Rohlen found that it was in the vocational schools, rather than the academic ones, where disorderly conduct was to be found. This is where he found delinquency among youths, too, and although socioeconomic factors may play a part, Rohlen's work would suggest that a lack of such purpose may leave a void of ambition, despite attempts to make vocational schools more attractive. During the years since Rohlen's study the violence in middle schools has become a significant problem, and the reasons would seem to be comparable. In the system which has developed there is no satisfactory place for students who lag behind. The success of the egalitarian principle in the early stages of schooling may make the pill of hierarchical sorting more difficult to swallow for those who fall behind.

In fact the two principles of equality and hierarchy vie for attention throughout the school career of Japanese children. Classmates are among the most equal relations that a Japanese person will encounter in his or her entire life, and many adults retain ties with their school or university friends through regular reunions, even for old primary school companions. Women, in particular, may never again form such intimate relations in later life, and they will turn to old school friends with their deepest worries. On the other hand, relations between classes are strictly hierarchical, and interaction between members of different ones reflect these differences. For example, club activities, which are held on the school premises, begin to train children in the less formal aspects of close hierarchical relations.

These clubs, which are common-interest groups covering activities such as sports, music and other hobbies, form something of an antidote to the uniformity of the system because they allow a degree of individual expression among all the communal activities of Japanese schools, both in the choice of activity and in the chance children have to choose their companions. Their membership typically cuts across classes so that seniors help to train juniors in the pursuits involved. Members of the same club may spend a lot of time together, and become very close, but if they are from different grades they will address one another as senior and junior, and their behaviour together will resemble that described in the previous chapter as appropriate for seniors and juniors in various other walks of life. In fact in many schools these hierarchical relations are more marked than in several arenas of adult society.

The relations between pupils and their teachers are also hierarchical. In most Japanese schools classes are large (up to 45 students) so that there is only limited opportunity for close relationships to develop in the classroom, but some teachers take part in club activities and thus provide role models in areas of common interest. Closer relationships may also develop between children and the tutors who take their after-school classes, and these smaller groups have been likened to a more traditional form of education which existed in the Tokugawa period. Some teachers arrange trips and outings for their private pupils, and the groups which come together for work may also find themselves playing together as well.

One of the criticisms of the system has been that children have little time left for informal play once they begin to prepare seriously for university or school entrance exams. For the children involved, their closest friendships are often with members of the same tutorial groups, and with these they may spend several hours a week travelling to and from their classes. Some tutors try to create the atmosphere of a club for this after-school study, and one such teacher of my acquaintance provides all his pupils with brightly coloured 'club' bags in which to carry their books around. He also arranges for the pupils to stay overnight together at the school for special sessions, and takes them on trips together, walking or ski-ing as the season dictates. The children involved attend several classes a week, so much of their social life will be tied up with groups such as these, and it will be here that they enjoy informal play as well as hard work.

A division has already been made clear between those children whose parents are able to send them to classes after school and those who are not. A further division arises as the children who do not attend begin to engage in other activities. For Kobe, Rohlen calls these the 'city' activities – going out with friends, riding motor bikes, visiting coffee shops, 'dating'. All these are low-status activities for academically orientated high school students. They are usually found among those who leave after middle school, when such activities were not allowed. Those who are involved have usually given up on the race for university entrance and their parents are probably not pushing them either. Serious students return home after their classes, and late at night they are to be found at their desks. Sports will even have to take low priority in the lives of the most dedicated. Their rewards come later.

UNIVERSITY AND JUNIOR COLLEGE

Once a place has been gained in a university, the quality of career that a student can expect is fairly clearly decided, whatever the outcome of the degree. This means that the pressure which preceded university entrance is relieved and young people can relax and enjoy their studies or their social life during this period. In anthropological terms this period can be interpreted as part of a transition from childhood to adulthood. Many of the characteristics described long ago by Van Gennep of rites of initiation in general are present here. They include ordeals, education and freedom from social constraints. Japanese university students have successfully negotiated the ordeals of the entrance examinations, they have filled themselves full of 'education' and they are at last allowed to develop a sense of freedom. Their contemporaries in employment seem to have to take their freedom by having a period of rebellion against adult society, symbolised, for example, in unconventional clothes and hairstyles, but for students there is also a chance for political rebellion and some of their most spectacular activities, such as those expressing opposition to Narita airport, have been reported in the international press. More recently, however, students have become less and less interested in politics, and more interested in international travel as a means to dabble in freedom from the constraints of Japanese society.

About one-third of the graduates from high school go on to higher education in Japan at present, but there is a big difference at this stage between the courses chosen by boys and by girls. Four-year degree courses are the most common ones embarked upon for boys, and in 1991, 72 per cent of university students were boys. The two-year course of a junior college is popular with girls, and more than 90 per cent of their enrolment in the same year was from girls. For the latter, education and home economics are likely subjects of study. The proportion of all students of higher education in universities, as opposed to junior colleges, is 81 per cent (Figures from the *Statistical Handbook of Japan* 1992).

Until this stage, boys and girls move through the system in more or less equal numbers, girls often having the edge over boys for high school entrance, but attitudes tend to be different from an earlier stage. Boys are much more likely to be striving towards entry into the best university they can manage, whereas girls are generally more relaxed. It is not seen as advantageous for girls to be more qualified than prospective husbands, and marriage is still the chief goal of a majority of women. Nevertheless, if girls are willing to make the effort, there are few hurdles put in their way on the basis of their gender, and an academic career is a definite possibility for women. In any case, the mothers of the next generation are probably among the highest qualified in the world.

There is little anthropological work available on the lives of university students, although a useful book to refer to is *Higher Education in Japan* (1971) by Nagai Michio, a Tokyo University professor who became Minister of Education. There is no doubt that the experience of having attended university gives adults an edge in the employment market over their contemporaries who completed their education in high school. The period spent in university may be a time for experiment and political protest (see, for example, Steinhoff 1984), but most of these radical activists knuckle down to become conforming citizens once they join the ranks of the employed.

EDUCATIONAL REFORM

It should be pointed out at this stage that many Japanese people are unhappy with their education system. It provides a very high standard of average education, so that Japanese children compare more than favourably with their contemporaries in other countries. However, there are various criticisms which have been made of the Japanese system, and observers from societies which place more emphasis on individual development have been particularly shocked by the apparent emphasis on uniformity. The pressures of the exam system have been blamed for a number of evils, and big business has been charged with compounding the problem by selecting graduates only from the top universities. There seems to be a move away from this policy by up-and-coming middle-sized companies, and reports in the Japanese press would suggest that some companies are benefiting from a more adventurous selection process.

From the point of view of the education system itself, a process of reform has been underway since 1970, although progress is slow. An advisory council was set up by the Prime Minister in 1984 to chart a more specific course, and its first report was submitted in June 1985. It proposes a greater emphasis on individuality, creativity and choice, among other things, but it has been the subject of much controversy and debate. The variety of views expressed, together with the range of arguments put forward to support them, would seem to militate against any immediate action of a drastic kind, although certain less controversial aspects of the report are gradually being implemented. The discussion is vaguely reminiscent of that which surrounded ideas for reforming the family system in the Meiji period, and it may well run on for just as long.

During visits to primary schools in 1994, I was told about innovations such as 'team teaching' and 'streaming' within classes. The teachers I met also used other English words to describe activities which they had been practising for many years, but which they said they had modified to take more into account than they felt they had done previously the individuality and creativity of their charges. They also emphasised the way that children could often choose between a range of options for the work they did: topics for essay writing, themes for poetry, subjects for their painting classes. In practice, as I looked around the schools I visited, they seemed little changed from the time in 1986–7 when my own children experienced the system, but these primary schools had impressed me at the time with the care and attention they gave to the individual needs of the pupils. These pupils also achieve much success in international comparisons of their progress, and it is probably not at this stage that much in the way of reform is needed.

CONCLUSION

Education is an issue of great interest in Japan today, and it is no coincidence that high-level discussions about it remind one of debates on the family. The issue is again one of concern about the maintenance of order, control and Japaneseness, and a fear of the dangers associated with internationalism and too much freedom. In many ways the education system and even the examination entrance system, have taken over roles which used to be played by the family, and the new nuclear family has slotted into a place within that system. Continuity is still an important principle underlying Japanese thinking, and where the family has lost its former role in that respect, education has taken over and opened up new avenues. On a national level there is concern that there should continue to be a specifically Japanese culture to be passed on and that this will not evaporate with the competing concern for Japan to become internationalised.

This chapter has emphasised the fate of only a proportion of the Japanese population in discussing in so much detail the exigencies of the university entrance system. Nearly 60 per cent of the population takes up employment at an earlier stage. The emphasis here reflects issues which concern the Japanese media, however, and so effectively reach the majority of the population through newspapers and television. Discussions about education may be seen as having a wider influence than that received by children attending school. It seems likely, in view of what has been said, that experiences with the system now contribute a very important measure of status, not only for the individuals who go through the system, but for their families, too.

REFERENCES

Cummings, William K., *Education and Equality in Japan* (Princeton University Press, Princeton, New Jersey, 1980)

Fukuzawa, Rebecca E., 'The Path to Adulthood According to Japanese Middle Schools', *Journal of Japanese Studies*, vol. 20, no. 1 (1994), pp. 61–86

Goodman, Roger, *Japan's 'International Youth': The Emergence of a New Class of Schoolchildren* (Clarendon Press, Oxford, 1990)

Hendry, Joy, 'St. Valentine and St. Nicholas in Japan: Some Less Academic Aspects of Japanese School Life', *Japan Forum*, vol. 3, no. 2 (1991), pp. 313–23

Krauss, E.S., T.P. Rohlen and P.G. Steinhoff, *Conflict in Japan* (University of Hawaii Press, Honolulu, 1984)

LeTendre, Gerald, 'Guiding Them On: Teaching, Hierarchy and Social Organization in Japanese Middle Schools', *Journal of Japanese Studies*, vol. 20, no. 1 (1994), pp. 37–59

Lock, Margaret, 'A Nation at Risk: Interpretations of School Refusal in Japan', in M. Lock and D. Gordon (eds), *Biomedicine Examined* (Kluwer Academic Publishers, Dordrecht, Boston: 1988), pp. 377–414

Ohki, Emiko, 'Pre-kindergarten "Education" is Flourishing in Tokyo', *Japan Education Journal*, vol. 27 (1986), p. 10

Rohlen, Thomas P., *Japan's High Schools* (University of California Press, Berkeley, 1983)

Steinhoff, Patricia G. 'Student Conflict', in E.S. Krauss, T.P. Rohlen and P.G. Steinhoff, *Conflict in Japan* (University of Hawaii Press, Honolulu, 1984), pp. 174–213

Vogel, Ezra F., *Japan's New Middle Class* (University of California Press, Berkeley, 2nd edition, 1971), Chapter 3

White, Merry, *The Japanese Overseas: Can They Go Home Again?* (The Free Press, New York, 1988)

FURTHER READING

Beauchamp, Edward R. (ed.), *Learning to be Japanese* (Linnet Books, Hamden, Connecticut, 1978)

Dore, Ronald, *The Diploma Disease* (Allen and Unwin, London, 1976), Chapter 3

———, *City Life in Japan: A Study of a Tokyo Ward* (University of California Press, Berkeley, 1958), Chapter 12

———, *Education in Tokugawa Japan* (The Athlone Press, London, 1984)

Kobayashi, Tetsuya, *Schools, Society and Progress in Japan* (Pergamon Press, Oxford, 1976)

Nagai, Michio, *Higher Education in Japan: Its Take-off and Crash* (University of Tokyo Press, Tokyo, 1971)

Passin, Herbert, *Society and Education in Japan* (Columbia University Press, New York, 1965)

Singleton, John, *Nichū: A Japanese School* (Holt, Rinehart and Winston, New York, 1967)

White, Merry, *The Japanese Educational Challenge: A Committment to Children* (The Free Press, New York, 1987)

———, *The Material Child: Coming of Age in Japan and America* (The Free Press, New York, 1993)

7 Religious influences

INTRODUCTION

In this chapter and the next we temporarily leave the world of Japanese institutions which may readily be compared with their counterparts elsewhere, and plunge into a very different cosmological system. At this stage the reader with some anthropological background will have a definite advantage, for religion in Japan may much more easily be compared with any number of indigenous religions around the world than with the great traditions which are discussed in 'religious studies' or 'comparative religion'. What should be included under the term 'religion' in Japan remains open to discussion, and it has been argued that to the Japanese themselves even their language and their cultural identity are endowed with sacred qualities.[1]

One of the problems is that Japan has been influenced by a great number of religious traditions. Another is that religion pervades many spheres which others might call secular and it cannot easily be separated from them. It is thus sometimes difficult to draw a line between the 'religious' and the 'secular', a problem not infrequently encountered by anthropologists and one which is reflected in their writings. Also, the English language tends to distinguish between magic, science and religion in a way which reflects a European philosophical heritage, being based largely on developments arising out of the work of Newton and Descartes. This clearly affected the work of some of the early 'armchair' anthropologists. It is, however, impossible to make such clear distinctions in other cultural contexts, as some Western scientists, who have encountered oriental culture, have begun to realise (e.g., Capra 1983).

The content of this chapter may, therefore, include areas which are not immediately recognisable as 'religious' from an outside point of view, and readers may be surprised to find references to books about medical anthropology in the reading list. On a global scale, however, explanations of misfortune, including illness, are frequently couched in supernatural terms, with supernatural remedies, and anthropological work in Japan would suggest that these are by no means absent there. Other aspects of Japanese epistemology will emerge in the pages which follow, although there is no space here to present a comprehensive 'world view'. The chapter is divided into sections which consider various religious influences, both separately and in some of their syncretic forms.

Another problem in coming to terms with Japanese religion relates to the question of belief. Many Japanese people claim to be non-religious, if asked directly. They have no strict allegiance to a particular religious organisation, and if asked whether they believe in a god or gods, they may well reply 'no', or 'only if I want something'. The same people may, however, be observed practising a variety of 'religious' activities in the course of their lives, and Shinto and Buddhism, the two main Japanese religions, claimed in 1991 to have nearly 107 million and 96 million followers respectively when the total population of Japan is only 124 million.[2]

Again, the problem seems to arise from a completely different understanding and expectation associated with the concepts of religion and belief. When religion is something quite distinct from the other affairs of life, one can talk about believing in it, or otherwise, and members of the world of Western philosophy are accustomed to this approach. Indeed, Japanese refer to members of particular sects or other religious groups, as 'believers'. When religious ideas pervade all areas of society, as is the case in many traditional worlds, the use of the word 'belief' is less appropriate, because there is really much less opportunity for choice.[3] Japan is an interesting case because Western philosophy is taught in Japanese schools, yet for many Japanese the world they know is based on an epistemology quite different from the one that they learn about in school books. Probably the best way of elucidating this is to present some of the evidence.

SHINTŌ

The most ancient and all-pervasive religious influence in Japan is that which has come to be known as Shintō. This is the name given to the indigenous elements of Japanese religion which can be traced back to the pre-historical times described briefly in Chapter 1. Much of Shintō may have been imported, but it is Shintō which is associated

with the mythology of Japan's creation and the supernatural ancestors of Japan's imperial line. It is Shintō which is the very foundation
of Japan's identity as a nation. During the warring years leading up
to and including World War II, Shintō doctrine, developed and prop-
agated by a specially created state Shintō office, sought to inspire
Japanese people with nationalistic fervour. This state Shintō was
dismantled by the Allied Occupation as having been responsible for
much of Japan's aggression, and the post-war Constitution included
a clause separating religion from the state.

Some Japanese still refer to Shintō activities as superstition, but
the disrepute into which it fell has failed to eradicate Shintō rites and
festivals, as we saw in Chapter 4. Indeed, these have been increasing
in the last couple of decades, and the funeral of the Shōwa Emperor,
as well as the enthronement of the new one, was conducted with
secular rites for the outside world, but also embodied the Shintō rites
which were designed to follow ancient custom. A comprehensive
study of the relationship between Shintō and state from the Meiji
Restoration to the end of the Shōwa era is to be found in Hardacre
(1989).

The word Shintō was chosen to correspond to the names of other
religions as these became influential in the Japanese world, and
it translates literally as 'the way of the *kami*', where the character
for 'the way' (pronounced *tō* or *dō)* is the same one used for arts and
life-paths such as in jū*dō*, bushi*dō* (the Samurai way), and sho*dō*
(calligraphy). *Kami*, another reading of the character for *shin*, is a
word which has been translated as 'gods', but it is also applied to
natural objects which are regarded as sacred, such as trees, mountains, seas, birds and animals, as well as to some human beings,
usually but not always after they have died. The mythological characters who appeared in Chapter 1 are *kami*, and their supposed
descendant, the Emperor, was regarded as having divine qualities
until the present incumbent formally renounced them during the
Occupation.

One of the most evident manifestations of Shintō all over the
country is to be found in the shrines which form the centre of the
neighbourhood festivals described in Chapter 4. These buildings are
maintained by the local people who in turn come under the protection
of the particular deity who is remembered there. This *kami* is called
the *ujigami*, the *kami* of the local *uji*, which in ancient times used to be
a local unit of related families. These days, however, the relationship
of common residence is enough to elicit protection, and members of
a community are supposed to share the benefits and duties of this

relationship. Annual festivals illustrate the strength of such support, as residents of all ages participate in the customary celebrations, and such events provide a good example of how 'religious' activity may be intermingled (or not) with the other interpretations mentioned in Chapter 4.

Other Shintō shrines are associated with deities with special powers, rather than with specific geographical areas. The larger ones have a resident priest or priests, sometimes aided by shrine maidens called *miko*, who are unmarried daughters of priests, or parishioners who also dance for the *kami*. Together, they take care of visitors, who may be very numerous at the most famous shrines. One such is the Izumo shrine in Shimane prefecture, where the deity is supposed to help cement marriages, so that it is visited almost constantly by young couples. There are shrines all over Japan where the deity is supposed to help with learning, and these are visited by schoolchildren and parents. The most famous and sacred shrine is the one at Ise, where the nation's founding ancestress, Amaterasu, is remembered, and this is the one that agemate groups used to save up to visit at least once in their lives.

People visit shrines for particular reasons, and they visit them at particular times, such as New Year, or for the age celebrations which will be described in the following chapter. They also visit them as tourists. In all cases, the behaviour is much the same. They enter the shrine compound, wash their hands and mouth, if there is a source of running water for the purpose, and approach the front of the shrine. Here they make a monetary offering, ring the bell to attract the attention of the deity, clap their hands and bow their heads in prayer. Afterwards it is customary to buy a charm or amulet for the Shintō shelf at home, or to write one's prayer on an appropriate receptacle at the shrine. On special occasions, a ritual may be performed by one or more priests, and this usually involves four main elements: offerings, purification, prayer and a ritual feast of some sort, even if it is only a drink of sake.

In general, Shintō is concerned with notions of pollution and purity, as can be seen from the ritual elements outlined above. The washing on entry to a shrine purifies a person from the pollution of the outside world, ritually marking the sacred inside of the shrine compound, as the removal of shoes marks the inside of a house. A further 'inside' is found in the shrine building itself, although most visitors will not penetrate this far, except for special celebrations, and it is rather the area of the priests and their assistants. For a special ritual, a further rite of purification initiates the proceedings, and this is accomplished by the shaking of a decorated staff over the participants. Local communities invite priests to carry out similar purification rituals annually for their shrines.

In the Shintō order of things, death, injury, disease, menstrual blood and childbirth are regarded as polluting. Thus the bereaved, and women who have recently given birth, are not supposed to enter a shrine compound for a definite pollution period. In the house of the deceased, a white sheet of paper is hung up over the Shintō shelf to protect it from this pollution, and a warning notice should be displayed on the outer door of the house during the mourning period. Salt is regarded as a purifying agent, and it is customary to present small packets of salt to guests at a funeral. In fact, in most houses Shintō is divorced entirely from dealing with the dead because at this time families turn to the other major religion, namely Buddhism. On the whole, Shintō ritual is associated with celebrations of life and its development, with the harvest and fertility, and with house-building and the community.

BUDDHISM

Buddhism, which was introduced into Japan around the sixth century AD, has developed a large number of Japanese sects and sub-sects. Their doctrines are now very different from the original Indian variety of Buddhism, as they are from the interpretations of the Chinese sages who transmitted the religion to Japan. Several times over the centuries efforts have been made to amalgamate Shintō ideas with Japanese Buddhism, for example, by explaining *kami* as manifestations of Buddhas and Bodhisattvas, and most Japanese people can without conflict practice both Buddhist and Shintō rites. Sometimes these are even combined. Buddhist edifices are usually called temples, as opposed to Shintō shrines, with correspondingly different Japanese words, but there are places where both exist on the same site, and priests of either religion may officiate in the buildings of the other.

However, Buddhism has also maintained a separate identity, and this has not been tainted by the disrepute into which Shintō fell in the post-war years. Buddhism appears sufficiently self-contained to be described as a 'religion' or 'faith'. The Chinese script used to write it comprises two characters: one is the character for Buddha; the other, also used in Christianity and Confucianism, literally translates as 'teaching', and Buddhist texts and sutras give it a body of dogma which Shintō lacked until very recently. Many of the sects have doctrines of enlightenment, of escape from the constant cycle of reincarnation: one may strive to become either a Buddha or, by refraining from nirvana in order to help others, a Bodhisattva.

Ordinary people are often unaware of such doctrine, however. They refer to their recently deceased relatives as 'Buddhas' (*hotoke*) anyway, and turn to Buddhist priests for funerals and the memorial rites which they understand will bring their souls safely to a secure state as ancestors. Such memorials are held at regular intervals for up to 33 or even 60 years after death, when some people feel that their ancestors become converted into *kami*. There is an excellent anthropological study of this aspect of Japanese religion by Robert Smith (1974), and a collection of essays which appeared shortly afterwards compares the attention paid to Japanese ancestors with that found in Africa and other parts of East Asia (Newell 1976).

Japanese families with deceased relatives to remember usually have a Buddhist altar (*butsudan*) in the house, as described in Chapter 2. They will also have affiliation with a particular Buddhist temple in the area, although they may not share this affiliation with their neighbours as they do in the case of the local Shintō shrine. Buddhist affiliations tend to be on a household level, rather than a community one. The physical remains of the family ancestors may be buried in a graveyard associated with the temple, or they may be stored in urns in a purpose-built *nōkotsudō* somewhere in the vicinity of their residence. This is often the site of dancing at the annual summer *bon* festival when people travel all over Japan to visit the families of their ancestors.

Some families visit their temples to make offerings and to attend meetings at particular times of year, particularly the spring and autumn equinoxes and New Year, as well as the *bon* summer festival, but many more receive the priest at their houses, and then only for funerals and memorial services. Members of the newer Buddhist movements, such as Sōka Gakkai, attend their temples regularly, but for most Japanese families their original affiliations were established by their forbears during the Tokugawa period and they do not have any great personal commitment. At that time it was compulsory for everyone to be registered at a Buddhist temple, a system which dated back to the anti-Christian purges of the late sixteenth century.

The temples themselves are organised in a hierarchical way, with a chief temple for each of the main sects, usually in Nara or Kyoto, and branch main temples in the provincial capitals which service the smaller local temples. This system made it possible to register the whole population, and some temples still have their records of the local populace going back for 200 years or more. Until the Second

World War, the temples owned enough land to support themselves, but since the post-war land reform removed much of this source of income, their activities have had to diversify. A traditional occupation of Buddhist priests in the Tokugawa period was teaching, and many temples ran schools for the local children. Some priests now have teaching and other jobs in the wider community, others have set up youth hostels, courses for schoolchildren and kindergartens within the temple premises.

Like Shintō shrines, there are also Buddhist temples associated with special needs, and some of these have been developed as important sources of income in recent years. One example was given in Chapter 2 where, in the context of a discussion about the problems of old people, it was mentioned that temples all over the country have become associated with people praying for a quick death so that they will not be a burden to their relatives. Another example is of temples where mothers may pray for the souls of their aborted babies. This may involve the purchase of a small statue of the Buddha Jizō, and such temples may organise regular ritual activities for the bereaved parents. Abortion is a common form of birth control in Japan, and women seem to be encouraged to attribute misfortune which may befall them later to the actions of the aggrieved souls whose lives they terminated – an interesting phenomenon since Buddhism is officially opposed to the taking of life. LaFleur specifically addresses this question in his book *Liquid Life* (1992), and the phenomenon has been discussed by anthropologists Mary Picone (1986), who looks at the commercialisation of Buddhism more generally, and Emiko Ohnuki-Tierney (1984).

In practice, the activity of a lay person visiting a Buddhist temple is not much different from one who visits a Shintō shrine. In front of the altar, hands are held together silently, rather than clapped, and there may well be images of the Buddhist figure being invoked. Purification is usually with the smoke of incense rather than with water, and the receptacle is not necessarily at the entrance to the temple, as is the water at a Shintō shrine. But a variety of amulets and talismans are usually on sale here too, and it is again possible to have one's prayers written on an appropriate receptacle and hung in the buildings. It is also common to purchase a printed version of one's fortune to tie onto a convenient tree. A special rite would involve priests clothed rather differently from the Shintō ones, and the esoteric interpretation of events would be distinct. However, many of the ritual elements are directly comparable from the point of view of a lay participant.

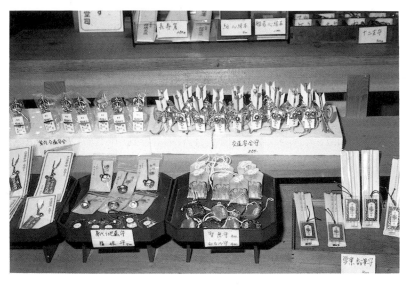

Figure 7.1   A selection of protective charms and amulets like these are available at shrines and temples.

One Buddhist sect which has become rather well known in the West, and which has particular functions with regard to modern Japanese companies, is Zen. This sect arose, like the rest, out of Chinese teachings, but it has flourished in Japan in association with indigenous aesthetic ideas, and it has become associated with various Japanese arts, such as the tea ceremony and flower arrangement, which will be discussed in Chapter 10. An essential element of Zen is a practice known as *zazen*, which is literally 'sitting meditation', and which involves sitting, usually cross-legged, for long periods of time during which one is supposed to remove oneself from all thoughts and bodily concerns. This kind of discipline is supposed to develop one's strength, or one's spirit (*seishin*), and several Japanese companies send their new employees for a period of *zazen* during their training (see, for example, Rohlen 1974; Kondo 1990: Chapter 3).

FOLK RELIGION AND TAOISM

Some religious figures in Japan make use of both Shintō and Buddhism, as well as drawing on ideas from Taoism. Taoism is rather like the Chinese equivalent of Shintō, in that it incorporates a variety of indigenous ideas about nature, so that it is not always possible to separate these various strands from each other. Such specialists may practise, among other things, geomancy, divination, healing and shamanism. They are usually consulted by individuals with particular requirements, for example, seeking explanations of misfortune such as illness or loss, or seeking advice about auspicious times for important events such as weddings, house building or funerals.

Such consultations are based on a largely Taoist view of the world in which time and space are not regarded as homogeneous.[4] In other words, there are good and bad times to do certain things. The simplest example of this notion is the six-day calendar commonly used in Japan in which one day is regarded as good for all endeavour, another is likewise bad, and the others are good and bad at certain times and for certain events. The calendar used by specialists is much more complex, however, and takes into consideration a number of other factors. These include the division of time according to the Chinese zodiac, which allocates hours and days to a cycle of animals in the same way as it allocates years. Time is also accorded one of the five elements, in its yin or yang aspect, so that the combination of factors on a particular day, at a particular time, will colour that occasion for any activity.

A similar set of notions about space, and particularly directions, involves the allocation of auspiciousness and inauspiciousness to spatial movements as well. These ideas are brought into play when a house is being designed, for example, and the direction it faces, as well as the design of the rooms, may well be decided in collaboration with a specialist in such lore. Similar discussions sometimes take place when journeys are planned, and the shrine visits made at New Year may be chosen according to directions which are thought to bring good luck for that year. One resort in the case of persistent misfortune is to examine the location of one's house or family graves, and a specialist may advise some considerable upheaval in order to alleviate the perceived problem.

The time (and place) of birth is supposed to affect the character and destiny of a person, as is their chosen name. Parents therefore often consult a specialist before deciding on a name. The issue turns on the number of strokes it takes to write the chosen characters, and a problem may be alleviated by keeping the pronunciation of a name, but choosing a different character to write it. Specialists are frequently consulted about the suitability of prospective marriages, and the combination of names and birth signs are carefully considered. Sometimes inauspicious aspects of a union can be overcome by changing the name of one of the partners. Politicians are also wont to consult specialists about their chances, and they too have been known to change their names on the advice of such a person.

Illness is another reason for such consultations, and healing may take a variety of forms. In Kyushu, for example, I witnessed specialists chanting themselves into trances during which they claimed to be able to discern the cause of an illness by entering the body of an afflicted person, even if that person were absent. They could then make recommendations for removing the irritant, whatever it happened to be, and sometimes a rite of exorcism would be performed. If the cause of illness was attributed to some outside supernatural agent, then recommendations would be made about how to pacify the offended spirit, *kami* or ancestor. Certain shrines and temples are associated with healing, sometimes of particular complaints, and people flock to the more popular ones to purchase talismans and other aids to recovery. Again they may write the nature of their desire on a wooden tablet, or even just a piece of paper, and hang it up.

Illness in Japan may be explained in terms of some polluting force, and it is not uncommon for a healing process to be described as puri-fication. The anthropologist Emiko Ohnuki-Tierney (1984) has discussed the medical roles of religion in Japan in the context of this kind of symbolism. As was mentioned in Chapter 2, she discusses the association of germs and disease with the 'dirt' of the 'outside' (*soto*) world as opposed to the 'clean' 'inside' (*uchi*) of the home. She also carried out an investigation of deities and Buddhas associated with healing, and comes to the conclusion that whether they be Shintō, Buddhist or Taoist, they are associated with marginality, or the boun-dary between inside and outside. This is the very area she associates with 'cultural germs' so that, as is commonly found in anthropological discussions of classification, the polluting and purifying forces fall between the important categories of society (cf. Douglas (1970), referred to in Chapter 3).

In my own research in Kyushu, I came to the conclusion that the specialists (known as *ogamiyasan*) who draw on Taoist ideas as well as those of Shintō and Buddhism, were consulted at times of change and therefore danger. Marriage, house-building and illness are all occasions when the usual order of things is threatened, and neigh-bours and relatives respond to these situations by making gifts, particularly of money. Disasters, such as fire or injury, meet with similar responses, both in the presentation of gifts and in the consul-tation of specialists to divine possible causes.

Ohnuki-Tierney points out that people usually consult regular biomedical doctors as well as religious specialists when they are ill, and talismans purchased in a shrine or temple frequently adorn hospital rooms. Japan also has a range of practitioners of Eastern medicine, which are discussed in some detail in another anthropological monograph by Margaret Lock (1980). Again, the author puts the medical systems available into a context of Japanese and generally oriental ideas about illness and its causes, and expectations about treatment and care. Together these two books go a long way towards breaking down the boundaries which exist in Western thought between magic, science and religion.

The attribution of illness to some outside polluting force, whether it be conceived of as germs or as some malevolent supernatural being, may be associated with the general concern with purity in Japanese religious and secular ritual. Visits to shrines and temples are often made for protective purposes, and houses may be purified if a source of pollution is suspected, perhaps through persistent disaster. On one such occasion, the specialist drew on the symbolic force of objects from Buddhist ritual for the deceased members of the house, and from Shintō ritual for the living members.

Roger Goodman's work discussed in the last chapter raises the ambiguity of attitudes towards 'returnee children' – on the one hand 'polluting' the educational system, dangerous beings in need of the purification provided by special classes and special schools, but also valued for their international experience. These attitudes resemble those more generally adopted towards the outsider or stranger, who may be seen as dangerous and polluting, or who may be a god bringing good fortune. The Japanese anthropologist, Yoshida Teigo (1981), has interpreted such attitudes in terms of anthropological theories about marginality, and mediation between 'this world and the next'.

In the context of the strong Japanese sense of *uchi* about themselves as a nation, and the recent emphasis on the importance to Japan of internationalisation, some parallels can be discerned between previous attitudes towards gods and contemporary ones towards foreigners. Thus the returnee children slot into a mediatory role between Japan and the outside world, and as John Knight (1992, referred to in Chapter 4) reports, a number of rural communities are seeking to offset their marginal position in contemporary Japan by installing international attractions. In the same way that people visit shrines and temples to approach the spiritual world, they may now seek to approach the outside, often equally mysterious, foreign world by visiting representations of it in Japan. This is a theme which will recur in Chapter 10.

CONFUCIANISM

The Confucian influence in Japan is of a rather different order to those discussed already. It has no priests and very few places of worship, but Confucian ideology has been called upon at various stages in Japanese history to support and justify codes of conduct and moral behaviour. Although in post-war Japan it has suffered something of the same fate as Shintō, in that it has been blamed as a bad, undemocratic influence, it has also been credited with responsibility for some of Japan's success. Introduced into Japan at approximately the same time as Buddhism, it greatly influenced the legal system from the seventh century until the Meiji Civil Code.

The family system, for example, drew much of its strength from the Confucian idea that stable families, rightly governed, lead to a stable and happy state. According to Confucian precepts, an individual needs training in the virtues of benevolent action, loyalty and filial piety in order to participate properly in five basic relationships. These are those between ruler and subject, father and son, husband and wife, elder brother and younger brother, and friend and friend. Rulers, and superiors generally, need to learn to inspire loyalty through benevolence. The only dyad in the group in which relations are equal is that between friends.

In Chinese practice, Confucian ideals underpinned the whole of the system of government. In Japan, the ideals which supported indigenous notions were most enthusiastically drawn upon, whereas those which conflicted with them brought about much discussion at an intellectual level without necessarily making much impact in practice. In the Tokugawa period, Samurai education was based upon Confucian texts, but there was plenty of argument, for example, about whether loyalty to a ruler should or should not take priority over filial piety in a situation of conflict. In the modern period the Japanese found a solution to the problem in the ingenious Shintō idea that all Japanese families are ultimately related as branches of the imperial line, so that loyalty to the Emperor could be seen as an extension of filial piety.

It is obviously a male-oriented scheme which conflicts with democratic ideals, and it is easily related to the system of hierarchical relations discussed in Chapter 5. However, it would seem that the Confucian influence, like others from outside Japan, including democracy, has been modified to fit in with indigenous ideas, rather than being solely responsible for the Japanese ideology of hierarchy. It is a 'teaching', like Buddhism, so it is accorded status on that basis, but it is much more a moral or ethical system than a system of religious practice, and it has been drawn on to build and support the ethics of both Buddhism and Shintō.

CHRISTIANITY

The influence of Christianity in Japan has also been a diffuse one rather than a story of success in attracting followers. The first influx of missionaries in Japan began in 1549, when Francis Xavier and his followers were rather successful in securing converts, but in 1640 Christians were banned by the Tokugawa regime, and some 37,000 were massacred brutally near Nagasaki. During the following two centuries all families were to be registered at a Buddhist temple, and except for a few 'hidden' communities in Kyushu (from one of which came the Nagasaski Mayor mentioned in Chapter 5), Christianity was virtually eliminated from the country. Since the mid-nineteenth century, when missionaries were allowed into Japan again, the converts have numbered less than 2 per cent of the population.

On the whole Japanese Christians tend to be individuals rather than whole families, and their children do not necessarily follow their example. It has become a 'personal religion', rather than an association of the continuing family, and some Christians are individuals who have moved for their employment away from their family and friends. One of the problems for Christianity in Japan is the exclusive nature of the religion. Other religious influences have always been readily accepted as long as they can be modified to fit in with the existing cosmology, and syncretism is an important facet of the Japanese world view. Christianity in its Western form demands the rejection of other religious ideas and practices, so that Christians are discouraged from helping to care for their local Shintō shrine, or carrying out Buddhist rites for their ancestors. Although Christians themselves may accept such demands, members of their families and communities are less able to understand such a seemingly selfish religion, and sometimes Christians are ostracised for their behaviour. A study of Christianity in Japan has recently been published by the anthropologist, David Lewis (1993).

There have been various movements to make Christianity more Japanese, and some churches have, for example, introduced memorial services for the ancestors of their parishioners which are held in the summer during the *bon* festival. These and other efforts have had some limited success, but on the whole the major influence of Christianity has been in other directions. There are, for example, a number of Christian kindergartens, schools and universities, which have a good reputation for their educational achievements, and there are also hospitals, homes for the aged, day nurseries and institutions for the handicapped, founded and administered by Christian organisations. Most towns have at least one Christian church in their midst, and it is not unusual for couples to request a Christian wedding, even though they are not practising the faith.

There have been other less obvious influences which ultimately derive from the Christian tradition, one example of which may be the reason for the practice of seeking Christian weddings. This is the modern use of the concept of 'love'. In pre-Meiji times, the Japanese word *ai* was used to apply to a love from a superior to an inferior, and there was another word which referred to simple physical attraction. Missionaries chose the first word *ai* to translate God's love for man, but they also used the word reciprocally to express man's love for God, and this levelling has spread to indicate the relations between lovers. Pop music has had a considerable influence on attitudes, and so have Western romantic literature and films, and the modern emphasis on 'love' as a basis for marriage is not necessarily directly related to Christian ideas, but the deeper meaning which has become attached to the concept cannot easily be derived from any other source, and there is certainly a prevailing ideology now that marriage in Japan, too, may acceptably be based on mutual love.

'NEW RELIGIONS'

If Christianity has provided a 'personal religion', which may answer the needs of individuals cut off from their families by virtue of the demands of the modern, industrialised society, there are various competing religious organisations which have been even more successful in this respect. Collectively known as the 'new' religions, they comprise a number of religious movements which have developed over the last century or so, often developing out of Buddhist or Shintō traditions already much more acceptable to Japanese ways of viewing the world. Typically, they have a charismatic leader who attracts followers to some new, hopeful way of life, and in this respect, they may be compared with millenarian movements which have arisen in many parts of the world in times of great social change.

In the Japanese case, they have been interpreted as providing a suitably traditional format for the changed circumstances of their adherents. Members join through their own personal volition, and this is in keeping with the post-war emphasis on individual rights, but in many cases they then establish long-term relationships of loyalty with a previous member of the group who will be expected to exercise the benevolence due in a traditional superior/inferior relationship. In time the new member will gather newer members, perhaps through having converted them, to whom he or she will in turn act as a benevolent superior. These close links provide security, and many of the converts are people who have been for some reason insecure before they joined the 'new' religion.

Apart from people who have moved away from their families and friends, a common example is of people who join religious groups because of persistent illness or misfortune. In this case, they may try several groups until they find one which appears to be effective. An anthropological work by Winston Davis (1980) discusses this phenomenon in considerable detail in a study of a religious group called Mahikari Kyokai. His book also provides fascinating illustrations of the way Japanese cosmology blurs our distinctions between mystical and scientific explanation, and Davis chooses to use the word 'magic' rather than religion to describe the activities of the people he studied.

Unlike Christianity, most of these 'new' religious groups tolerate the participation of their members in other religious rites, so there is less likelihood of alienating relatives and neighbours who expect cooperation in more traditional activities such as ancestor memorials or maintaining the local Shintō shrine. There is one very successful exception, however, and that is the group known as Sōka Gakkai, a modern manifestation of Nichiren Buddhism, which has also made converts in many countries other than Japan. The temples provide alternatives for all the Shintō rituals, and expect their members to destroy previous ancestral tablets when they join. It also has a political wing in the so-called 'Clean Government' Party (*Kōmeitō* which has had considerable success, particularly in local government. It claims to have several times as many followers in Japan as Christianity does, and statistics would suggest a multiple of at least three. Important studies of these 'new' religions include Hardacre (1986) and Earhart (1983).

CONCLUSION

This chapter has presented some of the religious influences in Japan in a rather *ad hoc* manner. The form of presentation is not inappropriate, however, for religious activity for many Japanese people may be carried out in a similarly *ad hoc* way. One of the overriding conclusions must be that syncretism is a strong characteristic of the Japanese case. Nevertheless, there are various underlying themes which run through the sections, or which link up with other chapters of the book, and this is again appropriate in the light of the opening remarks of the chapter about the difficulties of distinguishing between 'religious' and 'secular' areas of Japanese society. A very accessible book offering further detail is Ian Reader's *Religion in Contemporary Japan* (1991).

It should perhaps be added that there are Japanese people, particularly intellectuals, who claim to have no religious allegiances at all, who turn rather to Marxism or Maoism for a blueprint for life. Nevertheless, the majority of the population turns to Shintō for life crises, and to Buddhism for funerals. If we are to credit those who claim that the Japanese language, or 'Japaneseness', have become objects of religious observance, we are operating on a different level again. We are not talking here about 'teachings' or structured worship, but about cosmology, a shared view of the world, and such a level of analysis should indeed embrace all areas of life (and death). In the following chapter we turn to much more specific factors and look at rituals of the life cycle for members of Japanese society.

NOTES

1. Roy Andrew Miller in *The Japanese Language in Contemporary Japan* (American Enterprise Institute for Policy Research, Washington DC, 1977) argues that the Japanese endow their language with various mystical qualities, while Jan Swyngedouw (1986:9) summarises the ideas of the 'religion of Japaneseness'.
2. A 1981 survey carried out by the national broadcasting company, NHK, revealed that only about 33 per cent of Japanese claim to have a 'personal religion', yet over 60 per cent had prayed in times of distress and nearly 90 per cent visited ancestral tombs, 69 per cent regularly (Swyngedouw 1986:2–5; for further statistics, see Reader 1991).
3. Rodney Needham has discussed the problem of belief in a book entitled *Belief, Language and Experience* (Blackwell, Oxford, 1972).
4. This view was discussed in some detail by E. Durkheim and M. Mauss in *Primitive Classification* (Routledge and Kegan Paul, London, 1903).

REFERENCES

Capra, Fritjof, *The Tao of Physics* (Flamingo, London, 1983)
Davis, Winston, *Dōjō: Magic and Exorcism in Modern Japan* (Stanford University Press, Stanford, 1980)

————, *Japanese Religion and Society: Paradigms of Structure and Change* (Albany: State University of New York Press, 1992)

Earhart, H. Byron, *The New Religions of Japan* (Ann Arbor: Michigan, Papers in Japanese Studies no. 9, 1983)

Hardacre, Helen, *Shintō and the State 1868–1988* (Princeton University Press, Princeton, 1989)

Kondo, Dorinne K., *Crafting Selves: Power, Gender and Discourses of Identity in a Japanese Workplace* (Chicago University Press, Chicago, 1990)

LaFleur, William R., *Liquid Life: Abortion and Buddhism in Japan* (Princeton University Press, Princeton, 1992)

Lewis, David, *The Unseen Face of Japan* (Monarch Books, Tunbridge Wells, 1993)

Lock, Margaret, *East Asian Medicine in Urban Japan* (University of California Press, Berkeley, 1980)

Newell, William H. (ed.), *Ancestors* (Mouton, The Hague, 1976)

Ohnuki-Tierney, Emiko, *Illness and Culture in Contemporary Japan* (Cambridge University Press, Cambridge, 1984)

Picone, Mary, 'Buddhist Popular Manuals and the Contemporary Commercialisation of Religion in Japan' in Joy Hendry and Jonathan Webber (eds), *Interpreting Japanese Society* (Journal of the Anthropological Society of Oxford Occasional Publication, no. 5, Oxford, 1986), pp. 157–65

Reader, Ian, *Religion in Contemporary Japan* (Mcmillan and University of Hawaii, 1991)

Rohlen, Thomas P., *For Harmony and Strength: Japanese White Collar Organization in Anthropological Perspective* (University of California Press, Berkeley, 1974)

Smith, Robert, *Ancestor Worship in Contemporary Japan* (Stanford University Press, Stanford, 1974)

Swyngedouw, Jan, 'Religion in Contemporary Japanese Society', in *The Japan Foundation Newsletter* vol. 13, no. 4 (1986), pp. 1–14

Yoshida, Teigo, 'The Stranger as God: The Place of the Outsider in Japanese Folk Religion' *Ethnology*, vol. 20, no. 2, pp. 87–99

FURTHER READING

Bocking, Brian, 'Religion in Japan since 1945', in F. Whaling (ed.), *Religion in Today's World: 1945 to Present Day* (T. and T. Clark, Edinburgh, 1987)

Bellah, Robert, *Tokugawa Religion: The Values of Pre-industrial Japan* (Free Press, Glencoe, Illinois 1957; reprint: Beacon Press, Boston, 1970)

Blacker, Carmen, *The Catalpa Bow: A Study of Shamanistic Practices in Japan* (George Allen and Unwin, London, 1975)

Earhart, H. Byron, *Japanese Religion: Unity and Diversity* (Wadsworth Publishing Company, Belmont, California, 1982)

Hardacre, Helen, *Lay Buddhism in Contemporary Japan* (Princeton University Press, Princeton, 1984)

————, *Kurozumikyō and the New Religions of Japan* (Princeton University Press, Princeton, 1986)

Hori, Ichiro, Ikado Fujio, Wakimoto Tsuneya and Yanagawa Keichi, *Japanese Religion: A Survey by the Agency for Cultural Affairs*, trans. B.A. Yeshiva and David Reid (Kodansha International, Tokyo, 1972)

Morioka, Kiyomi, *Religion in Changing Japanese Society* (University of Tokyo Press, Tokyo, 1975)

RELATED NOVEL

Endo, Shusaku, *Silence* (Kodansha International, Tokyo, 1982)

8   Ritual and the life cycle

INTRODUCTION

In many anthropological studies ritual and religion are closely related, although in complex societies there is often no particular connection between them, and the term 'ritual' may also refer to behaviour, like etiquette, which is decided by society and where individuals have little choice about its execution. In Japan there is much behaviour which falls into this category, and some of it has already been described and discussed in previous chapters. In this chapter the focus will be on ritual associated with the life cycle, and on the passage of a Japanese through various stages of life (and death), as celebrated by society. Having discussed some of the religious influences in Japan, we will be in a position to see how great a part they play in this set of rites, and the various ways in which people are involved in religious practice.

Studies of rites associated with the life cycle are common in anthropological monographs of a particular people, for they aid an understanding of the system of classification underlying social interaction. These rites form a sub-group of the *rites de passage* identified at the turn of the century by Arnold Van Gennep as having many common characteristics in different societies. They often include, for example, distinct rites of separation from a previous state, rites of transition while the individuals are in a liminal in-between stage, and rites of incorporation into the new state. The complete set of *rites de passage* also includes rites of spatial transition, like those described in Chapter 3 accompanying moves between the inside and the outside of the house, and rites which celebrate the passage of time, like those associated with the New Year and other annual events.

The previous chapter focused on Japan's peculiar blend of religious influences, but the specific rituals covered in this chapter can easily be compared with rites of passage in many other parts of the world. Since the prime aim of this book is to elucidate Japan's systems of classification, however, an aim of this chapter will be to relate some of the events discussed to their wider context of social relations and their wider social significance. The rites will eventually be considered as a total system, in which marriage appears to play a pivotal role.

BIRTH AND CHILDHOOD

As in many societies, there is in Japan a great deal of ritual associated with the beginning of life. During a woman's pregnancy she will very likely observe a number of rituals, some of which have religious connections, but may also be given a 'scientific' basis. It should by now be evident that this combination arouses no sense of contradiction to the Japanese. A prime example is the use of a sash-type corset from the fifth month of pregnancy. This sash may be purchased from a shrine or a temple (see Ohnuki-Tierney 1984:138) and it is often signed with a character of good fortune by the prospective mother's gynaecologist, who is said to commend the use of such a garment as an aid to the ultimate recovery of the stomach muscles. Its acquisition may be celebrated by a public announcement of the expected birth, which is held on a Day of the Dog (according to the Chinese calendar), said to be in the hope that the child will be delivered as easily as dogs usually are. Mothers and grandmothers may also visit a variety of shrines and temples to pray and purchase amulets with this end in mind.

The birth itself usually takes place in hospital, but amulets may well be taken along by the grandmothers, if not by the parents themselves. A ritual which has little to do with medical attention is the careful preservation of the remains of the umbilical cord when it drops off the baby. This will be kept in a box by the mother, and may be presented to the child in due course when it leaves home to get married The return home from hospital may be marked by a naming ceremony, when the child's name will be written out and hung up in the *butsudan* or some other prominent place, and members of the immediate family, including both sets of grandparents when possible, will gather to celebrate the safe arrival of their new member. This is referred to in many parts of Japan as the 'seventh night' celebration, although it may not take place exactly that number of days after the birth.[1]

In some parts of Japan, the mother and baby are regarded as polluted after the birth, for a period which varies regionally. It is around 30 to 33 days, sometimes longer for girl babies than for boys, explained by my informants in Kyushu as due to the natural association of girls with the pollution of menstruation and childbirth. During this time neither the mother nor the child should enter a Shintō shrine, but the mother is also expected to rest while her body recovers, and refrain from housework, exercise and even reading and watching television. Usually at the end of this period, although it may be later, the baby is taken for its first visit to the local Shintō shrine. Members of Sōka Gakkai have a parallel rite in their own temples. Typically, the child is dressed in a special kimono, which may well be a present from one set of grandparents. Relatives, particularly grandmothers, and even neighbours, may witness this event or share in it by being given either rice cooked with red beans or specially prepared rice-cakes.

These two rites give the child a social existence as a member of an extended family and of a community, and the period of pollution can be interpreted both for the mother and the child as a period of transition in van Gennep's terms. Indeed, the mother's initial rite of donning the sash may be seen as her rite of separation from normal life, just as the visit to the shrine may be seen as a rite of incorporation for her back into normal life. For the baby, attention to the umbilical cord ritually marks a separation from the pre-birth state, and again, the visit to the shrine, usually to the community's protective deity, marks incorporation into social life. These rites have parallels in most societies, not least with the christening and a more ancient churching rite of Christian communities. The period of pollution and special care is also common, sometimes explained as due to the danger that a baby's new soul will slip away.

Another event usually accorded some importance during the first year of life is the first celebration of Girls' Day (on 3 March) for girls, and Boys' Day (on 5 May) for boys. For about a month before the day itself huge carp made out of cloth are hung out over the house to celebrate the birth of a boy, and inside are set up tiers of shelves with various symbolically appropriate decorations. For girls, these are splendid figures from the imperial court of the Heian period, together with sets of tiny accessories such as palanquins and tableware; for boys they are warrior armour and helmets, arrows and dolls depicting fierce heroes. When the day arrives, the child is dressed in some suitable finery, possibly the same garments as used to visit the shrine or temple, and relatives will gather to eat and drink in celebration of the new addition to their midst.

There is considerable symbolism attached to these events. The first child of each sex in a family is often given the most attention, and as main guests from the wedding, including the go-between, are often invited, the family gathering can also be interpreted as a celebration of the cementing of the marriage of the child's parents symbolised in the birth of a child. The displays are set up year after year, however, and although this is a secular ritual, the objects are treated with a certain amount of reverence. The two themes, the rich splendour of the Heian Court, and the brave ferocity of the Samurai armour, would also seem to serve an important symbolic role. They represent two major periods in Japan's history as well as two areas of dominant value, namely cultural treasure and military training, both of which have numerous sub-symbols, often also represented in contributory parts of the display.

As these objects are set up and discussed with children, year after year, the children learn some of the important values of their national heritage, and grow into the roles expected of members of such a nation. The carp, for example, symbolise courage in adversity because they swim upstream against the current and can even leap up waterfalls. It is said to be a quality boys should have, but, as we have already seen, children of both sexes in Japan are expected to work hard throughout their childhood years and strive for goals which may prove to be quite beyond their reach. In later life, both men and women in Japan are praised for qualities of endurance and persistence, even in the face of failure.

The display for Girls' Day features a lord and lady with a retinue of servants and attendants, but the most important symbolic element here is that they are all attired for a wedding. In the more expensive versions there are elaborate depictions of the betrothal gifts, carefully prepared and wrapped and accompanied by vehicles for their transport from one aristocratic house to another. There are also tiny models of the ceremonial food to be presented and consumed. Other elements of these displays represent other important values, and stories are often told about characters associated with them, renewing for adults and children alike familiar themes of their heritage, and emphasising for girls that marriage should be amongst their (if not the) chief goals in life.

Subsequent rites formally mark the progress of a child through various stages of development. A hundred days after birth there is a small ritual of 'first eating', associated in theory if not necessarily precisely in practice, with weaning. The first birthday is sometimes the occasion for a ritual associated with the child's first walking steps. Children of three, five and seven years are dressed up in smart clothes, often traditional Japanese garments, and taken to a Shintō shrine on 15 November each year, when they take part in a rite for their protection and future good fortune. They may also be given gifts by their neighbours, a glossy photograph usually records the occasion, and in some areas a party is held. This event seems to be an amalgamation of previous rites associated with the first wearing of various traditional Japanese garments, and it still provokes some considerable display of finery, especially for girls.

All these practices vary somewhat depending on the region, and the Japanese anthropologist, Sofue Takao, has suggested that social interaction with relatives and/or neighbours is a stronger motive for holding them than the 'supernatural effect' (Sofue 1965:159). The combination of social and supernatural is familiar from Chapter 4, when the community importance of Shintō festivals was described, and it will recur in Chapter 10. The Shintō ritual marks these occasions with an appropriate set of symbolic associations, but the exchange of

Figure 8.1 Children of seven, five and three years dress up in traditional garments to pray for good fortune in shrines all over Japan in November.

gifts and parties provides a good opportunity for families to express their longer-standing relationships. Some of my own informants spent so long on 15 November dressing their daughters, at the hairdresser and in the photographic studio, that they left no time for the shrine before they had to arrive at the restaurant they had booked for the occasion. However, they did make an excursion to the shrine a few days after the event.

From the time children enter school, in their seventh year, their life cycle celebrations not surprisingly become geared to the education system. They celebrate graduation from kindergarten, entrance to school, graduation from primary school, entry into middle school . . . and so on. The next public occasion is when they officially 'come of age', on 15 January after their twentieth birthday. They are now legally responsible for their own behaviour, and they may vote in local and national elections. Again, they dress up, some of the girls wearing very valuable kimonos, to attend a civic ceremony in their home town. They listen to speeches about the upright citizens they are expected to become, and reply with poems and essays about the adulthood which stands before them. Legally, they have become adults. In practice, this status is not complete until another rite has taken place.

MARRIAGE

As was suggested in Chapter 2, marriage is a most important event in the life of an individual, whether a member of a continuing family or not. Until a wedding has taken place, young people of both sexes in Japan have considerable freedom of action, and their families are quite tolerant of unusual lifestyles, travel, even career changes, as long as they settle down when they reach the age considered appropriate. This was for some time around twenty-four for girls and twenty-seven for boys, although it has been rising in the last few years, so that young people may get away with waiting another couple of years before members of their family get too worried. However, the idea of a cut-off age is still taken seriously (see Brinton 1992).

For boys, marriage may also make an implicit statement about staying in the family business or making a permanent commitment to his present employment. For girls, it is more likely to spell change, for although most will have been working until they marry, unless they can find a spouse and/or mother-in-law to support them, they usually expect to give up their job to take care of the home, or contribute to their husband's family concern. The latter would apply to a man if he were to be adopted into his future wife's family business as well, of course.

The means by which spouses are chosen are various, and this is a matter which has undergone much change in the modern period. In the old Tokugawa villages, young people chose one another on the basis of mutual attraction, and their parents usually knew one another already. With increased opportunities for mobility in the Meiji period, marriages were made over longer distances, and the Samurai custom of arranged marriages became almost universal. It was important to make a selection appropriate for the continuing house, and adults sought the help of a go-between who knew both parties well. As Western influence spread, however, the notion of 'love' marriages began to appeal to young people, and after the Second World War, marriage based on the mutual consent of the individuals became part of the new Constitution.

Nowadays, both types of marriage persist, and it is not even always possible to classify a particular marriage as 'love' or 'arranged', although people like to talk as though it were. Some people meet and decide to marry, although they may not call their relationship one of love; others claim to have fallen in love after a meeting arranged by a go-between. It is this meeting, called a *miai*, which characterises an 'arranged' marriage, and some couples even ask a senior to stage-manage a *miai* so that their old-fashioned parents will feel happy about the union. In fact, these arranged meetings have undergone considerable change since they were introduced to give the individuals a say in the choice of partner, and in the absence of any very clear courting patterns, many Japanese people see them as a convenient way of being introduced to prospective partners.

In the Meiji period, when marriage was seen much more as an alliance between houses, the young people had to be content with a mere glimpse of each other as they passed as if by chance in a public place such as the theatre, a shrine or a restaurant. Later, a private meeting would be arranged, with an opportunity to talk, and eventually the couple would even be left alone for a few minutes. Nowadays, such a meeting may be followed by 'dates', and the young people are much freer to refuse a suggestion than they were in the past. There is even a popular television programme which arranges such meetings in full view of an audience of millions.

Marriages based purely on 'love' were for long regarded with suspicion, for the meaning of the word used in this context for 'love' (*ren'ai*) has only recently begun to take on some of the long-term associations it has inherited from Christianity. Before that it was very much an expression of physical attraction, and as such was associated with weakness, or extra-marital affairs, to be separated therefore from the serious business of marriage, which was concerned with nobler sentiments such as duty and filial piety. It is still customary for parents to investigate the background of the potential spouses of their children, and detectives may even be hired for this purpose. It is also quite usual for a religious specialist to be consulted about compatibility, name combinations and the auspiciousness or otherwise of the proposed wedding day.

The mediatory role of the go-between is a common one in Japan in general, and many other arrangements are made in this way in a society which tries to avoid direct negotiation between strangers. There are, in fact, several aspects to this role. First of all, the go-between can bring together people totally unknown to one another and make a formal introduction. Second, he or she can act as a liaison between the two families, providing information for each about the other, and once a marriage is agreed, transmitting and co-ordinating their wishes about the details. The go-between can also break the bad news and avoid loss of face if the negotiations fall through. At the wedding itself, there is a ceremonial role to be played, particularly in introducing the two families to each other, and a successful superior may be asked to do this, even in a marriage otherwise arranged by the couple. Finally, there is the role of guarantor, and the go-between may be called upon to mediate again if the marriage breaks down.

Particularly in stable, continuing communities, marriage represents the amalgamation, to some extent, of two separate *uchi* groups, and the person or couple who successfully brings this about is ideally a member of an *uchi* group of both sides. Thus a relative, neighbour or work superior is an ideal person, and anybody may carry out this role. In practice, there are some people who are more successful at it than others, and some for whom it becomes almost a business, like the owner of a bridal-wear shop. In many other areas of Japanese society, negotiations between strangers are ideally carried out through an intermediary who has *uchi* connections, such as a shared old school or a common interest in some leisure activity. Perhaps for reasons such as these, marriages arranged by a go-between are still common, although love matches have been popular in Japan since the late 1940s.

Over the years there has been great variety in the type of ceremony chosen for the wedding itself. Some detailed examples are described in my book (Hendry 1981), but they are by no means exhaustive. There may be a religious ceremony, but this is not compulsory, and a wedding can just be a public gathering, as long as it is registered legally. Wedding halls have become very popular in recent years, typically providing a Shintō ceremony, a reception, and even the photographs, gifts and other smaller accessories of the occasion. Edwards (1989) has a detailed description of one such place, where he was employed during fieldwork, and he analyses the elements of the ceremony as a window to understanding Japanese attitudes to gender and the person. Another study focuses on the commercial aspects of the wedding industry from the back-stage, and the author, Ofra Goldstein-Gidoni, who worked as a dresser, chose the title 'Packaged Weddings, Packaged Brides' for her thesis.

Churches are sometimes chosen, too, as already mentioned, and members of Sōka Gakkai have their own Buddhist service. In large country houses, weddings may be held in front of the ancestors at the *butsudan*, with several receptions to accommodate all the guests who need to be entertained. Some couples even choose to take the whole wedding party on a package deal to Guam, Hawaii or even Australia for their nuptial celebrations, and these are said to be less expensive, even including the air fares, than holding the same event in an upmarket urban wedding hall.

The crux of the wedding, however it is celebrated, is a sharing of cups of sake between the bride and groom, and afterwards between each of them and the other's parents. The two families then drink together. Symbolically, the couple is joined together, but they join each other's families, too, and the two families become linked through them. In stable communities, these families will call on each other for aid and ceremonial companionship in the future. The bride usually wears a head-dress which is said to symbolise the hiding of horns of jealousy, and her white undergarment is supposed to represent the clean slate she brings to her new life. It is also common for brides to change their clothes during the reception and a likely outfit these days is the white dress of Christian weddings. The modern ceremony includes an exchange of rings, too, and a multi-layered (often empty) wedding cake is usually cut and distributed.

An exchange of betrothal gifts usually precedes the actual wedding ceremony, and it is also common for girls (or *yōshi* – adopted sons-in-law) to take a large trousseau with them when they marry. The objects used on all these occasions have much symbolic association, largely concerned with long life, happiness and fecundity for the couple. Common symbols used in all manner of ways are the turtle and the crane, both representing long life. The betrothal gifts typically include expensive kimonos or a large sum of money, which equals (and may exceed) the expenses of the trousseau. This is likely to comprise items for the future home, such as furniture, electrical equipment, clothes and even vehicles. Families see these gifts for a daughter or son going to be adopted into another family as the settlement of their share of the inheritance.

The occasion is also an unrivalled opportunity for display, and since wedding guests usually include all of one's important acquaintances, it gives families an excellent chance to demonstrate their material wealth to the world at large. Particularly in times of change, such an event makes possible the confirmation of aspirations to a status higher than one's parents held, and little expense is spared. Indeed, many families save for years for the weddings of their children and the total average cost in 1993, including engagement ring, nuptials and honeymoon, was estimated to be just over 8.3 million yen (more than £55,000 by the current rate of exchange) (Japan Pictorial 1994). In more ways than one, marriage represents the redefinition and confirmation of status for the families as well as for the individuals becoming linked.

YEARS OF CALAMITY *(YAKUDOSHI)*

The only individual ceremonial occasions during the middle part of adult life are those associated with certain years of age when people are thought to be particularly vulnerable to illness or other misfortune. The major ages involved are 33 for women and 41 or 42 for men, although there are a number of less important years as well, and the preceding and following years should also be treated with some caution. Traditionally, Japanese people counted themselves a year older from 1 January, starting with the age of one at birth, and this method is still used for *yakudoshi*. Thus, a New Year visit to a shrine is an appropriate time to purchase a protective amulet, or even ask for a rite of protection to be performed by a Shintō priest, and certain shrines are said to specialise in this. In some areas a party is held, and appropriate gifts will be given.

Several anthropologists have mentioned these 'years of calamity', but the most comprehensive discussions are to be found in Norbeck (1955) and Lewis (1986). Both discuss the various reasons given for taking care at these times, and Lewis tries to estimate the number of people in the city where he worked who actually participate in the observances. He asserts that attempts to obtain statistics are unreliable because people who have yet to reach their major *yakudoshi* may say they will do nothing but change their minds when the time comes. Nevertheless, he finds that more than half of his sample admits to paying some kind of attention to these supposedly calamitous years, and several of his informants did pay attention after saying that they would not.

He also notes an interesting tendency for people to cite pseudo-scientific explanations for *yakudoshi* observances referring, for example, to changes in the body which are supposed to take place at these times. Other explanations are concerned with the Chinese calendar, discussed in the last chapter, and with homonyms where the words for the most serious ages also have inauspicious alternative meanings. The 'scientific' ideas seem to be most acceptable, although events which are attributed to lack of care during *yakudoshi* include disasters like the death of relatives, which could not possibly be explained in such a way. Lewis sees notions of years of calamity as structurally compatible with ideas of pollution and purity and with a Japanese cultural emphasis on age. They certainly also help the collective blur between science and religion in a Japanese view.

RETIREMENT AND OLD AGE

According to the Chinese calendar, the precise combination of animal and element which characterises any particular year returns only once every 60 years, and a life cycle celebration recognises this by marking the return of the year of a person's birth at 61. There are various ways in which this occasion may be celebrated. For academics, for example, a *festschrift* may be published. Within the family, gifts may be given and a party held. It is not uncommon for another visit to a shrine to be made, and this year is also a *yakudoshi* for men. In some areas this is said to be the time to pass on the household to the next generation, and the age is said to imply a return to dependence, this time on one's children rather than on one's parents.

During the later years of life, there are a number of celebrations again for those who reach particular ages. The ages of 77 and 88 are often chosen, and the names of the celebrations are formed out of an adjustment of the characters used to write those numbers. A similar process applies for the 99th birthday. The anthropologist Thomas Crump has cited the names of these celebrations as an example of the way Japanese use their originally Chinese script in many symbolic ways, attributing a mystical quality to the use of numbers which resembles that of the Pythagoreans, but which we have largely lost in our Platonic scientific world (Crump 1986:91). The use of stroke-counting methods for choosing names is another example of this idea.

DEATH AND MEMORIAL CELEBRATIONS

The ritual associated with death in Japan is usually carried out by a Buddhist priest. There are secular ceremonies, and there are Shintō rites for exclusively Shintō families, the Emperor and members of the imperial family, but by far the most common arrangement is to turn to Buddhism. The body is prepared, with the help of close relatives, and dressed in a white garment, as at birth and marriage, but fastened the opposite way from usual. Many of the activities associated with death, funerals and memorials make use of this symbolism of reversal, and generally this class of ceremonial can be opposed to that used on happy occasions during life. It is also customary, for example, for large wreaths to be erected outside the house of the deceased, and these are only distinguishable from those used in front of new shops and business ventures by their use of colours of mourning, such as blue, yellow and green, rather than colours of celebration, such as red, orange and purple.

On the evening after the death, it is customary for friends, neighbours and other associates to call on the bereaved family and express their condolences. The closest neighbours usually help to prepare the house for these visits, erecting drapes and other equipment, which may belong to the *chōnai*, to convert the main room of the house into an altar, decorated also with lanterns given by close relatives. These same neighbours also take over many other practical tasks, allowing the family to mourn, and greet their many visitors. If the house is too small, the family may request the services of a local temple, where they receive visits, and often sit up all night with the body, which they then accompany to the crematorium the following day.

The funeral itself is then held back in the home of the deceased, or in the temple, the urn of ashes taking the central place. A Buddhist priest will officiate, and his chanting is often relayed by loudspeaker out of the house to the people who are unable to fit inside. All the various associates of the deceased will attend, and burning incense is passed round so that each can add a pinch to the fire as a token of farewell. The close neighbours serve tea and snacks and keep a record of who attends and how much money they give (so that the family can eventually reciprocate accordingly). They also hand out a card of acknowledgement from the chief mourners, sometimes accompanied by a handkerchief and/or a small packet of salt, which is to purify the visitors from the pollution of death. It is also said to repel the soul of the deceased, which may be reluctant to go on its journey into the afterlife and could 'stick' to a living person.

The family of the deceased is regarded as particularly polluted at this time, and like the recent mother, they should not enter a Shintō shrine. It is also customary to paste up a white sheet of paper over the Shintō god-shelf in the house, and most families also put up a notice on their front door to indicate that they are under pollution restrictions. These include dietary prohibitions on meat and fish. Further rites should be held for the soul of the dead every seven days for a total of 49 days, when the pollution period officially comes to an end. In practice the rites at the end of one week, when a posthumous name is given, one month – on the same date as the death – and 49 days, are those most strictly observed, and a Buddhist priest usually visits the house on each of these occasions.

Further memorials of a similar nature are held after 100 days, after one year, and again after 3, 7, 13, 25, 33, and 50 years, although the final memorial seems to vary depending on the Buddhist sect and the region. Robert Smith (1974) discusses these rites in some detail. Essentially they are said to be for the care of the soul. Typically, relatives of the deceased gather in the house where the ancestral tablets are held, a Buddhist priest comes round and chants before the *butsudan*, and special vegetarian food is served. A visit may also be made to the graveyard or the mausoleum where the remains are kept. In some areas the last of these rites becomes a celebration with food usually reserved for happy occasions, since the deceased is then said to have become a *kami*. After this, the individual ancestral tablet should be destroyed, and the deceased should join the general ranks of 'ancestors' of the house, which are remembered annually at the summer *bon* festival.

SYNCRETIC ASPECTS OF LIFE CYCLE CEREMONIES

From the point of view of ordinary people taking part in ceremonies of life and death, some quite striking parallels and oppositions emerge. Considering the series of rites which are celebrated following birth and death, we find that they fall at approximately the same intervals. In both cases a rite is held after seven days, after a month, after 100 days and after one year. The length of the pollution period is different, but the same term is used for its lifting, and in both cases it is said to be associated with a concern for the soul; in the baby's case that it should become securely attached; in the case of the dead, that it should be firmly separated.

The annual ceremonies are not dissimilar either. For a child they occur after three, five and seven years, and an older rite of attaining adulthood which used to take place at 13 is still remembered in some areas. There is a *yakudoshi* for men at 25, and the major one for women is 33. Several of these years therefore correspond quite well with the memorial rites after death at 3, 7, 13, 25 and 33, and in some areas these actually continue until 61, which would correspond with the 'return of the calendar' celebration of official retirement. Progress through life thus has a parallel with the supposed progress of the soul through the afterlife until it becomes a fully-fledged ancestor and/or *kami*.

These rites are clearly distinguished from each other, however, in various symbolic ways. The food served is a good example. It has been mentioned that vegetarian food is prepared for memorials, but there are also special foods of celebration which are used on happy occasions. These include red beans, spring lobster and sea bream, the last because its name, *tai*, is part of *omedetai*, the Japanese word for 'congratulations'. Gifts are also presented in different wrappings. For all events of celebration, including others not necessarily associated with the life cycle, the envelope or paper is imprinted with a representation of a small piece of abalone, originally to indicate to the recipient that the donor was not polluted (which would prohibit the use of fish or shellfish), and brightly coloured strings or markings. For a memorial gift, the colours will be the black, blues or greens of mourning, and the motif a lotus flower. Parcels are wrapped differently, too.[2]

Where events are associated with some religious activity, the rites which accompany a person through life are usually associated with Shintō, whereas the memorials tend to be Buddhist. Neither the Shintō nor the Buddhist priest would be likely to present the situation in quite the way it has been presented here, as each religion, and indeed each sect, has its own view of life and death. However, from the point of view of the lay participant, it is not unreasonable to emphasise this opposition, even if all activities do not necessarily conform completely. It is interesting to note, also, that sickness, when the normal course of life is threatened, provokes recourse to the middle area of shamanistic and divinatory activity, which may be any combination of Shintō, Buddhism or Taoism.

I have developed this opposition further in my book on marriage in Japan, where I have also pointed out that Shintō is associated with the community as a whole, in that the community festivals are usually celebrated in connection with the local shrine, and Buddhism is more a concern of the continuing family, remembered at the Buddhist altar in the house. I have also argued there that marriage and its associated ritual tends to mediate between these oppositions in various ways, bringing family and community together to celebrate, involving attentions to the *butsudan*, as a bride leaves her own family to join a new one, as well as to the Shintō shrine which she visits in her new community. Marriage is also appropriately associated with the middle area of divinatory activity, since specialists are consulted about compatibility and suitable dates for the various rituals.

The argument is too long to do justice to here, and in any case, the situation may be different in an urban area, but the pivotal role that marriage seemed to play ceremonially is still reflected in the important place it has in the life cycle for both men and women. It allows its participants to make long-term statements about their own lives, and it finally confers full adult status on them, as they officially set up a new family of their own. It also provides an opportunity for the wider families involved to make visible adjustments to their own status, and to demonstrate to the world that they have done their duty by their children. We have also seen how the role of mediation in marriage and divorce can be related to the importance of mediation in other areas of social, economic and political life.

CONCLUSION

The previous chapter focused on Japan's various religious influences in turn, but by looking at a set of specific rituals in this chapter, we have been able to reveal the coherent way in which they intermesh indigenously. This chapter also helps to place Japan in a wider context since many of the rituals described here are directly comparable with those found elsewhere. The principles of rites of passage are very widely applicable, and Japan is certainly no exception, as reference to van Gennep would rapidly reveal.

NOTES

1. For further details of these and other rites described here see Hendry (1981) Chapter 6, and (1986) Chapter 1, where references are given to other descriptions of them.
2. Some other examples of these reversals are to be found in Matsunaga's article in Hendry and Webber (1986).

REFERENCES

Brinton, Mary, 'Christmas Cakes and Wedding Cakes: The Social Organisation of Japanese Women's Lifecourse', in T.S. Lebra (ed), *Japanese Social Organisation* (Hawaii University Press, Honolulu, 1992), pp. 79–107

Crump, Thomas, 'The Pythagorean View of Time and Space in Japan' in Joy Hendry and Jonathan Webber, *Interpreting Japanese Society* (Journal of the Anthropological Society of Oxford Occasional Publication, no. 5, Oxford 1986), pp. 88–99

Crump, T., *The Japanese Numbers Game* (Routledge, London, 1992)

Edwards, Walter, *Modern Japan Through Its Weddings: Gender, Person and Society in Ritual Perspective* (Stanford University Press, Stanford, 1989)

Gennep, Arnold van *The Rites of Passage* (Routledge and Kegan Paul, London and Henley, 1977)

Goldstein-Gidoni, Ofra, 'Packaged Weddings, Packaged Brides: the Japanese Ceremonial Occasions Industry' (PhD. thesis, University of London, 1992)

Hendry, Joy, *Marriage in Changing Japan* (Croom Helm, London, 1981)

———, *Becoming Japanese* (Manchester University Press, Manchester, 1986), Chapter 1

Hendry, Joy and Jonathan Webber (eds), *Interpreting Japanese Society* (Journal of the Anthropological Society of Oxford Occasional Publication, no. 5, Oxford, 1986)

Lewis, David, 'Years of Calamity: *yakudoshi* Observances in a City' in Joy Hendry and Jonathan Webber (eds), *Interpreting Japanese Society* (Journal of the Anthropological Society of Oxford Occasional Publication, no. 5, Oxford, 1986), pp. 166–88

Matsunaga, Kazuto, 'The Importance of the Left Hand in Two Types of Ritual Activity in a Japanese Village' in Joy Hendry and Jonathan Webber (eds) *Interpreting Japanese Society* (Journal of the Anthropological Society of Oxford Occasional Publications, no. 5, Oxford, 1986), pp. 147–56

Norbeck, Edward, '*Yakudoshi*: A Japanese Complex of Supernaturalistic Beliefs', *Southwestern Journal of Anthropology* vol. 11 (1955), pp. 105–20

Ohnuki-Tierney, Emiko, *Illness and Culture in Contemporary Japan* (Cambridge University Press, Cambridge, 1984)

Smith, Robert, *Ancestor Worship in Contemporary Japan* (Stanford University Press, Stanford, 1974)

Sofue, Takao, 'Childhood Ceremonies in Japan', *Ethnology*, vol. 4 (1965), pp. 148–64

FURTHER READING

Jeremy, M. and M.E. Robinson, *Ceremony and Symbolism in the Japanese Home* (Manchester University Press, Manchester, 1989)

Martinez, D.P. and Jan van Bremen (eds), *Ceremony and Ritual in Japan* (Routledge, London and New York, 1994)

RELATED NOVEL

Tanizaki, Junichiro, *The Makioka Sisters* (Picador, London, 1979)

FILMS

The Funeral (*Osōshiki*) (dir. Itami Juzo)
The Makioka Sisters (*Sasame Yuki*) (1958, 1984)

9 Careers and continuity
Opportunities for working life

INTRODUCTION

Having talked rather generally about a variety of influences on Japanese life, we come in this chapter (and to some extent in the next) to consider specific possibilities for the mundane business of making a living. In previous chapters the scene has been set with discussions of hierarchy and the importance of education, and here the aim will be to present some of the types of employment which are available. In Chapter 6 there was an emphasis on the importance of securing good employment on graduation from school, but we also pointed out in the last chapter that there is considerable tolerance for changes in employment until people reach marriageable age. Marriage represents a definite commitment to adulthood, and for men, in particular, this would seem often to include a commitment to employment at the same time. For women, it may alternatively spell the end of a career, but marriage is seen by many as a career in itself.

To some extent, this chapter will look at life courses for men and women separately, but it should be emphasised that in April 1986 a law came into effect in Japan which is supposed to ensure equal opportunities for men and women in employment. This law is supposed to 'oblige corporations to work actively to give equal opportunity to both sexes in recruiting, hiring, job assignments and promotion, and to eliminate discrimination by gender in some aspects of job training and welfare benefits, as well as in compulsory retirement age, terms of severance and dismissal'.[1] In practice, attitudes are still at some variance with this law, as they are with many other laws, and the situation shows little change to date, particularly in the practices of the larger corporations which have devised discriminatory ways to get around the law.

The chapter will open with a consideration of various types of employment and their characteristics, especially as described by anthropologists, and some statistics will be adduced to give an idea of how the population is distributed between the different arenas described. It will go on to discuss the role of unions, and some attention will also be paid to the social security provisions in Japan. There will be a discussion of male/female differences in expectations, practice and opportunities for careers, and this section should lead into the next chapter, where the actual occupations of women will be more widely represented in both leisure-time pursuits and employment in the entertainment industry.

COMPANY AND PUBLIC EMPLOYMENT

A common view presented of Japanese work life is that of the company employee (known in Japanese as the 'salaryman'). There have been several anthropological studies carried out in large companies or banks, and the picture they present is becoming rather familiar as Western businessmen seek to learn the secrets of Japanese success in the modern world. Their findings will be summarised here, but a clearer understanding could be obtained by looking at a specific example such as Rohlen's *For Harmony and Strength* (1974), Clark's *The Japanese Company* (1979) or one of the other references cited in the Further Reading at the end of the chapter (e.g., Abegglen 1958, Cole 1971, Dore 1973). Most of these remarks also apply to the employees of large public enterprises.

One of the chief characteristics of Japanese companies is that they tend to take over much more of their employees' lives than companies elsewhere are wont to do. They preferably recruit direct from school or university, and they provide training courses which inculcate company loyalty through songs and slogans as well as preparing employees for the particular tasks they must perform. Indeed, they seek to foster company loyalty before specific skills, for if the business of the company undergoes drastic change, they might expect their employees to turn their hands to quite different occupations. In this way, they are able to offer considerable security of employment, and since pay increases with years of service, as well as with seniority of work, it is common for men to stay in the same company all their lives.

Companies also provide many services and benefits to their employees. Pensions, health-care and bonuses are commonplace, but they often offer accommodation too. There are likely to be dormitories for unmarried workers, apartments for families, and even larger houses for senior employees, although many may choose to purchase their own property eventually. Company sports facilities are often also available, as are hobby clubs, and there may even be holiday sites in some attractive location by the sea or in the mountains. In return for all this, employees are expected to work hard and often late, to take few holidays and to spend much of their leisure time with colleagues, drinking in the local bars, playing sports together or going on office trips and outings with them.

The work group thus becomes another very close *uchi* group, and relations in many ways resemble those that were learned in the first such group in kindergarten. There is an emphasis, for example, on maintaining harmonious relations (as the title of Rohlen's book – the company motto where he worked – would imply), there is considerable peer pressure to comply with the expectations of the wider group, and the principles of reciprocity and cooperation underlie much of the daily interaction between colleagues. Members of the company are encouraged to share responsibility for it, and they are said to take a pride in being a small cog in an important big wheel. Like school life, company life is almost the whole life, and as mothers encourage children to look forward to attending kindergarten, school children are geared towards seeking employment in a big company.

Again, the individual is not neglected in this large group; long-term personal relations are established between peers joining at the same time, on the one hand, and between seniors and juniors, as described in Chapter 5, on the other. The ultimate inside group is of the former, and much social life will probably be spent with one's contemporaries, but these people are also one's rivals for promotion, and even closer relations are often established with specific superiors, and eventually inferiors. These are the personal relations of loyalty and benevolence on the parent/child model (*oyabun/kobun*). Such a superior will concern himself with the home life of his inferior, taking trouble to offer help in times of need, perhaps making the occasional loan, acting as ceremonial go-between at his wedding or even helping him to find a suitable wife if necessary. In return, the inferior is expected to give absolute loyalty to the superior and be available to support him any time the occasion should arise.

These relations were discussed in detail in Chapter 5, where the family was invoked as a model for company interaction, both for the hierarchical links, and for the way the individual is expected to put the wider *uchi* group before his own personal life. To a considerable extent, too, neighbourhood relations are replaced as men look to the company for recreation, support at life cycle celebrations, and maybe even political activity. Like the community's 'circulating notice board', there is a system of circulating ideas and proposals, which in theory gives everyone a chance to participate in decisions, although the seniority system probably affects the practical influence any specific employee may have in this respect. Nevertheless, it gives everyone a chance to express their views, and there is a balance here not unlike that in the traditional community between security and comfort on the one hand, and demands and obligations on the other.

Ideally, employees develop within such a framework throughout their working lives, and see their own interests as coinciding with those of the company. According to Rohlen's exposition of the official view, 'devotion to duty, perfected through greater self-discipline ... leads to ... an improved state of personal freedom and a sense of joy focused on fulfillment in one's work' (1974:52). There are echoes of Zen Buddhism here, as Rohlen points out, and this is part of a general Japanese concern with the development and strengthening of the 'spirit' (*seishin*). This reliance on spiritual strength was regarded as partly responsible for defeat in the Second World War, but here it has been rechannelled into peaceful, productive effort, and is therefore seen in a positive light.

Clark has investigated in more detail some of the ways in which reality departs from this idealised model of company relations. There is, for example, in any company a degree of labour mobility, and he has devoted a chapter to discussing this topic. His findings are consistent with the notion presented above that people are freer to change jobs before they marry, and he finds more fluidity among the employees taken after high school graduation than among those who completed university. There is also a category of temporary workers who are treated by big companies quite differently from the permanent employees, particularly at the 'blue-collar' end of the spectrum. The plight of one such group is described with poignant clarity by the journalist, Kamata Satoshi (1983), who posed as a seasonal worker for a period of six months to experience at first hand the life of an automobile factory, and subsequently published an account of his experience in diary form.

An ethnography which successfully probes and penetrates the ideology of a large enterprise is Noguchi's book (1990) about the National Railways which was mentioned in Chapter 2. He portrays the meaning of belonging to such a huge concern from the differing points of view of people at several different points in the structure. Despite the considerable dissatisfaction his informants were prone to express, there were a number of suicides during the uncertainty which surrounded the process of privatisation. Jeannie Lo's (1990) book about women working in a large manufacturing company clearly portrays the different expectations for women and for men, on the factory floor, in the office and in the company dormitories.

MEDIUM AND SMALL ENTERPRISES

In fact, the majority of Japanese employees work not in large corporations, but in medium and small enterprises with a maximum of 300 employees. Of manufacturing industries alone, 99.5 per cent fall into this category, and they account for 73.8 per cent of people employed in manufacturing. Of these enterprises 85 per cent employ fewer than 20 people, and nearly 50 per cent employ four or less. In wholesale and retail trade, 95.5 per cent of the total number of organisations employ less than 20 people, which accounts for 65 per cent of the employees.[2]

A large number of people, then, are employed in rather small enterprises which are entirely unable to provide the benefits and facilities described above. These smaller organisations are also much more vulnerable than the larger ones to changes in the economic climate; bankruptcy is not uncommon, and they are not really in a position to guarantee long-term employment in the way that large corporations are. Indeed, it is partly because the large corporations rely on smaller companies to act as suppliers and sub-contractors, which they can lay off if necessary, that they are able to maintain their own workforce in times of strain. It should be emphasised, however, that relations between companies are where possible long-term ones, showing a measure of the exchange of loyalty and benevolence which characterises Nakane's model of relations between people, as was mentioned briefly in Chapter 5.

For employees of these small enterprises, then, there are few of the material benefits large companies can provide, but there may well be a more real sense of family enterprise among them. The employer will usually know all the employees well, they will exchange gifts at important times like weddings and funerals, and they will know and respect intimate details of each other's lives. For example, when the head of a small paper factory near where I lived knocked his wife unconscious in a fight, not a word leaked out to the surrounding neighbourhood about the circumstances, although all the factory employees had watched him load her into the back of his car and drive her away to be admitted to hospital. In the same way, the employer will know of the families of the employees, and may well make allowances in times of particular need.

Perhaps more than within large companies, relations between employees may be based on the *oyabun/kobun* principle, and there is also more likelihood that employment will be gained in the first place through recommendation. Here, too, mediation is often used to bring together a person seeking employment and a prospective employer, and in the early days of industrialisation this type of arrangement was common in larger enterprises too. Typically, a young person seeking employment in a city would go to a relative who was already established there, and ask for help. Indeed, some city dwellers say they stopped visiting their home village because they were constantly pestered by such hopefuls. Nowadays, most firms recruit from school and university graduates, but a final year student may still choose to apply to a company where he has some connection rather than to a completely unknown one.

Kondo's (1990) ethnography of a small family confectionary business illustrates the relations which characterise this type of firm, and she also sets out to examine what the family ideology achieves in practice. She was, as expected, introduced to the firm through the mediation of a mutual friend, in fact her landlady, and this connection ensured her loyalty to her (benevolent) employer (Kondo 1990:202). She describes the various efforts made by the owners to maintain the family flavour of the company as it grew, through personal care of the younger employees from out of town to outings and celebratory meals. She also examines the extent to which these ploys are successful on the factory floor, and the reciprocal use of the notion of 'company as family' with its 'multiplicity of meanings' and uses which she describes as 'laced with contradiction, irony and compromise' (1990:218).

FAMILY OCCUPATIONS

Family employment has already been mentioned in Chapter 2 as a continuing tradition in some occupations, and it is by no means uncommon even in today's industrialised world. A variety of activities are pursued as family enterprises, although it is becoming more and more common than it used to be for individual members of such families to go out and work elsewhere. Formerly the pattern was for every member of a family to contribute as they could to the common enterprise, and they shared the benefits as they needed them, no one receiving an individual salary. Nowadays there is a move in some families towards dividing up the tasks clearly between the individual members and paying each one a regular fixed sum, although it is probably not uncommon for people to stand in for one another when necessary.

The kinds of occupation which are carried out as family concerns are those which entail the passing on of a particular skill or those which make use of family land or property. Thus, the potters in Moeran's *Lost Innocence* (1984) are a good example on both counts, for they pass on their potting skills to their sons, but they also need access to local land for their raw materials. Their success in marketing the pots to tourists no doubt encourages the younger generation to remain in the family business, as does the success with chrysanthemums in Kyushu, where I worked, and with family inns near the ski resort, as described by Okpyo Moon (1986) (as referred to in Chapter 2). Elsewhere, a traditional occupation may be pursued only by the older generation in a family, while the younger members go out to some other work elsewhere.

D.P. Martinez has recently described such a situation for families of Mie prefecture who dive for shellfish (Martinez 1993), and these again characterise the principles of family cooperation. The women are the divers, using no masks or artificial breathing apparatus. Instead, they weight themselves, to make descent to the seabed faster, relying on their menfolk to haul them back up to the boat before their breath runs out. The women usually work with their husbands, whose job is incidentally less arduous, but the whole venture is only successful with the cooperation of both members of the party. Usually several families dive at once, so there is an element of neighbourly support here too. Many daughters prefer to seek employment elsewhere these days, however, so there would appear to be less continuity than is found in family enterprises elsewhere.

Small shops are often run as family concerns, and sometimes particular members of the family will again have specific roles within the enterprise. One store may provide a delivery service, operated by one of their sons, and shops which provide gas cylinders for domestic use and undertake to change them when they run out perhaps allocate the responsibility to a young, strong member of the family. Farmers, too, tend to divide up their roles these days, and rice and more traditional crops may be the responsibility of the older couple, while innovations will fall to the younger couple. It is commonly the case in some areas that the men of farming families will go off to find piece-work during the slack season, leaving the women to cope with the household. In many of these cases, neighbourhood cooperation may play an important part in the smooth running of their economic as well as social lives.

Doctors were mentioned in Chapter 2 as another example of a profession which may be run as a family concern. There are many small, private clinics and hospitals, and these are not infrequently run by a father and his son or sons. In the more traditional arrangement, one son, usually the eldest, would be chosen to succeed, but a pair of brothers with different specialities can be quite a good team in a small local clinic, for example, and if either of them should marry a doctor, too, she can be incorporated into the practice. Otherwise, wives, or even daughters, may help with the administration, or perhaps work as nurses or assistants in the hospital.

In these examples, the principle continues to some extent of employing any member of the family who happens to be available for a task in hand, and some individuals may spend time away and then return to the home enterprise. This custom provides some degree of flexibility both for the family enterprise, which may have busy and slack periods, and also for the labour market in general which can thereby more easily accommodate fluctuating demands.

The low unemployment figures in Japan (2.7 per cent in 1993) are also to some extent related to this system, as persons seeking employment are only registered as unemployed if they are not able to work even one hour a month, and helping in a family business counts as employment. Such an arrangement therefore also answers needs taken care of elsewhere by a social security system, and in Japan it has been blamed as a disincentive for adequate development of social security services.

LABOUR UNIONS

Labour unions in Japan are usually organised first by the enterprise to which their members belong, and only second by industry (the one major exception being the seamen's union, which is only organised by industry). Thus all the permanent members of a particular enterprise comprise one union, regardless of their skills, and there are no outsiders in the group. There are then nationwide federations of unions for a particular industry, which superficially resemble those found in Western countries, but these are composed rather loosely of the many small autonomous unions, over which they have little authority, as opposed to being the national unions with local branches which are found elsewhere. Ultimately, members of unions put their own enterprises before the union as a whole, and these factors have worked against the development of working-class consciousness in Japan. There is also more mobility within companies, and union leaders can

Figure 9.1 These statues, which stand in front of Tateyama hospital, depict physically the family line which has headed the establishment since it was founded.

easily be promoted to management positions, perhaps because they have shown this potential for leadership or because their superiors feel they will then cause less trouble for the enterprise as a whole.

Negotiations and demonstrations typically take place within one enterprise, and often enough at predictable times. Workers are very susceptible to arguments about the damage excessive action could do to the firm and therefore to their own interests, and their usually fairly reasonable demands are likely to be met. The way in which large companies recruit general employees, whom they then train for particular jobs, is partly responsible for this system, for there is consequently little attachment amongst workers to others who share their speciality. It seems such workers would prefer to be retrained with different skills rather than lose their jobs, if such a choice arose, and there are consequently no craft unions to object to the practice.

There are, of course, historical factors which may be cited to account for the system as a whole, and Martin Collick (1981) has summarised these succinctly. In the early days of industrialisation, at the turn of the century, the expanding industries were seeking incentives to encourage workers to move from their rural family occupations to work for them, and the all-embracing Japanese firm developed in this way to take care of the needs of their uprooted employees. Long service incentives were further developed to keep the employees in times of labour shortage, and these included the deliberate inculcation of a sense of company loyalty. The family model was used to depict the factory, and the employer took on the aspect of a benevolent (though authoritarian) father to whom loyalty was therefore expected. The model was familiar, and it seems to have persisted.

One of the effects of such a system is that there is little encouragement for employees of smaller firms to organise themselves into unions, although by international standards their wages and conditions of work may compare quite unfavourably with those of bigger enterprises. There is, however, a high value placed on good relations amongst co-workers, whatever their status, and the security of family-type relations may be regarded as contributing more to the quality of life than an increase in salary necessarily would.

Figures from the *Japan Statistical Yearbook* comparing total union participation from 1975 to 1991 show a steady decline from 34.4 per cent to 24.5 per cent, although the rate varies in different branches of industry. In 1983 (Ministry of Labour Survey) 35.8 per cent of workers in manufacturing industries were organised, for example, and in 1991 this had decreased to 29.9 per cent. The same survey already revealed low participation in unions for employees in construction (18.6 per cent) and wholesale/retail businesses (9.5 per cent), which had dropped further by 1991 to 17.3 and 8.8 respectively. The 1983 higher figures for transport and communications (59.6 per cent) had dropped dramatically to 46.1 per cent in 1991, although finance and insurance (49.5 per cent) had only slipped to 47.6 per cent.[3]

Public employees are organised on a different basis, however, and some of their unions have been much more antagonistic than the enterprise ones. Teachers, for example, are organised on a national basis. They have limited rights to negotiate, and much of their action has been highly political, expressing dissatisfaction with the rigidity of the centralised system. The employees of National Railways were in a similar position before it was privatised. Since public employees are ultimately employed by the government, their unions provide forums for the expression of left-wing dissatisfactions which may have only a passing relationship to the specific issues they use as vehicles at any one time.

SOCIAL SECURITY PROVISIONS

It will probably have become evident that security is a major concern of Japanese people at various levels of society. In Chapter 4 we discussed the combination of security and obligation which characterises membership in a close community, and we referred back to that remark earlier in this chapter in commenting on the all-embracing nature of the large Japanese firm. For smaller firms in Japan, and particularly for family enterprises, the community often still provides a fair degree of security of this type. Families themselves are also often to be found taking care of their unemployed and their ageing members. The face-to-face *uchi* group is where people seek their closest ties, and it is where people turn first in times of need. Even when people must be admitted to hospital, they try whenever possible to take a relative with them to attend to their most personal requirements, and there is generally something of an aversion to putting oneself entirely in the hands of strangers.

It is probably not surprising then that although a national social security system exists in Japan, and it has been continually developing its services throughout the post-war period of economic expansion, particularly since 1973, in some respects it still operates rather as a last resort used only when all else fails. The system is administered at a local level, however, and in line with similar developments in other countries, it is actually moving towards encouraging self-help within the community. One of the problems has been that a multiplicity of public and private schemes are available for social insurance, health coverage and pension plans, so that administration has been complicated and sometimes difficult for the most needy beneficiaries to understand. Recently a 'basic pension' plan has been introduced to reduce this confusion. Health coverage is required by law. 'Livelihood assistance' is paid out to the most needy families (1.015 million persons in fiscal 1990, a substantial drop from 1.47 million in 1983).[4]

Institutions of social welfare have been growing rapidly in the post-war period, however, and there are facilities in most areas for welfare for the aged, rehabilitation and care for the mentally and physically handicapped, and institutions for child welfare, including day nurseries. The last have been increasingly popular as nuclear families have become more common so that the system of leaving small children in the care of a grandparent is less often viable. Old people's homes have also increased in number, although many still regard them as a poor alternative to family life, as discussed in Chapter 2, and day-care facilities seem to be preferred where there is a chance to continue living with children who may be out working. Roger Goodman has carried out some recent research on children's homes in Japan and this should be published in the near future. For further detail about the types of old people's homes available and the lifestyle they offer, see Kinoshita and Kiefer (1993) and Bethel (1992), cited in Chapter 2.

WOMEN'S CAREERS

Since the Equal Employment Opportunities Bill was passed in April 1986, the whole of this chapter should in theory be applicable to men and women alike. In practice, the participation of women in the labour market is rather different, and this section will summarise the way in which a woman's working life may differ from that of a man, and why. The situation is not the same in all fields, and it will be instructive to consider the first three sections of the chapter again separately. An attempt will then be made to consider both the expectations of women with regard to careers and the opportunities open to them.

In large companies women have fared rather badly with respect to salary and benefits. They are employed, it is true, but most are employed on a short-term basis to carry out less prestigious tasks than their male colleagues, and they are expected to leave on marriage, or at least when they become pregnant. If they fail to marry, or decide not to have children, they may continue to be employed, but their opportunities for advancement have on the whole been severely limited. A few companies have recently been employing women among their university graduate intake, with the intention of treating them in the same way as their male counterparts, but as yet few women have advanced to high positions in company employment. For example, in 1986 a woman was made branch manager of a bank for the first time in Japan.

In response to the Equal Employment Opportunities Law, companies were obliged to offer opportunities to men and women alike in terms of advertising vacancies and starting pay, but according to Lam (1993) some interview the women only after the male applicants have been exhausted, and many companies have apparently created a two-track system. This obliges female recruits to make an irreversible choice between regular, clerical work with low pay and little chance of training and advancement, or a managerial track which involves undertaking to accept mobility, in other words, to transfer to another part of the country if the company should request this.

Since most Japanese women hope eventually to marry, and they see such a commitment as causing possible difficulties in their future family life, they are reluctant to choose the managerial track. A book by Jeannie Lo (1990) about women in the Brother company portrays very clearly the situation for a woman in a regular office career who fails to find a marriage partner. She may work for the same company for many years, but there is virtually no possibility for promotion. Indeed, according to the anthropologist James McLendon (1983), who describes the role of women in a large trading company, the main intention of many of the women who join large prestigious companies is to find good husbands.

In medium and particularly small enterprises, women may have similar intentions, but they are often treated rather better. In many cases they may start by carrying out more menial tasks than the men with whom they work, but the closer relations often make it possible for women to exercise their abilities more fully, and there is also more opportunity for them to leave for a few child-bearing years and then return to a similar job. Many women choose to work 'part-time', an epithet which may in the Japanese case apply to a virtually nine-to-five job, but there is no obligation to stay on after 5 p.m. to go drinking with colleagues, as there may be for 'full-time' employees, who might also be asked regularly to stay late. The case of women in a small confectionary firm and this part-time status is discussed in Kondo 1990.

In fact, women account for 40 per cent of the Japanese workforce, and a graph of women's workforce participation by age shows a clear 'M' curve, rising almost as high in the post-child-bearing years as it does in the younger ones. The proportion of married women in the workforce rose from 38.6 per cent in 1965 to 59.5 per cent in 1983. Many of these employees are in the medium- or small-enterprise sector, but the figure is somewhat misleading, for previously, married women were often working in their homes.

Family occupations account for one section of these women, and traditionally all members of the family were expected to participate in a family enterprise, regardless of their gender, but it should also be noted that many women take piece-work into the home when they are caring for small children. This is often a rather poorly paid occupation, and there is probably an element of exploitation here, but women find it convenient to be able to pick up and put down their work as they are able. Some make a career of such work, dressmakers and cosmetic saleswomen being good examples. A case of the latter is described in some detail in *Letters from Sachiko*.[5] In other cases women of the house are carrying on a family occupation, while the men go out to more lucrative employment elsewhere. Sometimes these are locally noted crafts such as fan-, doll- or lantern-making, and the women are thereby keeping such local specialities available.

Figure 9.2   A local branch manager looks over the work of some of her subordinates in a provincial bank. This woman was Japan's first female branch manager, appointed autumn 1986.

In family occupations, women usually play an important part, although this will obviously vary from one family to another. In my own research in Kyushu I asked a number of families about who made important decisions and who took care of the money, and the answers varied widely (for details see Hendry 1981). The decisions were often said to be made after family discussion, a pattern comparable to company practice, but some said that men had the last word. In direct observation of such discussions, I noticed that women often appeared to allow men to make the final decision, but they were rather skilful at manipulating the situation. The family purse was sometimes taken care of by men and sometimes by women, and in urban areas this seems commonly to be a woman's role. Women are almost always responsible for cooking, cleaning and washing, although grandfathers quite often find themselves looking after small children for a substantial part of the day.

In the farming families of my acquaintance, it was generally younger men who operated the machines such as tractors, planters and combine harvesters, while women were left to deal by hand with the spaces in their small fields that the machines could not reach. Elsewhere, however, women have been left to attend to the farm work without the men of the family, who commute to work in nearby towns, and they have proved quite capable of taking advantage of modern machinery. Women have always played a vital role in the diving families described by Martinez (1993), but tasks are generally divided, at least ideally, on the basis of gender in many traditional occupations. In another fishing community described by Arne Kalland (1981), taboos surrounding women until quite recently excluded them entirely from the boats. A glance at any of the anthropological monographs on Japanese communities will illustrate further these patterns of female employment in the family.

It must also be pointed out, however, that women are expected to marry in Japanese society, as elsewhere, and unless they are the eldest in a family with no sons, they have also been expected to leave home and take up the occupation of their new family. In modern families, there is no longer necessarily a family occupation to pursue, but women are generally expected to be the ones to fit into the new situation which is why so many refuse to commit themselves to a managerial track in company employment. It should already be clear that Japanese women take very seriously the roles of wife and mother, and probably a majority feel that they should be at home during the early child-rearing years. The business of rearing children is regarded almost as a profession in itself by some mothers.

Some men feel that their wives should dedicate themselves entirely to the home, and wives whose economic circumstances allow it may well agree. In the late 1980s I spent some time doing research with a group of housewives in a provincial seaside town south of Tokyo and several of them, although highly educated, had chosen the 'profession' of housewife for their career while their children needed them. They explained that this gave them much more control over their own lives than trying to continue working outside the home, and they occupied themselves when their children were at school or kindergarten by attending classes: cooking, knitting, tennis and sewing, mostly activities which could help them keep a better home.

On the other hand, some women embark upon a career which they want to continue, and if they choose to marry, they will need to find a husband and preferably a mother-in-law who will cooperate. Particularly for professional women, it is becoming more and more acceptable to do this (see, for example, Hendry 1992) as they may well lose their chances of promotion if they break off to have children, and the figures for proportions of women in various occupations bears this out. For example, in professional and technical occupations, which include nursing and kindergarten teachers, 41.3 per cent are women, whereas there are only 8.3 per cent in managerial and 'official' positions, although this last figure has risen from 5 per cent in 1980.[6] Women in teaching, both at school and university level, and in medicine, law and other professions are still much better able to combine a career with marriage than are their counterparts who enter the world of big business.

In the early 1990s, there does seem to be an increase in the number of young women who reject marriage altogether as an option, particularly if they have strong feminist inclinations. This allows them to participate more freely in the workforce, and the Equal Employment Opportunities Law ensures that there are pathways for them to follow, even in big companies. Such women argue that if men want to share their lives they must meet them halfway, as indeed they are expected to do in other industrialised countries, and contribute equally in the running of the home and the rearing of children. There are also some examples of families who are trying to follow this route, but they still remain comparatively few in number.

Whatever their situation, women in Japan tend to think very carefully about the kind of lifestyle they would like to have and the best way to achieve their ambitions. For many, the ideal of being a full-time housewife, married to the employee of a prestigious company sounds much more attractive than working away in a small family business. For one thing, they would have exclusive care of their own children rather than leaving it to a parent-in-law. For another, they would be free for much of the day to organise their own time. In preparation for finding such a man, then, they pursue just enough education but not too much, which explains why there are so many more women than men in the two-year junior colleges. They then seek some suitably short-term employment, and if this can be in one of the prestigious companies, it obviously increases their chances of making the match they are after. There are various other accomplishments with which they can equip themselves, but these come into the subject matter of the next chapter.

This kind of preparation may sound rather callous to those of us who are brought up entirely under the spell of the syndrome of romantic love, but Japanese women tend to be very practical when planning their lives, and it seems appropriate that this discussion should come into this chapter, under careers, rather than in a discussion exclusively about marriage. An exchange of personal histories usually precedes an introduction for marriage, and there is no doubt that young women bear this prospect in mind when they plan their lives. In fact, most people probably marry into families with backgrounds rather similar to their own. This is certainly what their parents usually hope they will do and it is also the aim that go-betweens pursue.

CONCLUSION

This chapter has presented some of the opportunities available for the working lives of men and women in Japan. It has by no means been comprehensive, but it has, I hope, been somewhat representative. The next chapter deals with arts, entertainment and leisure, and of course, for those involved in creating them, these areas may offer alternative ways of making a living. In Chapter 10 I set out to demonstrate some of the possibilities for women which have not yet been touched upon.

NOTES

1. The *Japan Foundation Newsletter*, vol. 13, no. 3 (1985), p. 14
2. Figures from the *Japan Statistical Yearbook* (1992).
3. The 1983 figures are from *Facts and Figures of Japan* (Foreign Press Center, Tokyo, 1985), and the 1991 ones from the *Japan Statistical Yearbook* (1992).
4. *Japan Statistical Yearbook* (1992).
5. This is a fictionalised and annotated collection of letters by James Trager, but based on a real correspondence between his Japanese wife and her sisters in Japan. It does not ring true as intimate female Japanese correspondence, but there is much of interest in it about the life of a Japanese housewife turned businesswoman.
6. *Japan Statistical Yearbook* (1992).

REFERENCES

Clark, Rodney, *The Japanese Company* (Yale University Press, New Haven, 1979)

Collick, Martin, 'A Different Society', in Howard Smith (ed.), *Inside Japan* (British Broadcasting Association, London, 1981), pp. 9–58

Hendry, Joy, 'Generational Diversity in a Family Life-History: Two Academic Women', in Susanne Formanek and Sepp Linhart (eds), *Japanese Biographies: Life Histories, Life Cycles, Life Stages* (Austrian Academy of Science, Vienna, 1992), pp. 113–35

——, *Marriage in Changing Japan* (Croom Helm, London, 1981)

Kalland, Arne, *Shingu: A Study of a Japanese Fishing Community* (Scandinavian Institute of Asian Studies Monograph Series, no. 44, Curzon Press, London 1981)

Kondo, Dorinne, *Crafting Selves: Power, Gender, and Discourses of Identity in a Japanese Workplace*, (Chicago and London: University of Chicago Press, 1990).

Lam, Alice, 'Equal Employment Opportunities for Japanese Women: Changing Company Practice', in Janet Hunter (ed.), *Japanese Women Working* (Routledge, London, 1993), pp. 197–223

Lo, Jeannie, *Office Ladies, Factory Women: Life and Work at a Japanese Company* (M.E. Sharpe, New York, 1990)

McLendon, James, 'The Office: Way Station or Blind Alley', in David Plath (ed.), *Work and Lifecourse in Japan* (State University of New York Press, Albany, 1983), pp. 156–82

Martinez, D.P., 'Women as Bosses: Perceptions of the Ama and their Work', in Janet Hunter (ed.) *Japanese Women Working* (Routledge, London, 1993), pp. 181–96

Moeran, Brian, *Lost innocence: Folk Craft Potters of Onta, Japan* (University of California Press, Berkeley, 1984)

Noguchi, Paul H., *Delayed Departures, Overdue Arrivals: Industrial Familialism and the Japanese National Railways* (University of Hawaii Press, Honolulu, 1990)

Rohlen, Thomas P., *For Harmony and Strength: Japanese White Collar Organization in Anthropological Perspective* (University of California Press, Berkeley, 1974)

FURTHER READING

Abegglen, James C., *The Japanese Factory: Aspects of its Social Organization* (The Free Press, Glencoe, Illinois, 1958)

Brinton, Mary, 'Christmas Cakes and Wedding Cakes: The Social Organisation of Japanese Women's Lifecourse', in T.S. Lebra (ed.), *Japanese Social Organisation* (Hawaii University Press, Honolulu, 1992), pp.79–107

Cole, Robert E., *Japanese Blue Collar: The Changing Tradition* (University of California Press, Berkeley, 1971)

Dore R.P., *City Life in Japan* (University of California Press, Berkeley, Los Angeles, London, 1971)

——, *British Factory, Japanese Factory* (University of California Press, Berkeley, 1973)

Imamura, Anne E., *Urban Japanese Housewives* (University of Hawaii Press, Honolulu, 1987)

Kinzley, M.Dean, *Industrial Harmony in Modern Japan: The Invention of a Tradition* (Routledge, London, 1991)

Lebra, Takie Sugiyama, *Japanese Women: Constraint and Fulfilment* (University of Hawaii Press, Honolulu, 1984)

Nakane, Chie, *Japanese Society* (Pelican, Harmondsworth, 1973)

Plath, David (ed.), *Work and Lifecourse in Japan* (State University of New York Press, Albany, 1983)

Saso, Mary, *Women in the Japanese Workplace* (Hilary Shipman, London, 1990)

RELATED NOVELS AND LIGHT READING

Kamata, Satoshi, *Japan in the Passing Lane: An Insider's Account of Life in a Japanese Auto Factory*, trans. Tatsuro Akimoto (Allen and Unwin, London, 1983)

Keita, Genji, *The Lucky One (and other humorous stories)*, (trans. Hugh Cortazzi (*The Japan Times*, Tokyo, 1980)

Trager, James, *Letters from Sachiko: A Japanese Woman's View of Life in the Land of the Economic Miracle* (Abacus, London, 1984)

FILM

High and Low (Ten to Chi) (Dir. Kurosawa Akira)

10 Arts, entertainment and leisure

INTRODUCTION

Art and entertainment may be related to society in a variety of ways. One may, for example, take an historical approach (like Mason 1993, referred to in Chapter 1) and look to art for an expression of the periods through which a people has passed, seeking within that approach an understanding of influences and cultural changes which have taken place. One may also seek through art to understand something about the social organisation of the people producing it, and one may look for the symbolic meaning with which their work is imbued, whether it is there intentionally or not. In many cases, one may also seek to understand a people's religious and philosophical ideas through the art which represents them, and through collective ideas about what constitutes art, and how it should be produced.

In Japan there are many and various arts and entertainments, and it is not possible here to discuss them all individually. An abundant literature in Western languages enables a reader to pursue an interest in particular Japanese arts, which have in modern times become an important medium for the expression of Japan's identity. They provide an attraction for visitors to the country, as well as a comfort to Japanese who feel swamped by outside influence, and they have for some time been exported to vastly different cultural areas. At the same time, Japan's artists have made an important contribution to international artistic fields such as music, fashion and film-making, and these contributions may be related to international or industrial society as well as to their Japanese origins.

This chapter will open with a brief consideration of arts in historical perspective, concentrating particularly on the social organisation of the artists themselves, and the changes which have occurred in modern times. There will then be two rather long sections on specific ways in which ordinary people are now involved with arts and entertainment, the first being somewhat more concerned with the world of women than men, and the second more with men than women, although in the latter case the artists and entertainers are usually women. Finally, there will be a section on a leisure activity popular with all Japanese people, regardless of gender or socioeconomic affiliations.

HISTORY AND SOCIAL ORGANISATION WITHIN THE ARTS

The arts, in many different forms, can provide us with tangible evidence of Japanese history, and we can look to material culture for an expression of the various influences which Japan has experienced over the centuries.[1] Some of the most striking examples are those associated with religion, such as the architecture of shrines and temples, the gardens in which they stand and the statues and paintings with which they are adorned. Some of the most prized modern articles of Japanese art, such as swords, kimonos and ceramics, were articles in daily use in former times, and Japanese paintings, literature and drama fill in some of the details of daily and ceremonial life of the times concerned. In this section, however, the concern will be rather with the place of artists in society, relations between them, and the changes these have undergone in recent times.

In pre-modern Japan, specific arts tended to be associated with groups of people who inhabited particular positions in Japanese society. Artistic skills and knowledge were transmitted from one generation to another through family lines, and through hierarchically organised groups which could usually only be penetrated by means of personal introduction and recommendation. Typically, such a group would be headed by a master, known as the *iemoto*, literally 'family source' or origin of the *ie*, and he would pass on his position to a son, or someone specially adopted for the purpose. The principle is, of course, the same one which operated throughout Japanese society, and families associated with some artistic forms still exemplify this *iemoto* system today.

In an article entitled 'Organisation and Authority in the Traditional Arts', P. G. O'Neill (1984) has succinctly summarised the historical basis for this system and the principles which characterise it, using examples particularly from the performing arts. According to him, the first known groups of this kind in the arts were families engaged in ancient court music and dances known as *gagaku*, which date back to at least the early eighth century. During the flourishing court culture of the Heian period, many artistic pursuits became popular and houses developed their own specialities in broad areas such as poetry, perfume-smelling, culinary arts and horseback archery. The ensuing medieval period witnessed the more formal establishment of lines which have persisted until the present day in, for example, flower arranging, *nō* drama and music for its accompaniment.

Nō was patronised throughout the Tokugawa period by the military leaders, who supported and formalised the *iemoto* system. A similar structure was used in the prolific schools of military skills, such as unarmed combat and swordsmanship, which are regarded as art forms, and in the entertainments of the townspeople, which include *kabuki* and puppet theatre as well as various forms of popular music, dancing and singing. The skills of games and pastimes such as Japanese chess and *go* were passed on in this way, too, as were arts such as painting, calligraphy and the tea ceremony. Despite the long historical span and the wide range of activities, O'Neill identifies five characteristics, some or all of which, he says, were shared by these artistic lines.

First, there is the principle of hereditary succession to the headship, already mentioned above. Second, the transmission of skills and secrets of the art is usually accomplished through demonstration and minute imitation, rather than by explanation and formal teaching. This form of learning is appropriate for the stylised, ritual forms which characterise much Japanese art even today. The third and fourth points run together. Most groups developed a 'permit' system which pupils were granted as they improved, and which eventually granted them the status of teachers (or leaders), so that there developed a hierarchical, pyramid-shaped organisation. Communication within the group would go up the hierarchy step by step, and the final point is that each member would develop a strong sense of loyalty and obligation to his immediate teacher, and through him to the *iemoto* and the whole school or house.

These patterns are, of course, familiar from previous chapters, and indeed 'schools of art' exemplify Nakane's inverted V model, with the most experienced members remaining for ever superior to their pupils, who usually remain loyal to them. As Nakane described, factions tend to occur when a master dies, leaving more than one contender for the ultimate superior position, and the different 'schools' within particular artistic fields usually represent splits of this kind which occurred when the succession was not clearly established. Less exalted artisan families passed on their skills in this way, too, and indeed, the principles are essentially those of the *ie* system described in Chapter 2.

As Japan entered the modern period, the former military patrons of the arts lost their wealth and power, and the whole economic base of the system went through considerable change. Theatrical performers and their supporting musicians have now come to depend on their appeal to the general public, and many of the other arts are supported by amateur pupils who pay to study them (see the next section). The *iemoto* system has survived better in some arts than in others, and O'Neill (1984:643) suggests that one of the factors affecting this is whether or not the art is a creative or developing one. If the emphasis is on the preservation of tradition, as in *nō* and the tea ceremony, the *iemoto* system tends to be maintained, although factions may still develop and lead to divisions within groups. If the art is more open to innovation, like flower arranging, dance and painting, it lends itself to the setting up of new lines, particularly where there is an abundance of paying pupils.

The *iemoto* system has come under fire from time to time, especially in the post-war period. It has been described as 'feudal' and artistically inhibiting, and an abundance of new forms of art and artistic cooperation have been tried out, influenced by many different countries. Some of these have made an impact, but the hierarchical structure of continuity dies hard, as has been shown in previous chapters, and many innovative Japanese artists have had to make their names abroad before they could be accepted in Japan. These include the conductor, Ozawa, the film-maker, Kurosawa and the architect, Kurokawa, to say nothing of John Lennon's wife, the notorious Yoko Ono, who never did return to reconcile herself with Japan.

It is not possible to discuss all the artistic movements of the last few decades in Japan, but a glance at a few publications should help to give a flavour for some of the trends, as well as directing the reader to areas of particular interest he or she may wish to follow up. In the world of theatre, for example, Brian Powell (1985) has argued that modern theatrical groups have now just about come full circle back to techniques which were Japanese before the influx of Western influence. The 'new theatre' groups which arose in reaction to the ritualised styles of *kabuki* and *nō* have in turn become the target of reaction by 'underground' groups, which have made a considerable impression in the outside world by drawing on some of the traditional techniques the first groups were rejecting.

An anthropological paper on this topic is Valentine's (1986) discussion of dance in Japan. He identifies various spatial and temporal characteristics of Japan's various forms of dance, which he relates to other arts and the wider social structure, and he then shows how these have influenced even the most up-to-date American dances performed regularly by young people at Harajuku in Tokyo, as well as another Western genre known as *modan dansu*. He notes also that spatial patterns reproduce patterns of hierarchy amongst the dancers, and he again claims to detect Japanese traditional patterns in the Western dance forms. The extent of the survival of the *iemoto* system in the dance world was illustrated in 1980 when a well-known dancer Hanayagi Genshū stabbed the leader of the most renowned school of dance in the neck as a protest against the whole system and the monopoly its families have over dance teaching and performing in Japan. She served eight months in prison.

In the literary world, aspiring writers used to need to attach themselves to a successful member of their profession to advise them and help them to publish their work. Thus, the house of a famous writer would often also become the meeting place of a literary circle, again organised hierarchically, although the initial attachment was more likely to be through introduction and merit, rather than kin relationship. Before the Second World War, it was said that writers had to endure '10 years of hardship' because they were not allowed to publish ahead of their superiors, but since the post-war boom in commercial publishing, a young writer may become famous and successful overnight. Yoshimoto Banana is a good recent case in point. Irena Powell (1983) documented changes in the post-war literary world in a book entitled *Writers and Society in Modern Japan*. The older system is portrayed in Ishiguro's novel, *An Artist of the Floating World* (1985).

It is perhaps as a reaction to the apparent disintegration of the older system that some of the artisan crafts, initially made for daily use, and often still produced by families which operate along the old *ie* lines, have become highly prized as *objets d'art*. The anthropologist Brian Moeran (1984) has discussed this folk craft movement in his book about a potting community, and talks of such objects inspiring a 'nostalgia' for the past, something he sees as an especially Japanese trait. In the modern world, much of the old order has been replaced by Western-inspired institutions, and little of the old material culture remains in daily life. Art is a form which enables people to maintain some apparent continuity and, as will be illustrated in the section which follows, this continuity may be more real than the mere persistence of objects.

ACCOMPLISHMENTS

Many members of modern Japanese society come into contact with 'the arts' in their own study of some particular accomplishment. It was mentioned in Chapter 6 that small children go to classes in non-academic subjects, and in Chapter 9 that women may study various things in preparation for marriage. Such study is by no means limited to these two categories, however, and the pursuit of accomplishments is a common leisure activity for Japanese men and women of all ages. Some take things more seriously than others, and those who devote themselves for years to a particular art may gradually accumulate the skills and abilities to become a teacher and master (or mistress). Others may attend a number of different classes during their lifetimes, or even at one time, as in the case of the girls preparing for marriage.

There are quite a number of arts which may be studied in this way and many of them express fundamental Japanese values, even if they were originally imported from elsewhere. Several, like flower arranging and some of the martial arts, are now taught in an international context, and have become widely known. Many are described as 'paths' or 'ways', using the second Chinese character of Shintō, referred to in Chapter 7, and sometimes pronounced *dō*. The examples given there were *bushidō* (the Samurai way), *judō* and *shodō* (calligraphy). It can be seen that the system of classification includes 'ways' which would not necessarily always be called 'arts' in an international view, but for the Japanese they share qualities which bring them together. By an outsider, the first could perhaps be classed as a career, the second as a sport and only the third as an art in a more limited sense. An understanding of their shared qualities reveals some of the principles which underlie Japanese thinking more generally.

First of all these are accomplishments which require a good deal of dedication and training. There is an underlying assumption that anyone could, with enough application, succeed in the pursuit of these arts. This assumption has already been met in the education chapter. Second, the method of learning is based largely on imitation and repetition, as mentioned by O'Neill. Much of the movement involved is ritualised, clearly decided, and a pupil strives to achieve perfection in conforming to expectations. Many hours are passed in repetitive routine. Perseverance and even suffering are an integral part of the process. It is only after many years of training and advancement that one could even contemplate introducing originality into one's work.

A good example of the principles involved is to be found in the process of acquiring the skills of carpentry, described with exquisite care to detail in Bill Coaldrake's book, *The Way of the Carpenter* (1990). A decade's apprenticeship involves several years of 'miscellaneous chores around the workshop' during which time the carpenter's tools are forbidden to the trainee. Nor is any instruction given. The learning is based on observation and the experience acquired by being steeped in the work as it happens. By the time the apprentice is allowed to tackle a job he will have watched his master and more advanced trainees until he is 'overcome with an overwhelming desire to use the tools himself' (1990:8). A similar process is described by Hori (1994) for the monks of the Rinzai Zen monastery.

Figure 10.1   This ballet teacher illustrates the principle of teaching by 'putting (the accomplishment) into the body'.

Third, one of the characteristics of all these pursuits is that they enable the participants to develop spiritual strength, or *seishin*, and the development of *seishin*, in turn, helps them to improve their skills. In this sense, these 'arts' are 'paths' or 'ways' through life, and they are thought to have value for helping ordinary people to cope with the demands and realities of everyday life. Taken to their limits, these 'ways' may absorb the whole person, as in the case of *bushidō* for the Samurai class of the Edo period or for the master of a particular pursuit. One of the aims is to reach a stage when one knows so well the movements required that one can transcend all thought about them, an idea familiar from Zen Buddhism, which has certainly influenced many of these pursuits.

An interesting anthropological analysis which illustrates all these ideas, and places them in a detailed symbolic structure, is an article by Dorinne Kondo (1985) on 'the way of tea'. The author points out that this highly ritualised version of host/guest interaction also embodies the importance of *tatemae*, the formal graces required to maintain harmonious interaction. During the various stages of the 'ideal typical' version of the ceremony which she chooses to describe, the participants are led increasingly from the mundane world through physical and symbolic space to a totally ritual climax, and back again. Various other arts form part of the process, as the guests move through gardens, into a particular form of architecture, and admire a scroll, a flower arrangement and the pots in which the tea is served. An elaborate form of the ceremony may also include a light meal, introducing the art of cooking as well. Everything follows a formal, ritualised style and, as Kondo puts it, 'it is by becoming one with the rules that the possibility of transcendence lies' (1985:302). A more comprehensive ethnographic account of Japanese tea ritual, which also puts it into an historical context, is to be found in a book by another anthropologist, Jennifer Anderson (1991).

It has already been mentioned that some big companies send their new employees out for a period of *zazen*, and some of the spirit associated with the pursuit of these accomplishments is invoked in the wider training methods adopted by these corporations. Rohlen's passage, quoted in the previous chapter, that 'devotion to duty, perfected through greater self-discipline . . . leads to . . . an improved state of personal freedom' could appropriately be applied to these accomplishments, too. The wives of these company men often spend much of their own time putting similar principles into practice in the pursuit of accomplishments such as flower arranging, cooking and the tea ceremony, which help them to create a calm, pleasant and harmonious home.

As their children grow older and require less of their attention, these women may be able to devote more and more of themselves to the development of personal skills, such as calligraphy, painting or music – the Japanese stringed instrument, the *koto,* is particularly popular, for example. In some urban neighbourhoods women will give classes to each other in the arts in which they have become most adept, and for some, these pastimes eventually become careers. In rural areas, the situation is sometimes reversed. Farming women in the area where I worked in Kyushu would gather once a week to study the folk songs which their grandparents used to sing while they went about their work.[2] The youth group, on the other hand, met to practice the ancient *utai* songs, originally from *nō* plays, but now used at weddings and other ceremonies.

The previously aristocratic arts have thus permeated most areas of the social structure in the modern world, and the mundane activities of the artisan class have been elevated to the ranks of art. Underlying principles of artistic endeavour are applied in the mundane life of the company employee, and also in the middle-class home. Moeran (1989) has argued that the concept of *seishin* and its associated value-laden vocabulary also runs through Western institutions such as baseball and advertising, as well as pottery aesthetics. Perhaps there is also an idea that the application of devotion, dedication and perseverance to whatever pursuit can lift it from the mundane to the realm of 'art', especially if the occupation can be related to the 'religion' of 'Japaneseness'.

It should be noted, however, that accomplishments in modern Japan are by no means limited to traditional pursuits, and there are schools of music, art and dance which aim specifically to impart non-Japanese notions to their pupils. An American school of free expression in painting is popular for children, as are ballet classes, and Western music has almost replaced the Japanese variety in regular schools and kindergartens. Knitting, sewing and tennis classes are popular amongst mothers, as mentioned in the previous chapter, and there is even a report of *karaoke* as another recent subject of study! These are often arts where individuality and spontaneity are said to have a greater chance to express themselves, although Moeran has gone to some lengths to show that Western concepts like spontaneity and individuality have only 'apparently' been brought into Japanese pursuits in their original form, whereas in reality these, too, have 'been neatly adopted and adapted into *seishin,* or "Japanese spirit"' (1989:263).

However, the development of such a wide range of artistic pursuits, with all their attendant 'schools', cannot but admit a Japanese version of individuality, as a visit to one of the abundant Japanese 'arts festivals' would readily confirm, for the traditional arts as well as those introduced from the West.

GEISHA AND THE WATER TRADE *(MIZU SHOBAI)*

To turn to a rather different aspect of Japanese entertainment, well known particularly amongst male visitors to Japan is the night life which they are pressed to enjoy. Typically this involves drinking and possibly eating, but invariably accompanied by attractive women who keep topping up their drinks, lighting their cigarettes and generally trying to make them feel relaxed and happy. The size and lavishness of the establishment is variable, as are the duties of the attendant women. It may be a swish nightclub with music and cabaret provided publicly, or in private rooms with artists who perform only for a particular party, and some of the attendant women may subsequently be available for more personal services. It may also be a tiny establishment with a few seats and a single owner/barmaid, whose chief role is to listen like a mother to the trials and tribulations of her treasured customers.

Many Japanese men have regular bars of this latter sort, and they visit them frequently, often in preference to returning home in the evenings. The barkeeper is addressed as *mama-san*, where *san* is a polite term of address, and *mama* is indeed a word also used for mothers. There have been several attempts at psychological explanation for this phenomenon, relating it to the way in which Japanese mothers indulge their small children, especially boys, but apart from any direct psychological effect, the emphasis on mother/child relations over the conjugal one probably has a part to play. At larger establishments, too, there is a *mama-san*, who is in charge of the other women, sometimes referred to as 'big sisters'. These larger places are usually chosen when groups of friends or workmates go out together, the more plush and expensive places being selected when guests are to be entertained at the company's expense.

Before any further generalisations are made on the basis of the male/female dichotomy, it should perhaps be pointed out that women who visit bars and nightclubs in Japan are also accorded attention and service, and they are not necessarily stigmatised for frequenting them, as they might be elsewhere. There are even 'host clubs', which employ men to serve their female patrons, dance with them and provide them with sexual services if that is what they require. The principles of these establishments include the idea of treating customers like guests and helping them to relax and enjoy themselves. It is more often men than women who seek entertainment in this way, and it would be extremely unlikely for a married couple to go out to such a place together, but young couples are seen more frequently these days, and mixed groups of employees drink together.

Many of these bars and nightclubs are to be found clustered together in narrow streets around the main stations in Japanese cities, and it is common for commuters to call in for a few drinks on their way home. Members of the same workplace may move together to a bar after work, and it is reported that it is possible to be much more frank with ones workmates when drinking together than it is in the formal atmosphere of the office or factory. An article in English describing these amusement areas (Linhart 1986) borrows the phrase of a Japanese sociologist in the subtitle: 'zones of evaporation between work and home'. He summarises the activities available, including gambling, *karaoke* and the buying of women, and he provides a brief historical setting, but he also argues that these entertainment areas provide relief from the stresses of the workplace in a society where the family is less well equipped to do this.

A veritable wealth of information about the seamier side of entertainment in Japanese cities is to be found in Ian Buruma's book, *A Japanese Mirror* (1985), and in Nick Bornoff's book, *The Pink Samurai* (1991). There would seem to be much less stigma attached to the pursuit of erotic entertainment in Japan, and 'respectable' company employees quite happily engage in all kinds of activities which their Western contemporaries (or, at least, their wives) might find distasteful. Japanese wives are supposed to turn a blind eye to these extra-marital activities, and many become accustomed to seeing their husbands regularly arrive home late and drunk. Men with the resources have even been accustomed to maintaining a mistress or two, as well as their family homes, although this practice, at least among politicians, is becoming less acceptable in recent years.

An abundance of violent and erotic books and films, albeit legally restricted, permit men to live vicariously even beyond the lives in which they are allowed to indulge, and Buruma argues that this and the sometimes excessive violence of films, comics and television programmes makes it possible for people to live in quiet and apparently uneventful harmony in the real world. Essentially, his thesis is that Japanese men (and women) are able to maintain the *tatemae* of harmonious existence with their friends, relatives and colleagues, partly because of the many possibilities for vicarious and fantasy violence and eroticism: 'What one sees on the screen, on stage or in the comic books is usually precisely the reverse of normal behaviour' (1985:225). For this reason, perhaps, Totto-chan, 'the little girl at the window' mentioned in Chapter 3, became a bestseller, because it was about a child who managed to escape the usually inevitable system.

From the point of view of the women who work in the 'water trade', they are often those who have failed in the pursuit of accepted family life. They may be divorced or separated from previous husbands, or they may never have married. They often have children whom they must bring up alone, and the work they do in the evenings will bring in a good income. Working as a hostess in a bar or night-club, without any commitment to providing further sexual services, pays quite well, and if a woman can raise the capital to set up her own bar, she may then establish the security of a regular clientele. One woman of my acquaintance gave up her job as a bank clerk to run a bar when her husband, who had had the same occupation, fell too ill to work. This way she was better able to make ends meet. Other women are the regular mistresses of men who help them financially, and they maintain long-term relations in the way described above.

At the aristocratic end of the scale, there are women who devote their lives to this world of entertainment, and they may have started training even before they reached puberty. These are the geisha, who have become well known in the wider world. An excellent anthropological account of the lives of some of the most accomplished Kyoto geisha is to be found in a book by Liza Crihfield Dalby (1983), who carried out research by training as a geisha herself for a period. She describes with great clarity and insight the lives of these artists, the relations between them, and the professional way in which they carry out their work.

Each geisha is highly accomplished in particular skills such as playing the *koto*, dancing or singing, but they all train for years in the more general arts of caring for their guests (or, strictly speaking, clients). Nothing is left to chance, and they learn how to walk gracefully, how to sit, stand up, pass through a door, how to listen, how to talk, how to laugh, and even how to cry when the occasion demands. They also learn how to serve drinks and all manner of snacks and food, although there are maids in the best establishments who prepare the refreshments and carry them to the guest room. Nowadays, there are very few real geisha left in Japan, and they are extremely expensive to hire. Thus the women who are involved tend to mix with an elite of Japanese men, and their own status in society to some extent reflects these associations.

Within particular tea houses, to which geisha become attached when they decide to take up such a career, the women organise themselves hierarchically in relations again based on the family model of mother/daughter or younger and older sisters. Each tea house has a 'mother' who takes ultimate responsibility for her charges, and each individual geisha is linked to a particular senior or 'elder sister', who helps with her training. Eventually she, too, will have a junior beneath her to whom she is expected to pass on her skills. These relationships are again long-term, and they illustrate the inverted V model quite well. Since less highly trained entertainers, such as hostesses, have modelled themselves to some extent on the geisha image, this could well help explain the wider use of the term *mama-san*, although there is no doubt something in the psychological explanations as well. Buruma (1985) traces the power of the motherly image back to the early Japanese mythology of Amaterasu Omikami and her relations.

Although the entertainment industry may be seen as a source of employment for women, who may well have chosen to be there and be earning well, it also has a less respectable past reputation. In times of economic hardship, it has been a well-known practice for a struggling family to 'sell' a daughter to a brothel, or geisha house, in order to feed the rest of the family. An outright payment would be made, which would represent several years of training and service for their daughter who would live in the house, but she would literally be expected to pay off her own debt to the brothel through her work. The film *Street of Shame* is a depiction of just such a brothel during the period of political discussions about legislation to terminate these practices, and it portrays the variety of ways in which women involved came to terms (or failed to come to terms) with their situation.

TRIPS AND TOURISM

Another very popular use of leisure time in Japan is the taking of trips of one sort or another. The country is scattered with attractions which range from the natural beauty of the landscape, often culturally elaborated with religious edifices to celebrate their splendour, or depicted in enclosed and miniature form in gardens, through artificially maintained traditional villages and wildlife sanctuaries, to the ultimate expressions of technological achievement such as those displayed at Disneyland and Japan's EXPO sites. There is also an extensive and efficient transport network. Planes, trains and ferries are usually more reliable over long distances than vehicles which use the overburdened roads, but all forms of transport are well patronised, and full to capacity over national holidays.

Activities are varied. For the younger generations, hiking, skiing and wind-surfing are popular; for their grandparents, visits to the abundant hot springs are still a favourite choice. For many, sightseeing is enough incentive to make a trip; for others, pilgrimages continue an ancient reason for travel. The anthropologist Nelson Graburn (1983) has written a comprehensive analysis of the Japanese propensity for trip-making, and he has chosen to entitle his study 'To Pray, Pay and Play', since these three elements are commonly included in any journey, whatever'its stated purpose. This is no doubt related to the fact that shrines and temples are often built beside places of special natural interest, so that a visit to any such place may well include a prayer at the shrine and the purchase of a protective charm to take home. Ian Reader's (1993) discussion of a specific pilgrimage in Shikoku emphasises the variety of reasons for making such a trip.

Companions for such trips are rather various too. Travel with peers is popular, and since the annual class outings start at kindergarten in Japan, most people grow up with the experience. Age-mate groups often travel together from my area of research in Kyushu, and this probably dates back at least to the nationally common custom of groups saving to send one or two of their members to the shrine of Amaterasu at Ise. Nowadays hot springs seem to be more popular, and even some foreign trips, but most of the villagers have also been to Ise. Company employees, who are said rarely to take all the holidays to which they are entitled, do however spend time away together, perhaps at the company's own accommodation. Housewives also form themselves into groups of companions for the purpose of travel, particularly once their children are grown up and their obligations to the home have slackened off. The lone traveller is rare, except perhaps for young people travelling abroad, and even then they tend to meet up with other Japanese in a similar situation.

The family holiday is becoming more popular, particularly at the seaside, but in general such trips tend to be much shorter than the two to three weeks which are common elsewhere. Nor will it usually involve more than the nuclear parent-children group. Two nights away is perhaps typical, and the father of the family will be itchy to get back to work after what he may well describe as 'family duty'. Families also go out on day trips from time to time, Sundays and national holidays being particularly popular, and they also travel together to visit the parents' own family homes at New Year or the *bon* summer festival. Otherwise individual members of the family tend to travel with their own peers or contemporaries.

Members of the family are not forgotten, however, and one of the main purposes of travel seems to be the purchase of a large number of presents to take back to those who remain behind. For a major trip, it is customary for friends and neighbours to organise a send-off with a gift of money, and these well-wishers are also remembered when the presents are purchased. According to Graburn (1983:45), the cost of the gift should be half the sum received. It is also important to bring back souvenirs of the trip, and most tourist resorts have developed their own specialities to cater to these two needs. Thus, the traveller still goes in part as a representative of his or her *uchi* group, or, in Graburn's words, 'is doing something positive on behalf of the whole group' (1983:58).

Another related *sine qua non* of the venture is to record all the highlights of the trip in photographic record. For this purpose, Japanese tourists are always willing to help out total strangers by taking photographs for them, because the required picture involves the whole travel group posing together in front of each major site or famous place visited. There is apparently no need to record the informal moments, and albums are really only interesting if one knows the people, partly because the site itself is often largely obscured by the group lined up in front of it. The chief object of the exercise seems to be to provide 'proof' that one has been to the places involved and generally to legitimise the event. As Graburn points out, photographs are a natural adjunct to the whole system of purchasing local goods for presents and souvenirs. Many famous sites also have stamps which one can collect as further 'proof' of one's visits.

Graburn (1983:63) interprets the behaviour of these Japanese tourists as a seeking of 'a nostalgic confirmation of their cultural landscape', and he argues that Japan enjoys a special concept of nostalgia including 'a dreaming of the homeland', or 'a somewhat sad longing for an ideal harmonious context'. The right group visiting the right sites and enjoying their group photographs afterwards is a perfect expression of this nostalgia, he argues. This is the same 'nostalgia' referred to above by Moeran in the context of the artistic value accorded crafts which reflect an older social order, and in Chapter 4 where reference was made to the ethnography of Martinez (1990) and Knight (1993) who talk of the way the rural, especially with some ancient religious association, has become an attraction to tourists. Arts, in this case 'folk arts', remind Japanese of their heritage in the

Figure 10.2 The Imperial Palace, which occupies a large area of land in the centre of Tokyo, forms a popular backdrop for photographs of groups visiting the city.

same way that ancient lore and nationally famous places do. Their beauty lies in the way they illustrate a recognisable social order and a shared value system.

As Knight also points out, however, recent attractions very often include international associations, and the theme of internationalisation is an important one for tourists. For one thing, foreign travel has become popular and quite affordable with the high relative value of the yen, and Japanese tourists are exploring the beauty spots of the world. The shortish holidays still taken by most people preclude multiple visits to faraway places, but couples on their honeymoon are a regular sight in Europe, as are larger groups of retired people. Northern Australia has become a possible destination for families.

Within Japan, too, there is a growing number of sites to visit which represent foreign countries and their attractions. Disneyland is an example which is extremely successful in Japan, though it is little changed from the American version, and we heard in Chapter 4 about the Danish Pavilion near Kyoto. There is also a Holland Village in Kyushu, where Dutch students studying Japanese may be seen walking in the streets, a Canada World in Hokkaido, which takes advantage of the similarity of scenery, and an English garden is being constructed in Mito. This last is to have a 'grotto', a 'secret garden', and an 'aromatic garden', incorporated at strategic points about the parkland, so it is not an unsophisticated venture. There is also a park not far from Tokyo which has reconstructed ⅕₅ size versions of a selection of famous world sites such as the Eiffel Tower, London Bridge and the World Trade Centre.

The recreation in miniature of Japanese mountains and lakes in gardens brings the distant, wild and possibly dangerous into a manageable or 'tamed' form, according to the Norweigan anthropologist, Arne Kalland (1992), who points out that although the Japanese express their love of nature, they are often afraid in totally wild parts of the country, as well as being guilty of considerable environmental damage. The reconstruction of foreign locations in Japan allows for a similar 'taming' process, I would argue, and at the same time helps Japanese people to resolve their ambiguous attitudes to the outside. It is this foreign world which has brought so much change to Japan, much of it good, but it is also still very much *soto* (or outside) from a mainstream Japanese point of view. Some people have an opportunity to work and study overseas, as we have seen in Chapter 6, but for many these tourist spots are a way of coming to terms with the increasing importance of the wider world in Japan.

CONCLUSION

In all the sections of this chapter we have been concerned again with considerable ritual activity. In the arts, in much entertainment and in the use of leisure, we find that events and activities are ritualised and predictable. The familiar distinction between *uchi* and *soto* is here again, and sometimes the ritual is helping to demarcate or reassign meaning to *uchi* groups. This takes place at different levels, of course, from the family at one end of the spectrum to the nation as a whole at the other. Japan uses her arts and customary forms of entertainment to impress the outside world, but it is still in these same arts and entertainment forms that individual Japanese often find satisfaction and spiritual strength. It is perhaps through them, and applying a Japanese approach to less familiar aspects of the world, that they hope to achieve a oneness with the environment as it is reconstituted, just as a oneness with 'nature' may be found in a culturally highly elaborated garden. Further issues of this sort are discussed in Asquith and Kalland, forthcoming.

NOTES

1. A succinct and readable article covering the major historical periods from the point of view of the visual arts is Chapter 6 in Hall and Beardsley (1965).
2. The ethnomusicologist, David Hughes (1991), has written about the contemporary interest in 'old and new' folk songs in Japan.

REFERENCES

Anderson, Jennifer L., *Japanese Tea Ritual* (State University of New York Press, Albany, 1991)
Buruma, Ian, *A Japanese Mirror* (Penguin Books, Harmondsworth, 1985)
Bornoff, Nick, *Pink Samurai: The Pursuit and Politics of Sex in Japan* (Grafton, 1991)
Coaldrake, William H., *The Way of the Carpenter* (Weatherhill, New York and Tokyo, 1990)
Dalby, Liza Crihfield, *Geisha* (University of California Press, Berkeley, 1983)
Graburn, Nelson, *To Pray, Pay and Play* (Centre des Hautes Etudes Touristiques Serie B, no. 26, 1983)
Hall, John Whitney and Richard K. Beardsley, *Twelve Doors to Japan* (McGraw-Hill, New York, 1965), Chapters 5 and 6
Hori, G. Victor Sogen, 'Teaching and Learning in the Rinzai Zen Monastery', *Journal of Japanese Studies*, vol. 20, no. 1 (1994), pp. 5–35
Hughes, David, 'Japanese "New Folk Songs" Old and New', *Asian Music*, vol. 22 no. 1 (1991), pp. 1–49
Kalland, Arne, 'Culture in Japanese Nature', in O.Bruun and A. Kalland (eds), *Asian Perceptions of Nature* (Nordic Proceedings in Asian Studies no. 3, Copenhagen, NIAS, 1992), pp. 218–33
Kondo, Dorinne, 'The Way of Tea: A Symbolic Analysis', *Man*, vol. 20, no. 2 (1985), pp. 287–306
Linhart, Sepp, '*Sakariba*: Zone of "Evaporation" between work and home', in Joy Hendry and Jonathan Webber, *Interpreting Japanese Society* (Journal of the Anthropological Society of Oxford Occasional Publication, no. 5, Oxford, 1986), pp. 198–210
Moeran, Brian, *Lost Innocence* (University of California Press, Berkeley, 1984)
——, *Language and Popular Culture* (Manchester University Press, Manchester, 1989)
O'Neill, P.G., 'Organization and Authority in the Traditional Arts', *Modern Asian Studies*, vol. 18, no. 4 (1984), pp. 631–45
Powell, Brian, 'Contemporary Theatre in Japan', *Perspectives on Japan*, vol. 6 (The Japan Information Centre, London, 1985), pp. 27–32

Powell, Irena, *Writers and Society in Modern Japan* (Macmillan, London, 1983)

Reader, Ian, 'Dead to the World: Pilgrims in Shikoku', in Ian Reader and Tony Walter (eds), *Pilgrimage in Popular Culture* (Macmillan, London, 1993)

Valentine, James, 'Dance Space, Time and Organisation: Aspects of Japanese Cultural Performance' in Joy Hendry and Jonathan Webber (eds) *Interpreting Japanese Society* (Journal of the Anthropological Society of Oxford Occasional Publication, no. 5, Oxford, 1986), pp. 111–28

FURTHER READING

Asquith, Pamela and Arne Kalland, *The Culture of Nature in Japan* (Curzon and Hawaii University Press, forthcoming)

Barrett, Gregory, *Archetypes in Japanese Film* (Associated University Presses, London and Toronto, 1989)

Ben-Ari, Eyal, 'Posing, Posturing and Photographic Prescences: A Rite of Passage in a Japanese Commuter Village', *Man* (n.s.) vol. 26 (1991), pp. 87–104

Havens, Thomas R.H., *Artist and Patron in Post-war Japan: Dance, Music and the Visual Arts 1955–1980* (Princeton University Press, Princeton, 1982)

Hayakawa Masao, *The Garden Art of Japan* (Weatherhill, New York and Heibonsha, Tokyo, 1973)

Katō, Shūichi, *Form, Style, Tradition: Reflections on Japanese Art and Society* (Kodansha International, Tokyo, 1981)

Matthew, Robert, *Japanese Science Fiction: A View of a Changing Society* (Routledge, London, 1989)

Powers, R.G. and H. Kato, *Handbook of Japanese Popular Culture* (Greenwood Press, New York, 1989)

Schodt, Frederick, *Manga! Manga! The World of Japanese Comics* (Kodansha International, Tokyo, 1983)

Tsunoda Ryūsaku, Wm. Theodore de Bary and Donald Keene, *Sources of Japanese Tradition* (Columbia University Press, New York, 1958)

NOVELS AND LIGHTER READING

Morley, John David, *Pictures from the Water Trade* (Andre Deutsch, London, 1985; Flamingo, London, 1985)

Kawabata, Yasunari, *Beauty and Sadness* (Penguin, Harmondsworth, 1979)

Ishiguro Kazuo, *An Artist of the Floating World*, (Faber and Faber, London, 1985)

FILMS

Street of Shame (*Akasen Chitai*) (dir. Mizoguchi Kenji)
Tampopo (dir. Itami Jūzō)

11 Politics and government

INTRODUCTION

This chapter and the next bring us finally into an area which will seem, superficially at least, very familiar to a Western reader, since Japan's political and legal systems have in the last century been twice modelled on Western prototypes. As outlined in Chapter 1, the Meiji period witnesses the establishment of a bicameral parliamentary system, influenced by Germany, France and England, and, during the Allied Occupation, this system underwent a thorough, American-style 'democratisation' process. The language of politics in Japan is thus easily rendered into English – indeed, the 1947 Constitution was first drafted in English – and Japan may take a recognisable position in international political arenas, which she regularly does.

Under the surface, however, Japan has its own way of doing things, just as any people has, and it is one of the aims of an anthropological approach to penetrate the deeper levels of operation behind the familiar facade. Unfortunately, especially in view of some of the recent corruption scandals, this is an area which has been little studied by anthropologists in Japan, except at the most local level of the community, although there has been a highly controversial attempt to probe beneath *The Enigma of Japanese Power* by a man with some anthropological background (van Wolferen 1989). Otherwise, we must rely for the wider system on the materials provided by political scientists, who are, of course, by no means unaware of the problem. We also have available the historical precedents discussed in Chapter 1, and by now a fair amount of information about other areas of Japanese society, which provides a context and a framework for approaching our last two topics.

This chapter will open with an outline of the system of government in Japan, describing its institutional components and the principles by which they operate. It will then move on to investigate the roles played by its human participants, the ways in which they ally themselves with each other for political purposes, and the ways in which they achieve support. Finally, it will turn to look at the role of the voting public, the extent to which they participate in political activities, the way they make decisions about political matters and the opportunities they have for moving into political arenas. Judiciary matters will be left for the following chapter, which will focus in on social control at a more microscopic level.

The second edition of this book goes to press at a time of some considerable political uncertainty. The long-standing conservative government was overturned in the summer of 1993 after 38 years in power, and the first Prime Minister of the new coalition which replaced it was forced to resign less than a year later in the wake of yet another corruption scandal, despite promising a clean-up. A minority administration then lasted a mere nine weeks, to be succeeded by a government with both conservative and left-wing elements, under a socialist Prime Minister. Legislation for electoral reform has been put through the Diet, but it has yet to be implemented, though constituency boundaries are in the process of being redrawn. However, there is a prevailing view amongst commentators[1] that the principles of Japanese politics have not yet been radically changed; so this chapter will hopefully stand the test of time.

GOVERNMENT INSTITUTIONS

Despite the role of the imperial line in providing the Japanese people with an identity and a unity, the Emperor, himself, has no political power. The Constitution declares him a symbol of the state, with duties confined to ceremonial and diplomatic affairs. Like the Queen of England, he opens parliament, attests the appointment of ministers and ambassadors, awards honours, and receives foreign royalty and ambassadors. He thus performs a role not unlike that of most of his predecessors, retaining the dignity of distance from the everyday political affairs of the nation. Members of his immediate family play similar, though necessarily subordinate, roles.

The active government has three branches, legislative, administrative and judiciary. Legislative power is in the hands of the Diet, a parliament composed of a House of Representatives and a House of Councillors, both since the Occupation comprising elected members. Administrative power falls to the Cabinet, a body of ministers, headed by the Prime Minister, responsible to the Diet, but supported by a very strong bureaucracy of civil servants. Judicial power is invested in the court system, headed by the Supreme Court. Judges are appointed by the Cabinet, with the exception of the Chief Justice, whose appointment is officially conferred by the Emperor, and the courts have the power to rule on the constitutionality of laws and orders.

The House of Representatives currently has 511 members from 130 districts who serve for a maximum term of four years, although an election may be held within that period. The reformed system is to have 500 seats, with 300 elected from new single constituencies and 200 from 11 regional constituencies, chosen by proportional representation from party lists. There are plenary sessions, which are presided over by a speaker to maintain order, and there are also smaller committees. The House of Councillors, the upper house, has 252 members, 152 from the prefectures, in numbers proportional to their populations, and 100 from a national constituency. They serve for a period of six years, but elections are held every three years for half the seats. Together the houses make laws, raise and spend public money, and designate the Prime Minister. The House of Representatives is more powerful in that it can overrule the House of Councillors under certain circumstances, although bills should usually be approved by both Houses before they become law.

The Cabinet of 18 ministers is chosen by the Prime Minister. Its work includes the administration of the law, the management of internal and external affairs, and the preparation and submission of the budget. It takes joint responsibility for its decisions which are ideally made by consensus agreement. In practice, full advantage is taken of the supporting bureaucracy which still has a very powerful role to play in Japanese political life, so that many Cabinet decisions may in fact be arrived at prior to meetings, especially in the Conference of Administrative Vice-Ministers, that is, the heads of government ministries. Serious dissent in the Cabinet is rare and usually leads to resignation or dismissal. However, the usual turnover of ministers is quite high, and this enables the Prime Minister to maintain the representation of different factions, and to reward the supporters who helped him to achieve his own position.

The bureaucratic staff of the ministries maintains a solid, stable base for the day-to-day administration of business, and the personnel represent the elite of the nation's potential, since they are usually recruited from the graduates of the best universities. This is a pattern which was established in 1887 with the introduction of an examination to select the best candidates. In the early modern period, before political parties were established, there was no clear distinction

Figure 11.1   The 'Diet' or Japanese parliament can be seen here through one of the gates of the Imperial Palace. In many ways the Western-type system of government operates with heavy Japanese modifications in practice, although the Emperor has no power.

between the higher-ranking bureaucrats and the political leaders who were in charge of decision-making, and even after the parties emerged, many of their leaders were recruited from the bureaucracy. Until the end of the Second World War, too, imperial prerogatives were exercised by the bureaucracy, which became particularly powerful again after party government was abandoned in 1932 and power was shared with the increasingly dominant military regime. After the war, the Americans removed the armed forces and encouraged the re-establishment of competing political parties, which had been merged into a single pro-government party in 1940. The bureaucracy has nevertheless remained powerful, both in policy formation and in the drafting of legislation. Indeed, some argue that it forms the central axis of the political system, and its power has increased in post-war years. It certainly plays a useful stabilising role in times of political uncertainty. It also still supplies a substantial number of candidates for political office among career bureaucrats who have served their years in the Civil Service.

At the local level, there are elected assemblies for the prefectures, cities, towns and 'villages', including Tokyo wards. The mayors and prefectural governors are elected separately. These units are responsible for a variety of local affairs, including some taxation, although financially they are mainly dependent on subsidies and other aid from central government. Ultimately, at the local level of the community, on the other hand, there is still often a fair degree of autonomy, as was described in Chapter 4. This feature of the local community has probably been rather persistent throughout several changes at higher levels, and it is no doubt related to the strong *uchi/soto* distinction in Japanese society.

ELECTORAL SYSTEM

Elections were introduced into Japan in 1889, but the franchise was at first limited to a small percentage of men, depending on qualifications of residence and tax assessment. In 1925, universal male suffrage was introduced for adults of 25 and over, but women were only given a vote in 1945, when the voting age was reduced to 20. Until 1945, too, it was only members of the House of Representatives who were elected, and the power of these was quite limited. Now, control of a majority of the seats in this House gives a party virtual control over the legislative and administrative branches of government, since the leader of the party in power becomes Prime Minister.

Elections for the House of Representatives are thus the most significant nationally, and they are also the ones which have over the years engendered the most controversy. Until the political reform of 1994, each constituency returned between three and five members, depending on its size. Everyone had one non-transferable vote, and the designated number of candidates who won the most votes were elected. One of the results of this system was that in districts with a dense population more votes were required for the election of one candidate than in districts with a sparse population. An extreme example of this disparity was to compare Chiba district 4, which in the 1983 election required an average of 499,763 votes to gain a seat, with Hyogo district 5, which required only 110,051. One vote in Hyogo 5 was thus equivalent to more than four votes in Chiba 4. In fact, the election was declared unconstitutional by the Supreme Court because of this disparity, as several previous elections had been. Another aspect of the system of returning more than one member from each district was that big parties could field more than one candidate if they had sufficient support but it was important to be able to gauge the size of the likely support available to make sure that putting up two or more candidates would not allow a candidate from another party to slip through by dividing the votes.

Prior to the 1986 election, eight new seats were created in the most populous districts, and seven removed from the least dense, but a more radical new system was finally put through, albeit in modified form, by the new coalition government elected in 1993. This system involves electing 300 of the members of the House of Representatives from single-seat constituencies and 200 from 11 regional constituencies by proportional representation. Each voter will be entitled to choose both an individual and a party, and politicians may have two chances to gain a seat. The constituency boundaries thus need to be redrawn, however, and as this edition goes to press, it remains to be seen how the system will work out.

Elections for the House of Councillors are less controversial. Most prefectures are larger and therefore include both urban and rural areas, but there is severe discrepancy in the value of a vote between different prefectures. The national constituency is evidently representative. In the 1983 election, a system of proportional representation was introduced in the national constituency, and voters are asked to select a party rather than a candidate. Perhaps partly for these reasons, and also because the candidates are less likely to be locally known figures, there is rather less excitement, but the House of Councillors also ultimately has less power.

Local elections, on the other hand, usually inspire enthusiasm. Candidates will be influential local figures, and the abundance of personal connections which they build up usually ensures a high level of support. In rural areas, in particular, there is often most interest in local elections since these relate more apparently to the real world. It also reflects the general emphasis in Japanese society on face-to-face interaction.

The figures for electoral participation bear out this emphasis on local interest. Voting is high in general in Japan, usually over 70 per cent for national elections, although it dropped a little in the period preceding the 1993 election, but the turn-out rate usually falls between 85 and 95 per cent for local elections. Rural areas also tend to have higher figures than urban ones, again probably because the candidates are likely to be known personally.

Campaigning is rather severely restricted. Activities may not begin until one month before the election, and there is an upper limit on the amount of money to be spent, the number of personnel who may be involved, the number of speeches which may be made, and the advertising and posters which may be put up. House calls and leaflets are prohibited. Instead the candidates and their supporters drive around the constituency in heavily decorated vehicles, topped with loud speakers, literally allowing their pleas for votes to echo around the district. From time to time, they stop and make speeches, sometimes setting up quite a display to attract attention before they start. These speeches tend to be very formal and uninformative, however, and it doesn't really seem to matter if they can't be heard. In rural areas, they stop beside fields and on hillsides, where their voices are carried off on the wind, but they ensure that the names on their cars are written large enough for the farmers to read.

Ultimately, the campaign probably plays only a minor part in attracting votes, although it may ensure that people have the appropriate names firmly in their heads when they go to the polls and they have to write the name of the candidate on the ballot paper. Politicians use different methods to ensure their support, and the voters use other criteria to make decisions about whom to support, but these factors will be considered in later sections. First, it is necessary to explain the party system in Japan.

THE PARTIES

Political parties have existed in Japan since 1874, although their names and the aims they represent have undergone a number of changes since that time and there have in fact been more than 165 parties. They provide an excellent example of an amalgamation of Western and Japanese principles of formation. The parties themselves may be described for the ideologies they espouse, and their activities may be described in terms of their pursuit or modification of those aims. Likewise, the behaviour of the politicians and other members of the parties may be interpreted in terms of their own personal development of ideals and principles. At the same time, political parties may also be seen as rather loose amalgamations of hierarchical groups which are formed along the traditional lines described in Chapter 5.

To start with the last, politicians and their supporters may be described as formed into groups based on links of personal allegiance. An aspiring politician thus finds one of the best courses of action is to seek alignment with an established politician and thereby become part of the wider group to which he belongs. The senior politician will then help the younger one indefinitely in exchange for support and unfailing loyalty. A series of dyadic relations of this sort ensures a solid base of support for any particular politician, who will in turn have similar relations with even more established politicians higher up the pyramid. These, in turn, can draw on an increasingly broad support group the higher up they go.

As Nakane pointed out, however, problems arise when a person at the peak of the pyramid resigns. Unless there is a clear method of choosing a successor, this leads to competition between his direct inferiors. It is at this stage that the group may split into factions headed by different members of the secondary level, and this is indeed what happens with political groups. On the other hand, political strength is often to be found in greater numbers, so that groups with different leaders will align themselves into a coalition in pursuit of this strength. Political parties in Japan are thus made up of such coalitions, fission and fusion usually being contained within a party, but occasionally splits will be serious or ideological enough to engender new parties. A spate of these emerged in the climate of political unrest which led up to the election in 1993 and there were more splits in 1994.

Until that time, there was a recognisable split between the right and left in Japanese politics, and the right had maintained power in Japan since 1948, although their overall majority had risen and fallen over the years. The largest right-wing party, the Liberal Democratic Party (LDP), represented an alliance forged in 1955 between the previous Liberal and Democratic (or Progressive) Parties, largely in response to a similar alliance in their major left-wing opposition, the Japan Socialist Party (JSP). At that time, the only other left-wing party was the Japan Communist Party (JCP), but since then there have been various realignments. The other major party is the *Kō-meitō*, or 'Clean Government Party', a middle-of-the-road group which was spawned by the 'new' religious movement Sōka Gakkai.

The Liberal Democratic Party, which lost power in 1993, was a 'catch-all' party, deriving its support from business, large and small, agriculturalists, professionals and some religious groups. Its parliamentary members were drawn from local politicians, businessmen, former secretaries and the family of Diet members, and another substantial proportion of them are those bureaucrats who move into politics after a career in one of the ministries. There were also smaller numbers of professional people, journalists and lawyers. Most of them have college backgrounds, many graduating from the prestigious

Tokyo University. Their average age was high, perhaps in their later 50s, and in the years preceding their defeat there was a growing division between the die-hard members of the old school and younger politicians who were advocating reform.

Except for elections, most of the party's business was run by the professional politicians, who chose a president every two years. He became Prime Minister, as long as the party was in power, although since one of his chief roles was maintaining the support of leaders of other factions, he ideally made as many decisions as possible in committees. The policies of this party thus tended to be rather vague and flexible, usually the result of compromise. After a series of scandals involving Prime Ministers, two new parties were spawned from this larger, somewhat amorphous amalgamation of groups, and one party was formed from scratch outside the LDP, in the space of just over a year.

The party created from scratch was the New Japan Party, formed in May 1992 with the specific aim of breaking up the existing party political structure, and it was its leader, Morihiro Hosokawa, who was elected first Prime Minister of the coalition which took power in 1993. The second grouping, an LDP faction led by Tsutomu Hata, who became the next Prime Minister, split off in June 1993 to form the Japan Renewal Party. This was preceded by about two weeks by a third group of young members of the LDP who formed a party translated into English as the 'New Harbinger', in June 1993. These defections were enough to bring down the LDP in the elections of the following month, although they had to form a coalition with the other opposition parties, and Hosokawa was forced to appoint a cabinet of representatives from these who had little experience of office.

Strongest in opposition had for long been the Japan Socialist Party, but this again has had as many hues as there are factions, and it has also experienced considerable trouble maintaining unity and strong leadership. Financial support comes from labour unions and a substantial proportion of the parliamentary members are former union leaders. Others have risen through local government, and again a good number are university-educated. The party had a heyday of strength in the 1950s, during the period of economic hardship, then its fortunes declined, particularly after the split-off of the Democratic Socialist Party (DSP) in 1960, but its election in 1986 of Takako Doi, the first female party leader in Japan, had a great revitalising effect. New parliamentary members in the next few years included professional people such as lawyers, teachers and academics, among them a large number of women, and in 1989, Doi led her party to success by winning the Upper House elections, and in the following year gaining 50 new seats in the Lower House.

The Democratic Socialist Party was founded in the 1960s by a substantial wing of the Japan Socialist Party, including 59 Diet members, who felt their politics should be more practical and less dogmatically oppositional. It has thus sometimes allied itself with the LDP on particular issues, especially at the level of local government, and, more recently, it joined an Association for Democratic Reform, also supported by Kōmeito and the United Social Democratic Party (USDP). The USDP came into existence in 1978 as a protest against the static nature of the entrenched leadership of the larger Japan Socialist Party from which it splintered. It tried rather unsuccessfully for several years to unite the opposition parties, and although it did not immediately make much impact, it did attract the votes of the younger population. In 1993, it regrouped with some of the younger members of the JSP to form a useful member of the Hosokawa coalition government, but disbanded in the spring of 1994.

The *Kōmeitō* or 'Clean Government Party' has wonderfully improbable-sounding ideals of purifying politics, doubling welfare payments and abolishing income tax, but it had until 1993 the third largest number of seats in both houses of the Diet (after the LDP and the JSP), and it is certainly a force to be reckoned with in urban local government. It was founded in 1964 as a political wing of Sōka Gakkai, which has similarly utopian ideals of salvation from illness and material misfortune, but the two were formally separated in 1970. The political party tried to broaden its membership, but it is still heavily dependent on the network of Sōka Gakkai members for politicians and grass-roots support.

The Japan Communist Party, which dates back to 1922, albeit in an illegal and much persecuted form before the Second World War, has remained an active minority throughout the post-war years. Its Marxist-Leninist approach was tempered with Maoism during the Chinese revolution, but in the 1960s it announced a new independent line. This again involved a considerable practical element, with free medical and legal services for the poor, and its factions have been relatively united since then. Its support had increased substantially by 1972, and since that time it has commanded about 10 per cent of the vote, although the number of seats this becomes varies according to the vagaries of the electoral system. It did not form part of the coalition of the 1993 election, however.

POLITICIANS AND THEIR PATHS TO SUCCESS

It was noted above that the election campaign itself probably plays only a minor part in attracting votes, and this section returns to the question of how politicians achieve support when they stand for election. There are, of course, several roads to success in this respect, and we cannot hope to cover all the various possibilities, but we can look at some of the most likely paths. In a country which values long-term personal allegiance, it is perhaps only to be expected that the necessary accumulation of support is unlikely to be achieved overnight.

In rural and provincial areas, in particular, people who become politicians tend to be well-known figures in the area. They often start their political careers in the local assembly, but before they enter politics at all, they have usually built up a reputation as persons of some considerable status in the community. This status is achieved in various ways. In the past, an important component was good local family connections, and a newcomer to the district would have little chance of political success. Nowadays, education can to some extent compensate for a lack of 'breeding', but an aspiring politician must also show some concern for community matters.

Typically, a businessman will begin by allocating funds to various needy local causes, and he will start also to sit on the committees of local organisations. These may be economically important, such as the local Chamber of Commerce, or they may be less directly related to business, such as the PTA associations or shrine wardens' organisations. Important projects in the area would be targets for their attention, and a few splendid achievements would certainly ensure long-term note. A farmer/politician in the area of Kyushu where I worked had initiated a huge project to excavate a vast area of hillside and convert it into tea fields, parcels of which were purchased on easy terms by many of the local farmers. Their enhanced standard of living, as the tea crops began to bring in a profit, ensured their political support for this innovator for many years to come.

In the same way, members of all the groups and organisations supported by this local leader would know and trust him. Moreover, in a Japanese context, they would feel obligated to him for his service to their interests. In return for his benevolence, they would expect to express their loyalty, and in the absence of any stronger loyalties, they would be likely to vote for him were he to stand for election. For in many parts of Japan, personal allegiance is still much stronger than party issues, and large support groups have been known to maintain their loyalty despite a change of party by their leader. The politician, for his part, gives his time and resources to as many support groups as he can afford. He attracts loyalty by dispensing benevolence, and by belonging to as many *uchi* groups as he can.

At the level of local elections, candidates do not stand for particular constituencies, but for the city, town or village at large. They are usually supported by the area in which they live, however, even if only for pragmatic reasons of self-interest, and neighbours would probably only vote elsewhere if they had a relative running who lived in a different district. When a politician comes to stand for the Diet, however, he may draw on a larger circle of connections, and his experience in local politics may stand him in good stead. With time, and political advancement, an individual politician will probably have less and less time for direct participation in local events, and it is here that he can make use of younger aspiring politicians to help him out. A wise national politician retains a solid base of support of this kind while he pursues his career at a national level.

In urban areas, where the sheer density and variety of population makes it difficult to build up personal allegiances of the kind found in rural and provincial areas, the 'supporters' club' or 'personal support group' (*kōenkai*) has become an institution, although these are found in rural areas too. The *kōenkai*'s aims are to foster and nurture support for a particular politician, to run the election campaigns, and to deal with the press, the police and the general public. It will also organise 'surgeries' when the politician is in the locality. For a successful Diet member, this organisation may have busy branches throughout the constituency, each with local subordinate politicians as officials. In some cases, these activities have been so successfully organised that the system has been called a 'political machine'. However, the *kōenkai* are also to a considerable extent a function of the multi-member constituency system which pits members of the same party against each other in one district, and since this is soon to be abolished, the motivation to form personal *kōenkai* will be removed.

By now, our individual politician has moved well into the area of the inverted V model, described above. He has not arrived there without incurring a number of debts and obligations, however, and he will have continuing commitments to his seniors and juniors throughout his political life. This is an important principle to understand about Japanese politics, because there is a great deal of reciprocal exchange involved, and this is sometimes described in critical terms by Western observers. Politicians are also usually personally associated with a

variety of interest groups on whose votes they can count, but in return they must respond to their requests, when necessary. Indeed, success in the polls depends on the maintenance of such support, as may the financial backing of an election campaign.

Political leadership in Japan thus depends less on oratorical skills and a charismatic personality than on strong links of personal allegiance and a reputation for loyalty and sincerity. It depends on length of service, connections with sources of funds, and an ability to deal diplomatically and effectively with any number of different demands and requests. As one rises higher in the ranks, it also depends on possessing the skill to maintain harmony among one's subordinates, who may be pressing for their own success. A politician must try to share his largesse with equanimity, and the role of the Prime Minister is, of course, paramount in this respect.

The conflicts between the traditional Japanese side of the game, and the imported Western rules by which it is ostensibly played, were harshly illustrated in the Lockheed scandal. Prime Minister Tanaka was imprisoned for falling foul of the law in an international deal, but he never lost his support groups, even when he was paralysed by a stroke. Since that time, there have been many more financial scandals, even one or two with sexual innuendos, and these have increasingly been shocking Japanese voters as well as foreign commentators. Indeed, it was in the wake of one of these that three new parties were formed in 1992.

The reader may have noticed the way in which the male pronoun has been used throughout this section so far. This is indeed intentional, for women find it very difficult to follow the usual male paths through politics in Japan. There are a few female political leaders, and their numbers are increasing, but they are rarely able to build up the kind of support network that a man can, and they tend to come into the system in different ways. They may, for example, simply inherit the support group of a deceased or incapacitated husband, father or brother. This is not out of keeping with the old *ie* principles of replacement by other members of the house, and women have sometimes been very successful in this way.

Women are often active members of *kōenkai,* particularly if their husbands or fathers are involved. They usually play supporting roles, however, and see their own ambitions as reflections of those of the men they support. Women who are politically active in their own right are more likely to be successful in left-wing parties, as the election of a woman as leader of the JSP has shown, although the JCP is perhaps even more open to advancement for women. Susan Pharr

(1981) has discussed political women in a variety of arenas, from student members of the Red Army to wives who devote their lives to their husbands' political careers. A few politicians, both men and women, first achieve fame and success in a completely different field, such as television, and then use their names to attract votes. This type of arrangement is more common in urban areas, where there is less likelihood of a locally known person accumulating votes.

POPULAR PARTICIPATION IN POLITICS

A corollary of the system of allegiances described above is that the voting behaviour of individuals is often determined not by individual choice, but by membership in some *uchi* group which demands loyalty. In the farming area where I worked, for example, local elections commanded support on kin or residential lines, and for national elections, decisions tended to be made according to occupational allegiances. The LDP is the party which farmers feel represents their interests, and if a local candidate shows some personal interest in one of the agricultural or horticultural specialist groups, then his faction would probably be chosen, although proximity of residence or some other long-term relationship would probably be a closer link. In any case, the community seems to agree on whom they should support, and after that they take little interest in the affairs of national politics.

These principles operate in similar ways for people in many different walks of life, and anthropologists have often referred only briefly to national politics in a community study on the grounds that little interest is shown. One's vote tends to be determined by one's position in society: one's occupational group, one's place of residence and one's personal and group allegiances. For those who become more actively involved in party politics, their hands are even more tied. They become part of the base of support and the complicated series of exchanges, so that not only their own vote but as many others as they can command become tied to the system they have joined.

This is not the end of political participation, however, and this chapter would be incomplete without a consideration of informal local political activity. For in many areas of Japanese life, people who perceive a need will band together with others who share their perception and take direct action of their own. This may or may not ultimately involve the lobbying of professional politicians. Sometimes people are able to solve their own problems at a local level, and this is in keeping with the general autonomy associated with the smallest political units. Otherwise the people concerned will become one of the interest groups on which a politician, should he help them achieve their goals, will be able to count for future support. In this case, they have allocated their vote in a most effective way.

It should be emphasised that at this level of local political activity women are often strong and effective participants, although they may be represented by a man in formal encounters, and they may well also be the instigators of such action. A well-known example of this kind of activity is to be found in the environmental protest groups which have reacted to the threat to their residential areas by the waste of large enterprises. These movements have been spectacular and successful enough to attract the attention of political scientists, and the study by McKean (1981) has documented the phenomenon from that point of view. A collection of essays published in the same year by Steiner, Krauss and Flanagan (1981) looks at the wider subject of *Political Opposition and Local Politics in Japan*.

From an anthropological point of view this kind of action represents another example of the force of face-to-face interaction in Japanese society. In the traditional community, it was usually more effective for neighbours to cooperate to achieve some goal which they shared than to appeal individually to the impersonal institutions of which they formed only a minor part. The continuing existence of fire-fighting corps, road-mending meetings and women's consumer groups attests to the way this preference for a degree of local autonomy persists. Even in new neighbourhoods, self-help groups are soon formed, and these draw on the social patterns which developed in older communities.

An excellent case study of such activity is to be found in the book by Eyal Ben Ari (1991) already referred to in Chapter 4. He analyses in some considerable detail the way members of a new community near Kyoto came together to solve the problems they were suffering due to a lack of services. He discusses the various options open to the residents, the way they themselves considered all the possibilities, and the means by which they eventually achieved their aims. The self-help group that they set up is a prototype also found elsewhere, and once established it can be activated for other purposes in the future. In effect, the new neighbours have drawn on one of the strengths of the old, relatively autonomous community, but they also make good use of their residents' links with the sophistications of the outside world.

At this level of politics in the smallest local unit, there are a number of anthropological sources which document political behaviour. This is the face-to-face level with which anthropology is particularly familiar, and several authors have analysed the paths to power and influence within the community. The study by Beardsley, Hall and Ward (1969) is a classic example of one community; that by Fukutake (1972, referred to in Chapter 4) is a more general survey of rural Japan. Moeran (1986) has discussed the role of drinking in political behaviour in a rural community in Kyushu, and the recent work of Ben-Ari (1991)and Bestor (1989) (also referred to in Chapter 4) fill a gap with regard to political behaviour in urban neighbourhoods.

CONCLUSION

This chapter has set out to show how a Western system of politics works in an alien culture. The institutions are quite recognisable, but the behaviour within them is not so clear. Indeed, some integral parts of the Japanese version of the system have been shown to be quite corrupt by the standards of the societies from which the framework was adopted, and this fact has increasingly been disturbing the Japanese voting public. Complaints are also persistently aired about the perfunctory role of the Japanese parliament. Nevertheless, for the most part, the system works quite well, and despite apparently catastrophic changes on the political front, Japan manages to maintain a rather powerful role on the international scene, albeit often heavily criticised by the United States and others. At the same time, it deals rather effectively with grass-roots demands and can incorporate new political movements.

NOTES

1. See, for example, articles published in the April 1994 edition of the *Japan Forum* by Iritani Toshio and Stephen Johnson.

REFERENCES

Beardsley, Richard K., John W. Hall and Robert E. Ward, *Village Japan* (University of Chicago Press, Chicago, 1959), Chapters 12 and 13

Ben-Ari, Eyal, *Changing Japanese Suburbia: A Study of Two Present Day Localities* (Kegan Paul International, Tokyo, 1991)

Bestor, Theodore, *Neighbourhood Tokyo* (Stanford University Press, Stanford, California, 1989), esp. Chapter 3.

Healey, Graham, 'Politics and Politicians', in Howard Smith (ed.), *Inside Japan* (British Broadcasting Association, London, 1981), pp. 155–86

Iritani, Toshio, 'The Emergence of the Hosokawa Coalition: A Significant Break in the Continuity of Japanese Politics?', *Japan Forum*, vol. 6, no. 1 (1994), pp. 1–7.

Johnson, Stephen, 'Continuity and Change in Japanese Electoral Patterns: The 1993 General Election in Yamanashi', *Japan Forum*, vol. 6, no. 1 (1994), pp. 8–20.

McKean, Margaret, *Environmental Politics and Citizen Politics in Japan* (California University Press, Berkeley, 1981)

Moeran, Brian, 'One Over the Seven: Sake Drinking in a Japanese Potting Community' in Joy Hendry and Jonathan Webber (eds), *Interpreting Japanese Society* (Journal of the Anthropoligical Society of Oxford Occasional Publication, no. 5, Oxford, 1986), pp. 226–42

Okimoto, Daniel I, and T.P. Rohlen, *Inside the Japanese System* (Stanford University Press, Stanford, 1988)

Pharr, Susan, J., *Political Women in Japan: The Search for a Place in Political Life* (University of California Press, Berkeley, 1981)

Steiner, K., E.S. Krauss and S.C. Flanagan, *Political Opposition and Local Politics in Japan* (Princeton University Press, Princeton, New Jersey, 1981)

Wolferen, Karel van, *The Enigma of Japanese Power* (Macmillan, London, 1989)

FURTHER READING

Abe, Hitoshi, Muneyuki Shindō and Sadafumi Kawato, *The Government and Politics of Japan*, trans. with an Introduction by James W. White (University of Tokyo Press, Tokyo, 1994)

Calder, Kent E., *Crisis and Compensation: Public Policy and Political Stability in Japan, 1949–1986* (Princeton University Press, Princeton, New Jersey, 1988)

Curtis, Gerald L., *The Japanese Way of Politics* (Columbia University Press, New York, 1988)

Flanagan, Scott C., S. Kohei, I. Miyake, B.M. Richardson and J. Watanabe, *The Japanese Voter* (Yale University Press, New Haven and London, 1991)

Hrebenar, Ronald J., *The Japanese Party System* (Westview Press, Boulder, Colorado, second edition, 1992)

Pempel, T., *Policy and Politics in Japan: Creative Conservatism* (Temple University Press, Philadelphia, 1982)

Stockwin, J.A.A., *Japan: Divided Politics in a Growth Economy* (Weidenfeld and Nicolson, London, second edition, 1982)

———, *Dynamic and Immobilist Politics in Japan* (University of Hawaii Press, Honolulu, 1988)

NOVEL

Mishima, Yukio, *After the Banquet* (Charles E. Tuttle, Tokyo, 1967)

FILM

A Taxing Woman (*Marusa no Onna*) (dir. Itami Jūzō)

12 The legal system and social control

INTRODUCTION

Social control is anthropological terminology for the mechanisms a society uses to maintain order in social life. There are usually mechanisms both to encourage behaviour which is approved by the society and to discourage that which is unacceptable, so that as they are brought into play they reinforce the values which underlie them. These mechanisms range from the spontaneous reactions of friends and neighbours, such as admiration, gossip or ostracism, to the highly organised system of honours and punishments which are distributed by agencies of the state in which the society is found. In a small-scale society, or close-knit group, the former are usually more effective in practice than the latter, whose part is greater the more complex and anonymous a society becomes.

In any particular society, the value system, or systems, on which mechanisms of social control are based, is inextricably tied up with other important aspects of the cosmology or world view of that society, so that an understanding of social control must be placed in the context of such information. Thus, for example, Evans Pritchard (1937) argued that beliefs about witchcraft play an important part in the social control of the Azande people of the Sudan, and elsewhere notions of ancestral or spiritual retribution have been shown to play a comparable role. Similarly, systems of law need a set of (usually moral) principles on which to be based, and these principles may or may not coincide with those underlying the more informal mechanisms.

In a complex society like Japan, there are understandably a large number of factors which play a part, and indeed, several of them have already been discussed in other contexts. These will be referred to during the course of the chapter. Much of the formal legal system will be superficially recognisable to a Western reader, as the political system was, largely because it was imported from Europe, but there is again a considerable discrepancy between the principles which were imported with it, and modified by the Allied Occupation, and the principles which underlie indigenous, less formal methods of social control. This chapter will briefly describe the official legal system and its enforcement, but it will also devote space to discussing the way it is used, or not used, and indeed some of the other ways in which order is achieved in Japanese society.

One important general aspect of social control should be mentioned here, because it raises an issue which has been of some topical interest amongst commentators on Japan. This is the area known as dispute resolution. In Simon Roberts' excellent introduction to legal anthropology, *Order and Dispute* (1979), he emphasises the importance of moving away from our ethnocentric ideas about law and its enforcement, and he starts instead with two 'simple assumptions' about society. First, 'that a degree of order and regularity *must* be maintained in any human group if the basic processes of life are to be sustained', and second, 'that quarrels will inevitably arise, and that these may disrupt that order if they are not resolved or at least contained'. He thus sets out to examine the ways in which people maintain order and deal with disputes (1979:13–14).

Roberts is particularly concerned with small-scale societies, but these assumptions would seem to be valid anywhere, at least at the face-to-face level. Indeed, it is usually assumed by anthropologists that quarrels are inevitable, and one aspect of social control is therefore concerned with the mechanisms which are available to deal with dispute. In the case of Japan, so much has been made of the strong value attached to harmony, as if this in itself would do away with disputes, that some commentators have reacted by placing an equally strong emphasis on conflict in Japanese society. The positive value attached to harmony is evidently an aspect of social control which must not be ignored, but it by no means ensures that there will be no conflict, as the fruits of this reaction make clear (see, for example, Eisenstadt and Ben-Ari 1990; Krauss *et al.*, 1984). We will return to this problem after presenting some aspects of social control, starting with the most conspicuous means of dispute resolution, the courts.

LAWS AND COURTS

Japan has had a set of written laws since the early eighth century, when the influx of influence from China included the basis of the

Taihō Code, which was promulgated in 702, and the subsequent Yōrō Code of 718. These formed the foundations of a formal legal system, although there were of course modifications to their content and administration over the centuries which followed, particularly in the degree to which they were made locally variable. For example, radical revisions took place in the early Tokugawa period, when a system which has been described as centralised feudal law was instigated by the shogunate. There were separate codes at that time for imperial court nobles, for *daimyō*, for Samurai and for commoners. Administration of the law was largely carried out by local magistrates, although serious disputes could be brought to the central offices of the shogunate.

This system was entirely inadequate for the international country Japan was becoming when she entered the Meiji period, however. Under pressure from foreign countries, which insisted on rights of extra-territoriality in view of the weaknesses of the Japanese legal system, scholars began to debate the possibilities of various European legal codes for the needs of the Japanese case. The Meiji codes were at first heavily influenced by the French system, even being drawn up under the guidance of an adviser from the French government, but there were later influences from Germany and England. Major revisions were, of course, introduced during the Allied Occupation after the Second World War, when the influences were largely from the United States. That these influences are foreign is starkly clear in the three main principles of the 1947 Constitution which, as we noted in Chapter 1, aimed to introduce the ideals of democracy. They are: sovereignty of the people, pacifism and a respect for basic human rights, which include equality, liberty and life.

These principles are almost completely at odds with previous Japanese values, as a glance back at Chapter 1 will make clear, although this does not mean that the aims which they represent are entirely inconsistent with the aims achieved in other ways in Japanese social relations. An article by the Japanese lawyer, Kawashima Takeyoshi (1967), discusses the problems of using just one of these notions in a Japanese context, namely that of 'human rights', and he argues that the traditional notion of the individual in Japan involved a variety of social obligations, but had no place for the notion of 'right'. 'This does not mean, however, that a sense of respect for the honor, life and feelings of other persons did not exist', he writes (1967:264-5). With the introduction of these alien values, there have of course been changes, but the present legal system represents another example of a Western-like exterior, with rather different workings on the ground.

It is interesting, then, that until a recent move to a new building, the Ministry of Justice in Tokyo had a Western-style brick exterior, but the inside had been completely rebuilt. Now the brick building stands in front of the new concrete construction.

Figure 12.1 The former Ministry of Justice in Tokyo has a brick front reflecting the Western influence in the Japanese legal system. Like the legal system, however, the inside is constructed in a completely different way.

As mentioned in the previous chapter, the 1947 Constitution also stipulates the separation of legislative, administrative and judicial powers, and the last, the subject of this section, is for the first time guaranteed independence of the others. As in the United States, it is headed by a Supreme Court, which has the ultimate power to decide on the constitutionality of any laws, orders or official acts, and to issue rules of practice and procedure. Under this there are eight high courts, 50 district courts, 570 summary courts and 50 family courts. The last operate at the same regional levels as the district courts, but cover problems of domestic relations, juvenile delinquency and the criminal cases of adults who have contributed to minors' cases. Other cases start in the summary courts, unless they involve sums of over 900,000 yen, when they go directly to the district courts. The higher courts are largely for cases of appeal from lower down.

Justice is in the hands of judges, a jury system having been tried and eventually rejected in the period preceding the Second World War. Courts are allowed considerable discretion in administering punishments set out in the Penal Code, however, and also in suspending execution of punishments where the circumstances seem to warrant this. As Kawashima points out, the Japanese view of the relationship between legal rules and the social world is rather different from the state of tension which is taken for granted in Western society. A statute is considered, he argues, to be like a sword handed down from the ancestors as a family treasure – not for actual use, but as a symbolic manifestation of the prestige of the family (1967:267).

One of the major features of this official Japanese system is the emphasis which is placed on compromise and conciliation. As a general rule, a judge seeks solutions to cases which satisfy both sides, and there is a reluctance to apply universal principles in which declarations are made about absolute right and wrong. Instead, the particular circumstances of each case are taken into consideration as far as possible, and a willingness to confess and apologise on the part of the accused will usually result in a fair measure of leniency. According to Japanese judges, the primary purpose of trials is to correct behaviour, not to punish it, and if an apology seems to be sincere, the aim is deemed to have been achieved.

In this, there is evidently considerable success. According to an article by John Haley (1982), the rate of conviction in cases which go to trial is 99.9 per cent, but in less than 3 per cent of those cases do the courts impose a prison sentence, and in 87 per cent of those cases, the terms are less than three years. Furthermore, two-thirds of the gaol sentences are regularly suspended, so that less than 2 per cent of all those convicted of a crime are ever imprisoned. It is thus in the interests of the defendant to be repentant, and as an indication of sincerity, he or she will often arrange to pay compensation to the victim of the crime before the case comes to trial, and the victim, in turn, writes a letter absolving the accused of further blame. A situation of at least superficial harmony has been restored, and the crime is seen to have been appeased.

Examples of cases of unrepentence are recounted in some detail in Norma Field's book *In the Realm of the Dying Emperor* (1991) which was discussed in Chapter 5. All three of her cases, the otherwise law-abiding supermarket owner in Okinawa who burned the Japanese national flag, the woman who did not want her husband divinised, and the Mayor of Nagasaki who criticised the Emperor as he lay dying, refused to repent their actions. Indeed, it was this refusal which made them notorious, and the result illustrates perfectly the way a system such as this closes in on people who refuse to toe the line.

ALTERNATIVE RESPONSES TO DISPUTE

Conciliation was a prominent feature of Tokugawa law, and the modern legal system also provides an official conciliation procedure as a well-used alternative to litigation and court trial. The conciliator may be a judge, alone, or he may be part of a lay committee, and if the parties can agree to a solution there will be no need to have a trial. If they fail to agree, the trial will follow. The classic work by Dan Henderson (1965) traces the development of this modern procedure from traditional practices, and discusses how it has changed in response to the changes in society. He also points out that there is still a strong tendency to solve disputes through informal conciliatory procedures outside of the courts altogether, and this is conducted much as it has been for centuries, except that lawyers and police officers now have roles to play as mediators (1965:184).

Divorce cases provide a good example of some possible mechanisms involved here, especially as the role of the mediator in marriage has already been discussed in Chapter 8. In Japan, it is simply necessary to register divorce in the same way that one registers marriage, with both parties signing the document, and in fact some 90 per cent of divorce cases are settled informally. It is likely that a third party will have been asked by the family to help settle practical matters, and this may be the same go-between who brought the couple together in the first place, or it may be another person respected by both sides of the family. In case this informal system breaks down, there is a conciliation procedure which the couple must go through before the case comes to court, and another 9 per cent of cases are settled in this way, leaving only 1 per cent actually to require a court appearance.

It was already mentioned briefly in Chapter 4 that mediation in the case of disputes is one of the roles of the head of a village or community. Indeed, it is generally thought preferable to solve problems within the confines of an *uchi* group such as this, since resorting to the outside world is seen to bring shame on the whole community. Thus, boundary disputes, for example, are thought best settled at this local level where possible, and Kawashima cites an example of a farmer whose whole house was subject to the local sanction of ostracism by the community because his father had sued another farmer about the boundaries of their land (1963:45).

Another well-publicised case in 1983 involved a family whose three-year-old son drowned in an irrigation pond while he was in the care of a neighbour. The bereaved family filed a suit involving sums totalling 28 million yen for negligence, not only against their neighbours, but also against a contractor who had deepened the pond without putting a fence round it, and against the city, the prefecture and the state. The district court ordered the neighbours to pay 5 million yen, but exonerated the other defendants. The case was given much publicity on radio and television, as well as in the newspapers. Within a few days, the family who had lost their son received between 500 and 600 anonymous phone calls and some 50 letters and postcards condemning them in abusive language for taking legal action against their neighbours, particularly because they had won their case. Moreover, the father of the family lost his job and the other children in the family were subjected to derision at school.

Meanwhile, the neighbours appealed. This action provoked a similar response from the general public, suggesting that appealing to the courts even in self-defence is regarded as inappropriate in the case of relations between neighbours. In fact, within a week of the first decision, the bereaved family succumbed to the social pressure and withdrew its case, but by this time they had done irreparable damage to their reputation and were forced to move out of the district. That the matter was a tragedy, no one could deny, but it was evidently not regarded as a solution to bring a dispute between neighbours into the public gaze in this way. It is likely that the whole community had anyway responded with gifts of sympathy to the bereaved family, and appealing to the impersonal machinery of the outside world would perhaps seem like a rejection of this community support.

There are other reasons, too, why individuals, companies and other parties involved in disputes will usually prefer to avoid the shame of a court case, whatever the outcome. The public apology that might be required entails an enormous loss of face, according to Haley (1982:275–6), who has pointed out the extensive practical consequences which may result since so much in Japanese life is dependent on one's personal reputation and connections. Thus, he explains, companies will prefer informally to pay enormous sums of compensation rather than make a public apology. Modern forms of *mura hachibu*, or village ostracism, for someone who loses their reputation in the community include the denial of loans, the boycotting of goods, and a general reluctance to have any further business dealings with them. This would be tolerable if the transacting of business could easily be set up again, but long-term relations are so important that they are on the whole treasured with care and caution.

The force of ostracism as a sanction was illustrated in Chapter 3, when children were learning that they really had little option but to conform with the expected behaviour in kindergartens, and it was described again in Chapter 4 as the traditional negative sanction for stepping out of line within a village community. In both cases, the sanction is particularly effective because it is little used, the threat of such an outcome usually being a sufficient deterrent. In a similar way, people can usually rely on their business partners to conform to expectations in the interest of maintaining their business links in the community, and Japanese contracts are typically rather informal affairs emphasising the importance of 'goodwill' between the parties involved.

Ideally, then, disputes should be solved privately, if necessary with the intervention of a trusted third party to act as a mediator, a role which we have already discussed as important in Chapter 8. There, the emphasis was on the bringing together of two previous strangers for the purpose of marriage, but it was pointed out that the role is found elsewhere since it is a method of bringing people from 'the outside' (*soto*) into one's *uchi* group. Introductions are important because in general one tries to conduct one's life within a circle of *uchi* relations, and in any activity one can only benefit from a personal connection or perhaps a letter of guarantee. In times of dispute, in particular, then, it is preferred to keep the affair within bounded limits.

POSITIVE METHODS OF MAINTAINING ORDER

From the above discussion it will have become apparent that relations in Japanese society are to a large extent based on personal connections and face-to-face interaction. The preservation of this arrangement, which has often been lost elsewhere in modern times, is evidently one of the positive aspects of the maintenance of order in Japanese life, and, in the complex industrialised society which Japan has become, it is no mean feat. Some of the ways in which this is still achieved, despite the anomie which afflicts many other industrialised countries, have already been discussed in previous chapters, but this is a good opportunity for a summary.

In the first place, there is the development from an early age of the importance of the *uchi* group, the 'inside' of security, as opposed to the unknown dangers of the outside world. This is accompanied by the idea, learned first in the home, but afterwards applied elsewhere, that one should put the needs of the *uchi* group before one's own. One's personal behaviour is also often representative of some wider group, whether it be the family, the school, the village or the company, and as a person goes about their life they are expected to remember how their own behaviour will reflect on the groups to which they belong. In Chapter 2, this principle was discussed as part of kindergarten training, where teachers make effective use of peer group pressure to see that the children behave in an orderly manner and develop a sense of responsibility to this wider entity of which they are part.

In the traditional community, too, similar principles operate effectively to ensure much controlled behaviour. One example is the 100 per cent tax payment which is usual when a community pays as a unit. In the past, neighbours would have had to make up the shortfall if an individual house defaulted. Today the ultimate responsibility rests with the individual or family concerned, but it is still regarded as letting down the whole community if one house doesn't pay. For similar reasons, every house usually participates in cooperative activities to take care of village property, to keep the roads mended and the shrine weeded. The continuing reciprocal relations between houses also help to keep channels of communication open and to minimise differences which may arise. As was pointed out in Chapter 4, membership in such a community involves an almost endless series of obligations and duties, but it also provides a considerable degree of security.

Living within a small-scale community such as this also ensures that informal sanctions such as gossip and ridicule are effective. One family has very little opportunity to behave in a way which is radically different from the others, and they would be subject to neighbourly disapproval if they stepped out of line. A practice which is common when people are trying to arrange marriages for their children would seem to play a part in ensuring good relations, at least on the surface. Families who have had a possible partner suggested for their son or daughter often travel to the community of the family concerned and ask amongst the neighbours and perhaps in the local shop what the family is like. Since marriage is regarded as so important in Japanese society, this possibility may well help to maintain amicable relations between neighbours.

The all-pervasive hierarchical principle is another effective example of how personal relations remain important. In many walks of life individuals can only proceed up a scale of advancement by remaining loyal to their superiors and cooperating within a structured situation. The maintenance of order is aided here because there are certain expectations between particular pairs of individuals who are bound up in long-term hierarchical relations. Usually the inferior is obliged to defer to the superior in cases of difference, but the superior is also expected to consult the inferior and take his feelings into consideration before making a decision.

This kind of relationship is based on the principles of *giri-ninjō*, which Noda (1976) describes as the old Japanese system of rules which preceded the modern legal system. *Giri* may be loosely translated as 'duty' and it refers to the various expectations which exist between particular sets of relations. In Chapter 2, for example, the expectations between parents and children were described, and there are similar sets between a teacher and pupil, a master and an apprentice, indeed between any pair of hierarchical relations of this kind. An important characteristic of this type of duty, however, is that the person to whom it is owed has no right to demand that it be fulfilled. A failure to fulfil such a duty would incur great loss of face, and this is usually sufficient incentive, but it would involve equal loss of face were the potential recipient to point this out.

Such a relationship is supposed to be based on feelings of affection, and the value of the relationship itself is supposedly greater than any of the actual duties by which it is marked. This affection is the human element of the relationship, the *ninjō*, and if anyone appears to act out of self-interest, rather than with human feeling, they would be subject to informal sanctions of disapproval. Some modern Japanese would perhaps deny that *giri-ninjō* relations are important in Japan today, but the makings of relations of this kind are still in evidence in the upbringing of children when their mothers teach them to think of others before they act, to refrain from behaviour which they would not like to receive and to give in to a younger child who is not yet old enough to understand. The rationale for such teaching brings us back to the value placed on harmony in social relations.

The value attached to harmony in Japan dates back at least to the Seventeen-Article Constitution of Prince Shotoku (574-622), which esteemed concord above all things as the subject of the First Article and the underlying theme of all the others (see Nakamura 1967 for more detail). The Japanese word for this concept is *wa*, which is also sometimes used to stand for Japan or Japaneseness, and which has a set of connotations rather different from those of the English word 'harmony'. Kawashima (1967:264) quotes from a book by Ono Seiichiro, in which harmony is described as consisting in 'not making distinctions; if a distinction between good and bad can be made, then there *wa* (harmony) does not exist'. This notion evidently underlies the behaviour of judges when they seek to conciliate rather than to apply universalistic principles of right and wrong. Recognising that there are two sides to a dispute, and seeking a compromise between the parties, helps resolve a conflict so that harmony may be restored.

THE POLICE SYSTEM

So far we have discussed rather diffuse methods of encouraging social order, and if Japan were a small-scale society, they might be sufficient. Even before industrialisation, however, Japan had enough problems in the control of her people to warrant an organised system of enforced order, and in the Tokugawa period this was carried out by members of the warrior class, under the official guidance of the local magistrates but, in effect, by means of the sword. The present policing system has been grafted on to the old one, but much of it has again been imported from the West. However, it has often been described as one of the most successful forces in the world.

The crime rate in Japan is extremely low, comparing favourably with most other industrialised countries in almost all categories of crime, and the arrest rate is correspondingly high. For example, in 1989, the rates per 100,000 population for homicide, rape, robbery and theft, respectively, were 1.1, 1.3, 1.3 and 1203.7 for Japan, as compared with 9.1, 12.1, 65.8 and 5077.9 for England and Wales, and 8.7, 38.1, 233 and 5544 for the United States. The arrest rates per 100 offences for the same list of crimes in the same year were 95.9, 83.6, 75.9, 41.7 in Japan, and only 68.3, 52.4, 26.0 and 18.0 in the United States. England and Wales again fell somewhere in between the two (*Facts and Figures of Japan*, 1993). Moreover, this success is achieved with a higher ratio of citizens to police than in most industrial nations.

Again, there are evidently diffuse forces of social control which are working with the police, and the title of an anthropological study of the Japanese police system gives away some of the secret. In *Police and Community in Japan* (Ames 1981), the author writes in the introduction, 'the police have not been moulded in a vacuum . . . they fit Japanese society like a glove fits the hand, and the societal hand has determined the form of the glove' (1981:1). Ames goes on to describe how the police adapt themselves to various areas of Japanese life, first to the cooperating regular communities, both rural and urban, then to non-conforming groups such as youthful protestors, disadvantaged minorities, and out-and-out gangsters. He also discusses the way in which police officers are trained and maintained.

The local police offices found in rural areas of Japan epitomise the idea of community policing, and they are often mentioned as playing an important role in the prevention of crime. Typically, one police officer lives with his family in a house behind the office, and he is expected to integrate himself into the life of the community. His work includes regular visits to all the houses and factories within the district, he keeps a record of the entire population and their valuables. He also spends a regular daily period at his desk for consultation purposes, and his wife is paid a monthly allowance to answer the phone and look after visitors when her husband is out. The officer is usually accorded a fairly high measure of prestige in the community, and he will be invited to attend local events of any importance. He gets to know the district and its workings very thoroughly, and the local population come to know and trust him.

Similar principles operate in the running of urban police boxes, but there is usually more work to be done, and several officers may be required to man one box. Again, regular visits are made to the families and enterprises in the area, and a record is kept of residents' details, such as those who work late and may be vulnerable or helpful in the observation of crime. The box is attended night and day for the reporting of crime or traffic accidents, and the local officer is often the first on the scene. There is also an important role in providing information and general help to the populace, and this may include the occasional loans of bus or train fares, the care of drunks, and general advice to those who drop in for a chat. The police box takes on something of the air of a social centre at times.

In both urban and rural areas, the work of the police is usually supplemented by crime prevention and road safety groups, which are formed voluntarily by local residents from a particular *chōnaikai* (see Chapter 4). Membership in such a group involves occasional service at certain times of the year when there is a festival or a crime prevention programme. There are often also particularly cooperative residents who will keep the police box informed about any suspicious activities in the area, and a few selected houses are chosen to distribute information from time to time. The police, rather like teachers in the earlier stages of school and kindergarten life, take pains to remain on the same side as their charges, and they benefit from a good measure of cooperation in return.

The principle of neighbours watching over each other has a historical precedent in Japan, which has been a controversial issue at times. In the early policing days of the Tokugawa period, order was maintained at a local level by neighbourhood groups of about five houses, *goningumi* or five-man groups, which were collectively responsible for order in the area where they lived. Thus, if one of the houses was up to no good, the others were expected to put pressure on the dissident to reform, or if that failed, they would report them to the higher authorities. The system was revived in wartime Japan for the purposes of government control, and it was criticised and abolished afterwards, but the principle of group responsibility for order at an informal level has by no means disappeared. It seems to work well as long as the arrangements are not abused by higher powers. It is of course the same principle again which is put to good use in schools.

This pattern is again only effective in face-to-face communities where neighbours know one another, and in some modern urban areas this is no longer the case. Nor is the harmonious picture we have described of police/community relations the only image Japan has to offer. In 1984, for example, there were several newspaper reports about corruption and crime amongst the police themselves, and there were some rather alarming increases in the figures, both for crimes committed and for those which remained unsolved. There is also a well-publicised Japanese riot squad, which is from time to time seen on international television dealing with student and other unrest, and there is a very active and highly organised underworld of gang activity.

ORGANISED CRIME

Gang activity is an interesting phenomenon at several levels. On one level, gang relations seem to epitomise the principles of social order, in that the hierarchical structure is firmly established and rigidly maintained so that relations are predictable and reliable. These relations are established at formal ceremonies, rather like marriages, when individual members become linked as father and son or as brothers through the sharing of cups of sake. The partners thus formed can rely on one another for support and loyalty, and they take their places according to the further relations of the superior in the wider ranking of the gang. These long-term relations provide security and a place to belong for many of society's misfits and drop-outs, and the *yakuza* gangs have been described positively as having a role to play in keeping even crime in order in Japan.

The gangs in themselves are not illegal. Each group maintains offices in the cities in which they operate, and they hold ceremonies such as funerals in full public gaze. As a rule, these *yakuza* gangs have legal 'front' occupations, and they live in peace with their neighbours, including the police. On another level, they live quite outside the law, however, since many of the undercover enterprises they run are illegal. Their interests include gambling, prostitution, extortion, peddling, pornography and 'protection', and their territories run as far afield as Europe, South East Asia, Hawaii and California.

They are also sometimes hired by legitimate enterprises for particular ends, for example by right-wing politicians to intimidate a left-wing group threatening trouble, or even by police to help with security during an important event. It would seem, then, that they also have a positive role to play in the maintenance of order at the lowest level of social life in Japan, and since they absorb many of society's misfits, they also provide a haven for people who have no other niche in the organised social world which is Japan.

At this third level, then, gangsters make it possible for even the underside of Japan to be kept in control. Their relations with the police are generally rather cordial, even when they are involved in an investigation, and in the eyes of the general public they are sometimes seen as rather romantic, especially as they epitomise the old principles of *giri-ninjō*. Ames (1981:124) suggests that this is just the *tatemae* of the situation, however, and the *honne* is that these people are just criminals with a glamorous facade. The police maintain good relations with them because this is the harmonious way to proceed. In reality, they would love to eradicate them, and they continually issue advice to the general public, through posters and the circulating neighbourhood notice board, about helping to stamp out their activities.

On the whole the gangs have been too highly organised to be cracked, but problems do arise when factional strife develops, as they do in other areas where the principle so succinctly described by Nakane obtains, and intergang warfare provides the police with legitimate reason for arresting members of the underworld. In 1991, new legislation was passed in the Diet in response to an escalation in the outbreaks of intergroup violence which was said to be making life intolerable for members of the public living or working near the offices and homes of these gangs. The aim of the law, which went into force in March 1992, is to curtail some of the more antisocial activities of these groups. It also outlines procedures for the general public who become victim to gang activities, and it aims too to help young people avoid being recruited. From the point of view of the gangsters, the new law violates their human rights and goes against the Japanese Constitution.

It will be interesting to see what kind of long-term effect these new laws have on the nature of underworld activity in Japan, especially since their activities are now apparently operating well outside the Japanese legal system.

Some excellent anthropological fieldwork has been carried out amongst members of the Japanese underworld by Jacob Raz (1992a, 1992b), and his publications are very revealing of their point of view. He focuses in particular on the itinerant branch of the *yakuza*, known as *tekiya*, who set up stalls at festivals and peddle food and wares, thereby creating a large part of the festival atmosphere. For this reason they see themselves as 'indispensible' to the 'Japaneseness' of this quintessentially Japanese event, located as it is at 'the heart of religious and community life' (1992a:105; 1992b:217–18). Raz also discusses the ways, through forms of self-presentation such as tattoos, style of dress and hair, in which members of the *yakuza* express their rejection of wider Japanese society, which many of them also perceive as having rejected them. Not a few are of Korean and Burakumin origins. Nevertheless, Raz emphasises the way these groups, unlike the American Mafia, operate wholly within a Japanese cultural context.

Another inside view of the *yakuza* world and its modern history is to be found in a fascinating book put together by the retired doctor, Saga Junichi, based on a series of interviews with a dying friend and patient who was *yakuza*. *The Gambler's Tale* is a very personal account, but it well illustrates many of the ideas discussed above, such as the long-term loyalty amongst members of gangs and their hierarchical relations, as well as the resourcefulness of their members, especially in the desperate post-war years. It also depicts life in a couple of Japanese prisons.

CONCLUSION

This *tatemae–honne* distinction runs throughout the legal system and social control in Japan. The whole Western-inspired arrangement was set up to satisfy the world at large that Japan was capable of operating on the same terms as other 'civilised' countries. Indeed, the system is there to respond to the needs of those who call upon its facilities. For the most part, however, it continues to function along the lines of more customary practices which have quite different moral underpinnings. At the level of interpersonal relations the *tatemae* situation is where possible one of harmony, although, of course, there will be situations of conflict inside and outside the *uchi* groups to which people belong. The compromises which are reached sound splendid arrangements, but the *honne* may well be that one or more of the participants had little choice but to agree, just as partners in a consensus decision may come away with something less than the satisfaction they will show on the surface. However, the ability to have a *tatemae* face for any situation is learned early in Japanese society, as was pointed out in Chapter 3, and this, too, is an important mechanism of social control. Indeed, it is perhaps one of the most effective of all.

To return, finally, to the problem mentioned at the beginning of the chapter of the opposing interpretations of Japanese society as either very harmonious, or as full of conflict, we find that we do indeed draw on a similar distinction. Ishida Takeshi (1984) has proposed a very plausible way of reconciling these two views by using the notions of *omote* and *ura*, literally 'front' and 'back', but corresponding rather well to the notions of *tatemae* and *honne*, in juxtaposition with the notions of *uchi* and *soto*. He argues that the *omote* or surface relations between members of the same *uchi* group should be harmonious, and conflict which might well exist at the *ura* or underneath level is usually solved implicitly. At the *omote* level of *soto* relations, however, there should be no concessions and no compromise – hence the strong views of conflict. Even here, however, at the *ura* level, negotiation is possible if neither party loses face.

This chapter has tended to emphasise the harmonious side of the paradigm, but then it is concerned with social control, not social disorder. Surface relations between outsiders may well lead to open conflict anywhere in the world, and it reveals little about the Japanese mechanisms of social control to dwell on that superficial level. At a practical level, Japanese people would seem to prefer where possible to establish and expand their *uchi* relations with the security that follows, even if this means the loss of a degree of freedom. It is important to remember, however, that there are also people in Japan, as elsewhere, who feel that the system is too stifling, and once they reject the system, they have no option but to choose a path of direct conflict (or exile).

REFERENCES

Ames, Walter L., *Police and Community in Japan* (University of California Press, Berkeley 1981)

Eisenstadt, S.N. and Eyal Ben-Ari (eds), *Japanese Models of Conflict Resolution* (Kegan Paul International, London and New York, 1990)

Evans-Pritchard, E.E., *Witchcraft, Oracles and Magic Among the Azande* (Clarendon Press, Oxford, 1937)
Haley, John O., 'Unsheathing the Sword: Law Without Sanctions', *Journal of Japanese Studies*, vol. 8, no. 2 (1982), pp. 265–81
Henderson, Dan Fenno, *Conciliation and Japanese Law*, 2 vols. (University of Washington Press, Seattle, 1965)
Ishida, Takeshi, 'Conflict and its Accommodation: *omote–ura* and *uchi-soto* Relations' in E.S. Krauss, T.P. Rohlen and P.G. Steinhoff, *Conflict in Japan* (University of Hawaii Press, Honolulu, 1984) pp. 16-38
Kawashima, Takeyoshi, 'Dispute Resolution in Contemporary Japan', in von Mehren (ed.), *Law in Japan: The Legal Order in a Changing Society* (Harvard University Press, Cambridge, Mass., 1963), pp.41–72
———, 'The Status of the Individual in the Notion of Law, Right, and Social Order in Japan', in Charles A. Moore (ed.), *The Japanese Mind: The Essentials of Japanese Philosophy and Culture* (The University Press of Hawaii, Honolulu, 1967)
Krauss, E.S, T.P. Rohlen and P.G. Steinhoff, *Conflict in Japan* (University of Hawaii Press, Honolulu, 1984)
Moore, Charles A. (ed.), *The Japanese Mind: The Essentials of Japanese Philosophy and Culture* (The University Press of Hawaii, Honolulu, 1967)
Nakamura, Hajime, 'Basic features of the Legal, Political and Economic Thought of Japan' in A. Moore (ed.), *The Japanese Mind: The Essentials of Japanese Philosophy and Culture* (The University Press of Hawaii, Honolulu, 1967)
Noda, Yoshiyuki, *Introduction to Japanese Law*, trans. and ed. Anthony H. Angelo (University of Tokyo Press, Tokyo, 1976)
Raz, Jacob, *Aspects of Otherness in Japanese Culture* (Institute for the Study of Languages and Cultures of Asia and Africa, Tokyo, 1992a)
———, 'Self-presentation and Performance in the *Yakuza* Way of Life', in Roger Goodman and Kirsten Refsing (eds), *Ideology and Practice in Modern Japan* (Routledge, London, 1992b), pp. 210–34
Roberts, Simon, *Order and Dispute* (Penguin, Harmondsworth, 1979)

FURTHER READING

Haley, John O., 'The Myth of the Reluctant Litigant', *Journal of Japanese Studies*, vol. 4, no. 2 (1978), pp. 359–90
Haley, John O., *Authority without Power: Law and the Japanese Paradox* (Oxford University Press, New York and Oxford, 1991)
Koschmann, J. Victor, 'The Idioms of Contemporary Japan VIII: *Tatemae to honne*', *The Japan Interpreter*, 9 (1974), pp. 98–104
Moeran, Brian, *Okubo Diary: Portrait of a Japanese Valley* (Stanford University Press, Stanford, 1985)
Oda Hiroshi, *Japanese Law* (Butterworth, London, 1992)
Parker, L. Craig, *The Japanese Police System Today: An American Perspective* (Kodansha International, Tokyo, 1984)
Ramseyer, J. Mark, 'Reluctant Litigant Revisited: Rationality and Disputes in Japan', *Journal of Japanese Studies*, vol. 14, no. 1 (1988), pp. 111–23.
Smith Robert J., *Japanese Society: Tradition, Self and the Social Order* (Cambridge University Press, Cambridge, 1984), Chapter 2

Upham, Frank, *Law and Social Change in Postwar Japan,* (Harvard University Press, Cambridge, Mass., 1987)
Von Mehren, A. (ed.), *Law in Japan: The Legal Order in a Changing Society* (Harvard University Press, Cambridge, Mass., 1963)

LIGHTER READING

Crichton, M., *Rising Sun* (Century Arrow, 1992)
Saga Junichi, *The Gambler's Tale* (Kodansha International, Tokyo, 1989)

Conclusion
Evaporating the inscrutability

At the beginning of this book the conclusion was anticipated as the place where some common features of different areas of Japanese society would be brought together. So far we have skimmed across an enormous range of topics pertaining to a very complex and complicated society. We have ranged from the microscopic to the macroscopic, and back again. We have grown up with a Japanese child, we have gone out to work, to play, to pray and to vote, and we have learned how to deal with disputes. The question now remains: have we succeeded in evaporating the inscrutability? In these last few pages, the aim will be to summarise a few important classificatory principles which have emerged again and again in the course of this book. It is my contention that an understanding of these principles will go a long way towards aiding an understanding of Japanese behaviour at any level.

First of all, it is important to reiterate the point made in the previous chapter that much social interaction takes place at a face-to-face level. Within the largest corporations, universities, political parties, gangs and even the self-defence forces, two related principles operate to ensure that most important transactions may be made between people who know and understand each other, who can rely on each other and predict each other's behaviour. The first principle is the hierarchical one, which we have been referring to as Nakane's inverted V principle, although it has been described by plenty of other people; namely that recruits to any large organisation, as well as many smaller ones, establish long-term links with a particular superior. In turn, these inferiors will become linked to newer recruits as their superiors, and the whole enterprise can be pictured as a series of personal, individual links.

The second principle is even more widespread. It is the principle of establishing and belonging to *uchi* groups. These may be represented for any individual as a series of concentric circles, with the smallest, most intimate group in the middle, and the largest probably being the *uchi* group of all Japanese people. The primary school curriculum reflects this model as children are taught in social studies about the family in the first year, the neighbourhood in the second, the wider city, town or village in the third, the prefecture in the fourth, Japan in the fifth, and only in the sixth year do they begin to learn about the rest of the world. As the attachments get larger, there is less likelihood of seeing an entire group together at any one time, but there are various symbolic ways in which they may be represented, and in which their members may make known their common allegiance. Flags, badges and company songs are but a few examples. In fact, an individual probably spends most of his or her life with members of the closer groups, but in appropriate circumstances, principles of behaviour can be applied to more distant acquaintances on the basis of common membership in an *uchi* group at any level.

The consequences of this emphasis on face-to-face interaction are various and far-reaching. They are also particularly amenable to social anthropological analysis because much of the training of social anthropologists involves the study of small-scale, face-to-face groups of the kind which the Japanese have managed to maintain. I have made this point rather forcibly in the introduction to *Interpreting Japanese Society* (Hendry and Webber 1986), a collection of papers written by anthropologists about Japan, and referred to often throughout this book. In particular, much of the effectiveness of mechanisms of social control relies, in the Japanese case, on principles which are more commonly found in small communities of Africa and South America than in the industrial societies with which Japan is usually compared.

These are diffuse sanctions like gossip, ridicule and ostracism as negative reactions to unacceptable behaviour, and prestige and status as positive benefits which accrue to those who live according to the shared value system. These sanctions lose their power if people are easily able to move out of a community or other *uchi* group but, as was pointed out in Chapter 12, Japanese society makes it very difficult to do this. Of course, in urban areas, the pressures are much less great within a residential area, and some occupations are more constraining than others in this respect, but for many, the opinion of neighbours, friends and workmates counts for a great deal. This is true of many peoples throughout the world, within their own face-to-face circles, but it is emphasised here because the importance of long-term relations is so pervasive in the case of Japan.

Operating to maintain these face-to-face relations, then, are further principles which we have already discussed at intervals throughout the book. One is reciprocity. Again, this is a universal characteristic of social interaction, particularly important in long-term relations. Appropriate exchanges are usually very clearly decided in any particular dyad, and an imbalance in material goods usually implies that there is something intangible like help or loyalty moving in the other direction in its place, although prestige and status are often demonstrated materially by the receipt of an excess of goods. It is not unusual for people in Japan to keep a record of the value of goods which have been received, so that an appropriate amount may be spent when the time comes to make a return. There are certain fixed occasions when gifts will be made, and regular exchanges serve to reconfirm the relationships.

At a non-material level, there are other clear expectations of reciprocity in pairs of relationships, the most striking being the exchange of loyalty for benevolence between an inferior and superior in many different circumstances. This type of exchange may not be manifest in packets and parcels, but it is none the less binding. These rules may be discussed in terms of 'debts' (*giri* and *on*) but some relationships might even be regarded as too close for the application of such cold-sounding concepts. As was pointed out in the previous chapter, the *ninjō* of human feelings must not be forgotten. This might seem like a let-out clause allowing for the neglect of reciprocity, but it is precisely in relations close enough for human feelings to be taken into consideration that the force of obligation actually seems to be strongest.

Another important principle in the maintenance of long-term relations is, of course, the hierarchical one itself. Along with the exchanges involved, there are also fixed rules about who defers to whom, how much and when such deference may be relaxed. The contextual nature of hierarchy is interesting in the Japanese case, as is the virtual guarantee that one is almost always in a position to be superior to someone as well as inferior to someone else. Possibly before they are even aware of such differences, almost any member of Japanese society automatically receives a certain amount of deference merely on the strength of his or her age, whether it be two years or 82 years, and as long as one remains within the value system, one usually accumulates further status by living through the normal experiences of life. This is particularly the case in long-term relations, which provides an incentive for maintaining them smoothly.

Much of the expression of deference may be rather elaborate role-play, but this is an essential part of the maintenance of harmony in social relations, another principle which is, of course, highly prized. This role-play is part of the exercise of *tatemae* in human relations, the presentation of an appropriate face for any particular situation, and this aspect of Japanese interaction again runs through most arenas. It helps to make possible the phenomenon of consensus decision-making, the appearance of an amazing degree of social order, even among society's misfits and cast-offs, and it also helps to make possible the communication of less pleasant things, which would be quite unspeakable in ordinary language, simply by adjustment in the use of the various levels of politeness available.

Equality must not be forgotten, of course, and this is another principle which is important in certain circumstances, as was illustrated particularly in the education chapter. The assumption which is made about the ability of any child to keep up with the class, given the right approach and a measure of persistence and perseverence, is fundamentally much more egalitarian than the emphasis on innate intelligence which is found in most Western countries, although it is not to be denied that Japanese teachers are aware of such differences. The same principle is found in the arts, when the study of any skill is expected to involve long and arduous training rather than being a 'talent' which one is encouraged to feel one either has or doesn't have. The 'automatic' aspects of hierarchy, like those based on age and experience, also temper the differences with an egalitarian quality. We have also seen the symbolic expression of equality in the kindergarten and in the neighbourhood.

The principle of cooperation is also given a high rating in a Japanese list of value priorities, and this emphasis on putting the needs of a group of some sort before one's own personal desires tends to sound unattractive to people brought up in a more individualistic society. The security gained through membership in such *uchi* groups necessarily involves a certain loss of individual freedom, but socialisation is such that the needs of the wider group are presented as one's own needs, and a certain sense of satisfaction seems to be associated with the contribution an individual can make to the workings of a larger endeavour. In fact, if the system works properly, there should be no need for the self-assertive aspect of individualism, since close relations and associates, in whatever arenas they operate, should be taking care to consider each other's interests.

With regard to the development of individuality, there is no reason why this should be denied, and indeed there are plenty of Japanese 'individuals' to disprove any theory which would attempt to suggest it could. To take but one example, the almost universal pursuit of arts and hobbies, from a very early age through to long past retirement from economically productive activities, provides members of Japanese society with an abundance of possibilities to pursue individual interests or select companions outside those with whom one must necessarily pass a good deal of time. The close bonds which are formed within face-to-face society also make possible a degree of deep understanding which may never be achieved in a more anonymous world, and the pervasive use of *tatemae* behaviour, and its apparently clear separation from *honne*, even offers the possibility of an ultimate freedom of individuality which is perhaps denied to people who fail to recognise such a distinction.

In the end, we have distilled out a small number of principles which are certainly not uniquely Japanese. The creation of us/them dichotomies – as we could term the *uchi/soto* distinction – is a feature of human society found all over the world. The separation of real feelings from one's 'face to the world' – as in the *tatemae/honne* distinction – is also a recognisable human practice, though the degree of social support it receives is a variable feature. Even the development of *seishin*, an inner spiritual strength, is a concept by no means alien to other cultural systems. What is unique – although only as unique as any other specific form of life – is the way particular combinations of these elements may be found in particular parts of Japanese society, and recognised as Japanese. It is to be hoped that this book will, by elaborating on these principles, help to lift the veil of inscrutability with which even the Japanese are accustomed to shroud their categories of thought.

Index

abacus 103
abalone 146
ability 103
abortion 121
academic performance 98
accidents 97
accommodation 150, 182
accomplishments 18, 164, 173–7
administration 59–61, 69, 86
administrative branch of
  government 188, 191, 207
admiration 204
adoption 26
adultery 37
adulthood 110, 138, 142, 145, 147,
  149
advertising 160, 176, 193, 217
Africa 120, 223
age 90–1, 118, 138, 143, 224, 226
  grades 64; mates 63–4, 118, 182;
    retirement 33, 64, 143, 146, 159,
    183, 226
agriculture 102, 200
ai 128
ainoko 82–3
Ainu people 7, 82
akarui 47
Allied Occupation 17, 23, 35, 81–2,
  187–8, 205–6; directives 27, 98,
  117
amae 55n4
Amaterasu 8, 9, 10, 30, 98, 118, 180,
  182
Ames, Walter L. 214, 217
amulets 118, 121–2, 134, 142, 181
ancestors 17, 24–5, 31, 34, 60, 127,

141; early 7; memorials 10, 29,
  146; supernatural 117; treasure
  208
ancestral retribution 124, 204;
  tablets 129, 145
Anderson, Jennifer 175
animals 80, 123
annual ceremonies 145
anthropology 1–3, 5, 58, 76, 92, 101,
  110, 115–16, 124, 133, 150, 163,
  189, 200–2; legal 205; medical 116;
  social 204–5, 218, 223
apartment complexes 58, 73, 89
apology 47, 49, 208, 210
appeals 207, 210
application for university 104–6
archeology, findings 5, 7, 79;
  remains 10
archery 170
architecture 12, 169, 175
armed forces 17, 190
artisans 15, 80, 170, 172, 176
artists 168, 171, 177, 179
arts 225–6; classes 103; culinary 170;
  early development of 12; and
  entertainment 172–85; export of
  18; festivals 177; modern 172;
  performing 169; and religion 168;
  schools 170; social organisation
  87, 168–72; and Zen Buddhism
  122
Ashikaga family 14
Asquith, Pamela 80
Association for Democratic Reform
  196
atomic bomb 17